DANCING IN THE DHARMA

DANCING IN THE DHARMA

The Life and Teachings of Ruth Denison

SANDY BOUCHER

BEACON PRESS

BOSTON

BEACON PRESS
25 Beacon Street
Boston, Massachusetts 02108-2892
www.beacon.org

Beacon Press books
are published under the auspices of
the Unitarian Universalist Association of Congregations.

09 08 07 06 8 7 6 5 4 3 2 1

This book is printed on acid-free paper that meets the uncoated paper
ANSI/NISO specifications for permanence as revised in 1992.

Composition by Wilsted & Taylor Publishing Services

Library of Congress Cataloging-in-Publication Data

Boucher, Sandy.
Dancing in the dharma : the life and teachings
of Ruth Denison / Sandy Boucher.
p. cm.
Includes bibliographical references and index.
ISBN 0-8070-7319-9 (pbk. : acid-free paper)
1. Denison, Ruth. 2. Buddhist women—United States—
Biography. 3. Spiritual biography—United States.
4. Women—Religious life—Buddhism. I. Title.

BQ734.D45B68 2005
294.3'092—dc22   2004021446

For Ruth and her many students

Perhaps it's a good thing that I'm not perfect,
... otherwise you might be looking for the
Buddha somewhere outside your own mind.

AJAHN CHAH

There is no such thing as master and student.
This is why the relationship works.

STEPHEN T. BUTTERFIELD

Contents

A Day in the Desert

On this April morning of 2003, in the high desert, I expected the beginning of summer's crushing heat. Instead, as I trudge the quarter-mile from Dukkha House, the women's dormitory, to Las Vegas House, where Ruth now lives, my hair whips around my head from the cold wind, and above me loom great piles of darkening cloud. I look out across the open stretch of Copper Mountain Mesa, a terrain sparse with creosote and desert sage, dotted with modest houses, part of the Mojave Desert of California. Ruth Denison's meditation center, Dhamma Dena, spreads out in one-story buildings and house trailers, their wood, stucco, stone, and painted metal blending into the vast monotonous landscape.

I am here once again to sit and talk with Ruth, to learn her history, travel with her the road that led through sites both physical and mental to this destination.

Outside the gate to Las Vegas House, I find cacti planted in gleaming white toilet bowls, sprouting magnificent cherry-red blossoms, and I stop to admire the gorgeous petals of these briefly blooming flowers. I open the gate of the chain-link fence, walk up the sandy driveway, and go in the back door of the green-shingled, one-story house. The previous owner installed the fence and wire security door. Ruth has so little fear that, for most of the period this center has existed, doors were never locked, and most of them still aren't.

The fence was useful, however, during the five-and-a-half years of her husband Henry's dying, when he lived here and was guarded by fierce dachshunds, eager to take a chunk out of your ankle when you came to visit him. Many times I trembled at the gate, menaced by scrabbling, growling little wiener dogs, as I called for someone to come out and hold them back so that I could go in and sit with Henry.

This morning no such guardians attack me. Ruth's latest dachsies are too old and tired to leap into watchdog mode.

Through the closed porch I go, and into the dark, narrow kitchen, calling, "Hello, I'm here!"

Ruth stands in the living room talking to Dhammapali, the woman returned from Burma, who will stay here for a time. Dhammapali gives me her brilliant smile while Ruth goes on instructing her. "Yah, while I am gone for the night, dahling, you stay here in my house. That will be nice for you, hmm? Later I show you how to feed the coyotes, and the rabbits, and the roadrunners."

"I can sleep in my van," Dhammapali offers.

Ruth objects. "No, dahling, you sleep in here so you can take care of the doggies."

She turns to point them out, curled on a large round pillow between the dining room and the living room. Tara, shaggy and gray-whiskered, sleeps. Nelli Belli Delli, a beautiful caramel-colored shorthair with a delicate pointed snout, looks up at us anxiously. She is a purebred who had been used for breeding—kept in a small cage all her life, impregnated regularly, giving birth and nursing—until she reached the end of her usefulness and would have been sold for vivisection, had she not had the extraordinary good fortune of being rescued by Ruth Denison.

Dhammapali, wearing a floppy sun hat, comes to squat and pet the dogs.

I have taken my usual place at the dining room table and begin unpacking tape recorder, microphone, and clipboard.

"Yes, dahling, you get settled there," Ruth directs. She sends me a piercing glance. "Did you have breakfast?"

I assure her that I did.

Ruth is a small, erect, wiry woman wearing black pants and top, her upper body swathed in a bright red coat-sweater. On her head rests one of her hats—this one like a white cotton muffin, pouchy above, and with a narrow brim, beneath which brown-blond curls rest on her forehead and over her ears. (As unusual as it is for an eighty-year-old to have brown hair, Ruth has proof that this trait runs in her family. A framed photo on the wall shows her with her *Mutti* [German for "Mom"]; it was taken in Germany when her mother was in her nineties and still had light-brown hair.)

"Now, dahling, I want you to sweep the porch." This to Dhammapali, who crouches next to the dogs. "And then will you go tell Jim to fix that back door? It is *dangling* on its hinges!"

Ruth moves quickly past the table where I sit, and something catches her eye. She lifts a letter from a stack of leaflets and mailers. "You see what they are doing to the environment, dahling? On the whole I think it is better for women to have more leading positions in government, hmm? But with this Gale Norton!" She slaps the letter with a flat hand, and brandishes it at me. "With her we have not a good thing! Oh, you wouldn't *believe* what she is doing!" She hands me the letter.

While I read the latest account of what Norton, President Bush's secretary of the interior, has done, Ruth ushers Dhammapali out the door and finds her a broom.

I plug in the tape recorder, attach the mike, and sit waiting. Any number of events may occur to postpone our interview. Jim, the temporary handyman, may arrive and need instruction about the door. The phone may ring. We may hear the squawking of the roadrunner, Ruth's favorite creature. Those of us who grew up on movie cartoons will remember the roadrunner in Warner Brothers Looney Tunes shorts. A big wacky bird with tufted head, he streaks across the ground, tail held stiffly straight up behind him, chased by Wile E. Coyote. Ruth has cultivated a relationship with a pair of roadrunners, and keeps little balls of ground meat in her refrigerator to feed them when they come. They are inordinately precious to her. The last time one arrived, when I was here, it came running into the living room through the open patio door, giving its scratchy call for food. "Ah, that is the mother," Ruth told me, "she comes for food for her babies." She fell to her knees to hold out a meatball to the visitor, who plucked it greedily. Ruth looked up at me, her face opening with the delight of a five-year-old. "*Look,*" she said, "she took it even from my fingers!"

Now she heads for the kitchen. "Shall I make you a cup of coffee, dahling?"

• • •

This is Ruth Denison, one of the pioneer teachers of Buddhism in the West. Born in Germany before the Second World War, she survived bombings and strafings, privation, injury, and disease. Then, in her late thirties and forties, after coming to the United States, she entered a second rigorous training: she studied with the greatest spiritual teachers of the mid-twentieth century, in India, Burma, Japan, and the United States, and emerged with the authorization to teach, conferred upon her by an esteemed Burmese Buddhist master.

Ruth brought a strongly female, body-centered approach to Buddhist practice, when this was seen as radical and subversive. She taught the very first women-only Buddhist meditation retreat, and has continued as a powerful teacher for women, as well as for her many male students. She introduced sensory-awareness techniques and movement into Buddhist meditation practice, shocking the more traditional practitioners and delighting many of her female students. For thirty years she has taught extensively in the United States and Europe, and helped in the establishment of meditation centers in Canada, Germany, Massachusetts, and California. As often happens with innovators, Ruth is now viewed with respect by the establishment that once marginalized her. More conventional teachers have adopted some of her practices, and these have become routine in many meditation settings. For countless women and men, Ruth has opened the door to spiritual practice. Buddhist leaders and historians acknowledge her importance in the introduction of Buddhadharma to the West.

Unpredictable and contradictory, she challenges her students with her ever-present love of life and boundless energy. She can act the high-handed Prussian general at one moment—ordering you around, snapping at you if you're slow or inattentive—and, at the next moment, melt your heart with her tender empathy for pain. She can plunge you down inside your deepest consciousness through her grasp of the truths of existence, then send you into spasms of annoyance by interrupting your concentration with verbal guidance. Her compassion is expressed in myriad ways, many of them subtle or hidden; her patience with neurosis and madness brings comfort and healing energy to many. No one just like Ruth Denison has ever walked the earth before.

After some initial resistance—for the task seemed daunting—I have set myself to present in some measure the astonishing life that Ruth Denison has led. I do this because she is a consummate teacher whose contribution deserves recognition, and because she has struck new ground in the great continuing drama of Buddhism's coming to the West. But I also honor a more personal urgency in telling Ruth's story, for it was she who set my feet upon the spiritual path some twenty-five years ago and has continued to inspire and vex me ever since. To understand my own complex relationship with this extraordinary woman, I needed to grasp her evolution, through all the circumstances and choices of her life, into the mature teacher I know today. In the research and writing of this book, I encountered myself at every juncture, resisting Ruth, criticizing her, judging her, as well as opening to the teachings embedded in her life—for I have never been the compliant, adoring student. Now she is old and I am getting older, and it has become crucial to me to grapple with the many paradoxes of her character and my own response to them, in order to come to understand the full range of my own spiritual path and awareness. What was it about Ruth and myself that drew me back, year after year, to sit and move and dance with her, even when I could so clearly see her faults?

For over twenty years I have been coming down here to the Mojave Desert to Ruth's meditation retreats. This last year I came not to meditate but to sit at her dining room table and encourage her to tell again the stories about her life that I've heard in the meditation hall and everywhere else at Dhamma Dena. I've learned in my years with Ruth that things often do not happen the way I think they should. In her teaching, and in her life, Ruth acts spontaneously; she is so fully committed to *this moment* that she may lose track of what she promised yesterday, or even of the prescribed schedule of events at a retreat. At first this evoked little fits of exasperation in me—until I discovered the obvious, that it was my own mind that was causing me to suffer. Then I began to understand that this was a great teaching for me: to let go of expectations, not to hold so tightly to my own precious agenda, to break the form and stay with the interest and joy of the present moment.

Now there is sweetness in simply being with Ruth in each activity. She teaches in her daily life as much as in her formal instruction. She cares so passionately about the details of ordinary existence, and tends so lovingly to all living and nonliving beings, that it feels like a stiff begrudging and holding-back to give in to impatience with her.

Our relationship has evolved in the last year of interviewing. At first Ruth was quite suspicious of this book-writing project, even though she officially approved of it. She tends to resist documentation of herself or her work, believing that she must be experienced in person to be known. But as I researched the context of her German youth, her years in Hollywood with Henry Denison, her fifteen years of training with major teachers during the spiritual renaissance of the sixties, we talked in depth about her life, revisiting painful periods, going deeper. Gradually she began to relax and accept this process of telling her story, began to trust my intention to present her, to the best of my ability, in her complexity.

We both understood that this would not result in a conventional biography, as my own story intertwines with Ruth's. Also, I did not have ten years and financial support to put toward verifying every name, date, or occurrence in her life. Some of the evidence has literally disappeared. For instance, the village where Ruth grew up in East Prussia no longer exists—it was long ago swallowed up into Poland. All her siblings and many of her associates, German and American, have died. In many instances I have had to rely on Ruth's sometimes faulty memory for details, and occasionally I have had to contend with her giving different versions of a story. The time line of Ruth's life I have pieced together from her own accounts, other people's versions of incidents, the dates of certain well-known world events. It is accurate in its most important junctures. Still, some of it wobbled into the shadows when I tried to pin it down, and so I surrendered to a certain freewheeling spirit in Ruth and myself that gives greater value to the verve and spirit of a story than to its exact location in time.

• • •

This morning I am here to get her talking once again about her life—something she does with great wit and gusto—and at some point we need to begin.

Ruth has opened her jar of expensive organic instant coffee and made us each a cup, lacing them with half & half. Now she brings both cups to the table and seats herself across from me. I clip the remote microphone to the collar of her red sweater, and we are ready.

While setting up, I was looking from dining room to living room, at a handsome bronze statue of Shiva, Hindu god of destruction and reproduction, dancing within a ring of fire, that stands on a sideboard. The image once belonged to Alan Watts, I recall. One of the myriad of students and colleagues and old friends of Ruth whom I have interviewed over these months had told me a story about Ruth and Watts. It seems like a good place to begin.

"I heard that when Alan Watts died, you were in India, and you did a temple dance for him. How did that happen?"

Ruth leans forward, smiles slowly, pulling up the memory.

The famous counterculture explicator of Eastern religions, Alan Watts, became a close friend of Ruth and Henry Denison in the 1960s. He often led seminars and gave talks in the living room of their house in the Hollywood Hills. Watts was the centerpiece of a group of friends that included psychologists and philosophers, Hindu gurus and Japanese Zen masters, exponents of LSD and marijuana, innovators and risk takers, who came to the parties and dinners at 2796 Creston Drive. The house, perched on a steep hill above a reservoir, had the feel of a Japanese country house, simple and elegant, quiet, gracious, the perfect setting for the informal salon that Henry and Ruth hosted.

"Yah, I danced a lot with Alan, in my own home," she begins. "And when he was there, there were always people like Dr. Janiger the psychiatrist, Werner Erhard, John Lilly and his wife Antoinette, and the two people who owned the bookstore on Wilshire who gave Alan the opportunity to have seminars in their shop. We would play Mozart—the whole opera, *Figaro* maybe, so we didn't have to put always new background music after dinner at the big table. People were sitting in front of the fireplace and talking.

"So the music played, and Alan was always like this . . ." Getting up, Ruth lifts her arms in a flowing, Isadora Duncan–like, interpretive gesture. ". . . and I played into his movements. The others were always sitting and talking, and discovering, and investigating, and projecting. But Alan and I would dance."

She pulls out the mailing that describes Gale Norton's deeds, turns it over, and begins to draw a diagram of the living room in their Hollywood house. "Here's the fireplace in that big room. Then our guests sat here, around it, there was a big couch, then here a couch and here a couch, and then was here the big long table. And here was space. But you could also move onto the terrace outside. Doors slid open, big windows in the dining room also opened, you could just step over the lower part, and you could dance outside. So Alan and I, we did go with the rhythm of *Figaro,* sometimes staccato, sometimes waltzlike, and sometimes a little bit declining in motion, kind of playing with each other. The others, they just thought that was the thing to do, yah?

"So I learned about his death while Henry and I were in a taxi in Delhi. It was a wonderment for me that he died, he wasn't that old, sixty-three?"

"I think he was actually just fifty-eight years old," I offer.

She blinks at me. "Really. That young?"

"Yes, well, according to his biographer, he was burning the candle at both ends."

We slip off into a wrangle about Alan Watts's vivid lifestyle, Ruth not wanting to believe the biographer's more compromising assertions. "I admired his greatness," she states. "He always had it."

And we return to the subject of his dancing.

"When I heard that he was dead, I saw myself dancing with him. And I learned a great deal with movement. I enjoyed it with him, it was very inspiring. He thought that I was sexy—he wrote it in his book—and earthy. And religious. Yah, sex is also religion. You can put it into religion too, if you offer it to the spirit."

In his autobiography, Alan Watts had described her as "a very blond fraulein who—after harrowing adventures—escaped from East Prussia during the Russian occupation. . . ." saying that she was "audaciously adventurous, sexy, practical, and religious."[1]

"I saw the good connection I had with him on that level," Ruth continues, "and also I was always happy when the people there enjoyed it."

She pauses, raises her coffee cup to drink.

"So you were in Delhi when you heard about his death?" I prompt. "Watts actually died in November of 1973."

"Yah, we are in the taxi, and I hear Henry reading me the letter, telling that Alan had died. Then we were both silent, and I let the pictures go by. Henry was very casual about it, I got almost angry with him. I felt him so superior about it, so unattached.

"We went back to the hotel. Henry was probably tired, he always liked to read the *Newsweek*. He would take a glass of wine, and maybe take the afternoon to sleep. That just wasn't my thing. I went off to wander in the streets, with Alan in my head. I was thinking about him, I heard the music, and was really sad, thinking about dying."

As Ruth talks, I watch her face, whose framework of wide forehead, deep-set eye sockets, and emphatic jutting chin has been carved and gullied by experience; her light eyes behind glasses gaze out with the guarded expression of one who has seen the depths of human character, and its heights. She looks ancient, a foremother chipped out of a granite block. Then suddenly, as at the arrival of the roadrunner, wrinkles burn away before the fire of enthusiasm, and her eyes beam interest.

"I was walking in the streets and I came by the Sarasvati temple, where I never had been. Sarasvati is the female deity of wisdom, you know. It was all marble floors, big columns and arches, there was no door. I go into it. There was a big hall, beautiful steps going up, lots of shoes there. It was open, one of those afternoon rituals probably, hmm? It was full with maybe three hundred people sitting there. I heard music, that kind of percussion music with a nice rhythm.

"I go in, they all sit on the floor, and maybe five people have these percussion instruments, rattles and all, and go with it." She claps a rhythm. "They were chanting, 'Shiva, Shiva' in a lovely rhythm. I go in and sit there too."

Ruth was fifty-one years old at the time. She was probably wearing the white sari given to her by the wife of Indian meditation teacher S. N. Goenka. Her long blond straight hair was caught up in a bun behind her head, and fell in bangs on her forehead. I have seen a photo of her draped in this sari, smiling coquettishly at the camera as she poses, one arm raised above her head, fingers clinking imaginary finger cymbals, before a painted backdrop of a tree and waterfall. This is the woman who sat herself down among the chanting Indians and began to meditate.

"I had good concentration, I could come to this moment where I feel that I am just a conduit, that my consciousness was everyway here, I didn't need to think what I wanted to do. I forgot my surrounding."

And then an amazing thing happened. Without planning to, Ruth stood up and began to dance.

"I had a little bit the ground rules for Indian dance, I could stand on one leg like Shiva does. I practiced it and imitated him at home a little—what should you do in a hotel? So I started doing that, according to the rhythm, and according to my own interpretation, and nobody looked, everybody continued chanting. Only the musicians looked at me, and as I had tuned in to them, they now tuned in to me. I had no qualms about it that there were people sitting or whether they were looking, not at all. While I danced, I held Alan before me, and also the Shiva. Alan had loved Shiva. When he died, after I came back, his wife Mary Jane sent to me the dancing Shiva that you see there in my living room." She points to the exquisite large statue. "Maybe an hour and a half I danced. I thought I was expressing Shiva—well I was expressing something. They felt that too.

"Then it was finished, and I sat down. Nothing happened. I started chanting with them again. The chanting ended about 7:00 p.m. From 3:00 p.m. it had been going. Then came to me the head of the musicians and the head of the temple. They offered me to stay there, and they told me it was a Shiva dance, hmm? They thought I was kind of an incarnation of that. They asked me where I taught, what school I was. I said, 'No, I just listened to the music.' That was even better for them. They showed me the living quarters in the temple and wanted me to be there.

"So, well, I had a husband at home, so I told them I had to go. I don't know if I walked or if they took me back to the hotel. But they were really bowing, and the people too. They put flowers on my feet. I was in wonderment.

"When I told Henry, he got excited about it. He said, 'Why don't you do that again tomorrow?' He accompanied me the next day to the temple. But I had not the courage to get up, I couldn't coordinate to the music, I was not anymore present."

We sit for a moment in silence, as I ponder this remarkable story. It is like others Ruth tells, of her entering a situation so completely that she acts without self-consciousness, and is recognized by the participants as a gifted being. It is ironic that in this spiritual practice in which we are "training to be nobody special," Ruth often points out how very special she is. This is only one of her contradictions. In other settings she stays modestly in the background, serving others, calling no attention to herself. Ruth's range of roles is mind-bogglingly broad, from interpretive dancer to gutsy laborer, from gracious hostess to wise teacher.

• • •

Twenty-three years ago, when I first encountered Ruth, I was nearing the end of a period in which I had devoted all my energies to the women's liberation movement. Political activism had engaged me for almost ten years, and I found myself depleted, in need of some kind of internal sustenance. My partner at the time persuaded me to go with her and other women down to Dhamma Dena. She had heard about the very first women's retreat there in 1979, and now she wanted us to participate in the second one, in 1980. I agreed, mildly intrigued by the idea of meditation. So we made the ten-hour drive from Berkeley south to the little town of Joshua Tree and up a dirt road onto Copper Mountain Mesa to Dhamma Dena. I had no idea what to expect.

During the following days I observed that Ruth Denison—who invited us to call her simply Ruth—participated in every detail of our experience. She rearranged our pillows and told us where to sit, she wrangled with the cook in the kitchen, complained when chores were not properly executed, sent people off to do errands or perform special manual tasks. She was everywhere at all times. At night the lamp in the little hut where she stayed would glow until dawn's light etched the distant mountains. And at the morning sitting she would arrive fresh and demanding, sweeping in in her long skirt adapted from the one worn by Zen monks, her blouse with its flowing sleeves, her little cap covering her hair.

In the tiny meditation hall, which Ruth called the *zendo,* echoing her many years of Japanese Zen training, we sat on pillows, practically knee to knee, while she taught us to pay attention to our breath. Then, in long concentrated sessions, she directed our attention to the sensations of the body, her guidance so precise and subtle that I perceived my physical being as I never had before. And then when it all felt too intense to bear, she would take us out into the desert to dance in a circle, honoring blue misty mountains far away at the horizon and flawless sky above. Or she told convoluted stories about her adventures with the desert creatures, which sometimes left us gasping with laughter, or about how this place called Dhamma Dena had been established. Or she spoke of Dharma, the teachings of Buddhism, which she said were very precious to her, and her eyes filled with tears.

One day she explained the reason for our meditation. Seated in front of the group of women, she leaned toward us with great urgency.

"We practice," she said, "to reduce the compulsiveness of our minds. We come to the body sensations, hmm? And what happens? We contact our root, our life force. Yah, we are holding the mind *here* where life unfolds, we train the mind to become quiet, we take away its noodlings so it has more ability to see and begin to understand." She opened both hands toward us, and her voice softened, "You see, my dear sisters, we come in this way to know ourselves, we touch our joys and our sorrows, we see those troublesome habits that run us raggedy. It is to our whole unfolding that we want to be present—yah, to all that we are experiencing right now, right here—and then is reestablished the natural order of the mind."

The natural order of the mind eluded me at that retreat. I was struggling with a body that did not want to sit still, with a mind that kept slithering away from the task at hand, with a rebellious spirit that did not want to be told what to do at every moment by this insistent German woman. Nevertheless, I sensed what was being offered to me. Ruth, through her instruction, led me to a profound contact with my physical/mental being; perhaps only as a child had I been so alive to every moment of my existence. At some points during that retreat, my attention to my actual living experience opened me to moments of transcendent clarity and peace. I became very excited as I began to understand that I could learn to live from *that* place in myself rather than fall back into the conceptual, distracted mind-state that generally ruled me. Ruth offered practices to achieve this consciousness, but I had had enough experience of my resistance and struggle at the retreat to know that I would have trouble performing them in my daily life. Could I do this thing? Could I learn to sit still and investigate my body/mind, in the search for awareness? Could I learn to bring my attentiveness to my every action? I was gripped by the ardor of knowing that I wanted to take on this task. I had no idea this was the beginning of a twenty-year practice and relationship. And I did not realize that I had had the great luck to find an absolutely authentic, deep, unique teacher of how to live.

• • •

Now in Las Vegas House in 2003, the phone rings, and we are back in the constant activity and interruptions of Ruth's daily life. Ruth jumps up to answer the call, and I lurch forward to unclip the mike from her collar before she hurries across the room to the telephone.

Listening to the voice at the other end, she lifts her hand. "Yah, Seimi, I called you to go to the airport to pick up. . . ."

Seimi is a man who has lived in and around Dhamma Dena since the seventies and who often does favors for Ruth. I know that she is asking him to pick up a Buddhist nun, and that he is objecting because the traveler insists on maintaining the rule that a Theravada nun cannot be alone with a person of the opposite sex.

Ruth's face wrinkles impishly. "No, Seimi, I have the solution! You can wear a wig and a dress. I have both here for you."

Now she is smiling outright, as Seimi apparently objects.

Ruth tells him, "Well, Henry always wanted to do that."

When she gets off the phone, she has not convinced Seimi, and comes back to the table chuckling.

"Yah," she says in mock objection, "it's true. Henry sometimes said he wanted to try dressing up as a woman."

Her husband was a patrician, bearded fellow who stood at least six feet four inches tall. Imagining him in dress and wig sends us both off into giggles. Henry and Ruth were married for forty years, their union a crucial element in Ruth's spiritual development. Henry had been a difficult man, by turns supportive and denigrating, charming and sarcastic, kind and cruel. It was he who first took her to Asia, where she connected with her spiritual teacher, and through him she encountered many other teachers. Throughout their relationship, Ruth never forgot the gifts Henry brought to her.

I get up to go to the bathroom and come back to find Ruth washing dishes at the sink. "Are you hungry, dahling? Do you want lunch?"

When I tell her I've brought my lunch of peanut butter sandwich and an apple with me from Dukkha House, she protests.

"I would have *made* you lunch. I have a nice avocado here. And some cheese."

Now I remember how important it is for her to nurture and serve her guests. I had brought the sandwich because some days we become so caught up in stories that Ruth completely forgets to eat, and I feel embarrassed to mention my own hunger. Now I am uncertain.

"Peanut butter!" she scoffs. "That is for breakfast only!"

"Okay," I agree, "I'll have a little avocado."

Preparing the food, she is reminded of a big "puja party" she and Henry hosted in the Hollywood house for Lama Govinda. (*Puja* is a Hindu prayer ritual.) Lama Govinda was a German-born seer whom they had studied with during an extended visit in Almora, a "hill station" in the foothills of the Himalayas in India. In 1971 Lama Govinda made a journey to the United States and Canada, and was hosted by

Henry and Ruth. It is the menu at the party that interests her, as she tells the story of a culinary coup.

"We had the fire in the fireplace, and he would give his sermons, hmm? I would always provide a nice little dinner. I had a very special dish that everybody was raving about, because it was green, it was cold, it was almost jelled. Here is how I made it. There was a party before, probably a big party, and there was leftover lettuce that was limpy and drowned in the dressing. Somebody helped me. I said, 'No don't throw it away, just put it all into one bowl and I will put it in the refrigerator.'"

Ruth is famous for her frugality. To one who suffered through the near-starvation of postwar German life, wasting food is sacrilegious. I wonder what is coming.

"Then next day I look at my bowl of leftover salad. You cannot serve that, but there is good stuff in it, you know, beautiful dressing, and nuts were in it. It wasn't foul, only limpy. I look around and there I see my blender. I brought the two together. I took the bowl out and put it in that apparatus, hmm? Pushed the button and it was grinding and blending. And out came a beautiful fresh light-green substance, like chocolate pudding cooked but not chilled yet. So I took two of my most elegant small crystal bowls and put it in, and put them in the refrigerator.

"In the evening, my party saw that on the table were two green bowls, a very special dish. Now they get the crackers and cheese and they start taking this, and they ask '*What* is this? *What* is this? Can you give us the recipe?' Well, I said, 'I think I put a little green spinach in, maybe I had some. I really cannot give you that recipe, it's quite a complicated thing, you know the French recipes.' Anyway, this was the big thing of the night. It was the *purée la verte, à la Française*. And they had a great time."

She brings me half an avocado and a lemon slice.

"Do you want bread, dahling?"

As we eat, we hear on the roof above us the first pats of raindrops, increasing to a steady drumming.

Ruth is ecstatic. "What a divine thing! We will have a big desert!"

She means that the high-desert foliage will put out new green leaves, and that delicate wildflowers in yellow and pink and white will dot the sandy soil.

Soon Jim arrives. He is a meditator staying here for six months before he leaves for India. They go to look at the sagging door. Standing just inside, out of the rain, they engage in a lengthy discussion of how to fix it, although Ruth has decided Jim should wait until the rain stops to do the work. This they disagree on, as he would just as soon work in the wet, but she prevails.

Seated at the table, I look at the end of this dining room that was Henry's place during his dying. A wood stove with black stovepipe dominates the corner, flanked by a standing Buddha on a table; before the window stands Henry's big black contour chair. Entering the house during those five-and-a-half years of his decline, having made one's way past the yapping dogs, one always found him sitting here. His mind had begun unraveling, until he was only intermittently present. Ruth encouraged people to come talk with him, because the contact kept him more alert. So I would sit across from Henry, a thin handsome man in pajamas, whose stillness and noble bearded head gave him the look of some dignified ancestor, and try to hold a conversation. Though much diminished, Henry still expressed the range of his contradictory character, at one moment warmly gracious—"It's so kind of you to come visit me," he would say, his eyes gentle and friendly—at the next, coldly contemptuous, after I had used some trite phrase such as "To tell the truth." "Well I would *hope* you are telling the truth—or else you must be lying," he would say, his eyes shooting me an icy challenge, and I would be left speechless.

Each foray into conversation had to be led by me, as Henry's attention span allowed for only one exchange, so our communication consisted of my questions or assertions and his responses, followed by silence while he stared at me with sometimes fierce, sometimes puzzled or distracted eyes. But no matter how difficult our half-hour had been—and no matter how withering Henry's sarcasm still was—I always hugged him and gave him a kiss before I left. He was, after all, still Henry, the man Ruth had adored and struggled with for forty years.

She returns from the back of the house. "I sent Jim away," she tells me. "He should not do that work in the rain." She sits down at the table again, and I reach for the mike to clip it on her. "He's a good one, you know."

Most of the work of the building, repairing, and maintaining of this meditation center over the years has been accomplished by visitors like Jim, who work off their room and board by laboring.

"He's fixed up that trailer in my backyard. Dahling, it will be wonderful when I am old and creaky. Someone can live there and help me out. Have you looked at it?"

I wonder if there really will come a time when Ruth cannot manage her high-energy life and will become dependent on the care of those around her. I can fall into the habit of thinking of her as she was in her fifties and sixties, always vigorous and strong, never tired. But she has confided in me that sometimes now she feels weary and wants to simplify her life. And there are moments when I am confronted with her physical fragility: at one retreat I took her to the emergency room. Working with scavenged bedclothes, she had picked up scabies and had to be treated for the resulting sores. When we came back to Las Vegas House, I offered to help her apply the healing lotion to those places she couldn't reach. Seeing her without her clothes, I was momentarily taken aback by the vulnerability of her slender, soft, old-woman's body, and I realized that despite her relentless energy, she is becoming more frail and transparent as she ages.

But Ruth returns me to the here and now, describing the remodeled trailer parked against the fence behind her house. The grounds of Dhamma Dena are dotted with house trailers, large and small, among the houses. Ruth has acquired them over the years, drafted retreatants to clean them out, furnished them with beds and chairs from Goodwill, lamps and fittings scavenged from trash night in Hollywood or brought from her own Hollywood house, and has made dormitory space and small private accommodations for special guests.

"The air conditioner, dahling, it was going to cost me a *fortune* to get it fixed up and attached! Jim drove up to San Francisco and bought materials at a place he knew there and did it for practically nothing. He is good. And he does things his own way—I can't tell him how."

"Maybe it's time to break," I suggest.

"Yah, maybe. . . ." She glances around the room, and I know she is identifying the plethora of tasks that will engage her for the rest of the afternoon.

"But maybe one more story?" I ask.

"Dahling, I don't know."

"How about the baby opossums?"

Ruth smiles. "Oh, you like that? Do you know there are two opossum stories?"

"Well I remember the one about the babies that you fed with an eyedropper."

She tilts her head coquettishly at me. "This is the other one!"

And I settle back to hear about this time when Ruth was still living in the Hollywood house.

"I saw him injured on the road, a young one. He was injured in his mouth. The lower jaw was pushed in the opposite direction of the upper, and it was like a cross there, he couldn't eat. And he would always go—" She makes a raspy, gasping sound. "So I picked him up and brought him to our house, and put him into the bottom of the shower, just to confine him and keep him safe. Then I began to feed him a little bit with mashed banana on my finger and put it in his mouth. Somehow his mouth kind of adjusted itself a little bit, by me doing this. And he became my pet.

"I was again alone. Henry was gone."

Henry was a seeker, who traveled the world searching for spiritual awareness. Often Ruth accompanied him, but sometimes she was left behind. Luckily she found a great deal to occupy her at home.

"I would sit at the table at breakfast and would have the 'possum. He is a nocturnal animal, he doesn't do much in the day, hmm? I would give him a piece of banana, but he would hardly eat anything because it was daylight.

"So then I put him on my shoulder, and I would do my porridge or what I was doing in the kitchen. I stand there and stir my soup or so, and he sits here on my shoulder, then he goes down along my arm with which I stir. I say, 'Oh! He falls down!'"

"In the soup?" I ask, and she laughs.

"No. Before it. But he *didn't* fall. He was hanging. He thought my arm was a branch. He has this long prehensile tail, and naked, it has no fur. So he was hanging there." She stands up to demonstrate stirring with an opossum on her arm. "Then I think I went to the table again and put him up there, and he crawled back onto me. So I walked with him in my house. And he was sitting on my shoulders in the day. No danger.

"Then I wanted a picture to send to Henry—I think he was gone for a year that time. So I dress up in my finery. I go to the photographer, and I hold the 'possum here on my arm once, and once he was on my neck. It gave me an idea. I thought, 'It is like a fur collar.' I let him rest there.

"I go to the car and he stays around my neck. But I want to go to the post office. He was quiet. It was daylight. Lo and behold, I advanced into the post office lobby. I held him with his tail here a little bit, but he was slummering, the eyes closed, he felt good there. I stand in line." We crack up, chortling, as I imagine the scene. "I stepped forward, and behind me were many people. And as I communicate with the one in front of me, the 'possum started moving. And they just *go!* The one before me turned around because the one behind me screamed. So I was suddenly the first one, and they were all around me!"

She gives herself up to laughter.

"But you know, dahling, everyone had fun at the end. And admired that perhaps, hmm?

"So I came home. First I brought some hay in at the bottom of the shower, so when I went on the toilet, opposite was the shower door, I opened it and talked to him. Or I would take him on the table and he eats his bananas and nuts, and he had a great time. Also in the bathtub I put him, and my student Elizabeth had an adopted child from Cambodia, a four- or five-year-old one. He liked to be in the bathtub with that baby. No water there."

We hear the renewed pulsing of rain on the roof, a loud enclosing sound.

"Wonderful!" she exclaims. "Yah, that will give a boost for the desert again."

"That's a great story," I say.

"It's not finished!" she tells me.

"So now finally I thought, he can eat, I started feeding him a little bit from outside, leaves and so on. I decided he has to be going back to nature. So, we had a gardener at that time, and the gardener built a box for me, the walls with wire, and a door in it. The wire gave him the feeling of the outside. I would sit him out on the hillside in the wire cage, and left it out a few days. Brought him the material he would eat. He had to eat outside, I stopped all the finery. And I began also to read about them and their habits, and so on.

"Then one day I opened the door. The first night he didn't go out. The second he was gone. Yah."

She looks at me with great satisfaction.

Darkness is entering the room from the storm outside. It's almost 5:00 p.m. already. I ask if it's time to stop now. But she is thinking of that hillside behind the Hollywood house, seeing it in her mind.

"You know it was wild when I first came there to Henry's house. They had made a big sign on the hills, fifty dollars reward for shooting a mountain lion. Yah. And deers were there, coming in our garden.

"You see, I fed the coyotes there in Hollywood too, just like I do here in the desert. I would carry down the bucket and had made steps in the hillside. One Zen *roshi* [head Zen teacher], the one who gave me the name Myodo—*myodo* means 'the bright way'—that roshi came down with me to see where I fed the coyotes, and he wrote about it in one of his newsletters. He was fascinated by my doing what I did, feeding them."

Another burst of sound beats at the roof. Ruth is delighted.

"Oh, that rain!"

Later she drives me in her old green Pontiac station wagon like a ponderous hearse, back to Dukkha House, while rain slashes across the windshield, bending the creosote bushes, soaking the earth.

Seated in Dukkha House, watching the downpour from a window, I smile at the rescue of the opossum. This tale speaks so strongly of Ruth's attitude to life. This is what she teaches: not to carelessly do the usual, conventional thing, but to see deeply into each situation and act to support and encourage living beings. First Ruth allowed herself to feel the suffering of the injured animal; then, instead of passing by or dropping it at an animal center, she gave her time, attention, and caring to nurse it back to health. And she did so with her eccentric imagination and humor. Every day, every moment, Ruth involves herself intimately with the whole complex web of life.

PART I

The Good Girl:
The German Years

CHAPTER TWO

First Inklings

To know Ruth, one has to start at the beginning of her life, in that place that so shaped her and determined her path: Germany. Even in her eighties, after living in the United States for over four decades, Ruth embodies certain traditional German values. Although she has spent months and years traveling and living in Asian cultures, practicing an Asian-based spirituality, Ruth resembles most strongly the German women of her generation. She insists on cleanliness and order; she holds strong opinions and expresses them forcefully; she believes in authority and respect for the teacher; she labors ceaselessly and expects others to do likewise; she respects efficiency and productivity. The foundation of her personality was laid in the land of her birth, and this structure underlies her approach to everything in life.

Beginning to think of telling Ruth's story, I was eager to follow the threads of her attitudes and capacities back to their source, to identify the roots of so much that has proved both inspiring, endearing, and difficult for me during my years of following and trying to apply her teachings. I surmised that her contradictions, the seeming paradoxes expressed in her life, had been prepared in the soil of her childhood and early adulthood. I realized I would have to immerse myself in histories of the Germany of the Second World War and before. Ruth herself had told many stories set in the land where she grew up, some of them mysterious or disturbing, and I knew I needed to discover a larger context into which to place those experiences.

Ruth was born in 1922, just after the First World War. Accounts of that period portray a Germany deeply scarred by the losses and humiliations of its defeat. But Ruth herself, as she grew from infancy into childhood, would have inhabited a more optimistic world, for, in the decade after the treaty that ended the war, German industrialists began to reopen their factories and create jobs, commerce thrived, and the country restored itself to prosperity. The Weimar Republic, established after the war, offered opportunities for creativity and freedom that spawned a liberal intelligentsia in Germany, which gave rise to striking achievements in literature, pictorial art, theater, and film. The republic also abolished restrictions on Jews, allowing them to participate in every sphere of public life.

East Prussia, where Ruth was born and spent her young life, was a region somewhat isolated and set apart from the rapid progress of the rest of the country. East Prussia was the northeasternmost province of Germany, separated from the rest of Germany by the Polish Corridor, a strip of land controlled by Poland. While it was politically and culturally part of Germany, geographically East Prussia floated like an island in a Polish sea. A near feudal economy still thrived in this remote province, where there were two categories of people, the gentry and those who worked for them. Ruth's father, Hermann Schaefer, had returned there after his service in the war, and become a Gartenmeister, who tended the gardens, greenhouses, and grounds of a feudal lord. Hermann married, and on September 29, 1922, his wife, Elisabeth, gave birth to their first child, whom they named Ruth Elisabeth. Three more children were to arrive in the next four years.

As Ruth told me her stories of childhood, I began to form a picture of a bucolic life, in which her father moved the family to a neighboring village and a farm of his own. There he specialized in the cultivation of vegetables and fruit trees, growing greenhouse vegetables to sell in wintertime, and hitching their two horses to the wagon to take produce to sell at market in the town. At home, her mother worked as a dressmaker, designing clothes for the neighbors and also sewing dresses for her three little daughters, shirts for her son.

Their home was a peaceful, industrious farm environment, where Ruth grew into a healthy toddler. After a short, painful, and temporarily crippling bout with infantile paralysis, she grew up running in the fields and meadows surrounding their farm, swimming in a lake with other children—and she learned to work hard in house and garden. Her mother told Ruth she was a "good girl," not like little sister Chrystel, who sometimes opposed her mother and refused to do as she was told. This mother, whom they called *Mutti*, was the dominant force in the house. Playful and enthusiastic on the one hand, dynamic, strict, and demanding on the other, she meted out swift and sometimes physical punishment for mistakes and disobedience.

Ruth developed an early relationship to God, whom she understood to reside up in the sky, and she reports feeling light, open, and joyful as she went about her duties, believing that by working hard she was "pleasing the Lord." Her mother would take the children to the Lutheran church in the village, but Ruth learned much of what she knew about God and Jesus in school. For an hour most mornings the teacher taught religion. Ruth was strongly impressed by the pictures of Biblical scenes, Christ and his disciples, camels and desert tents beside the Dead Sea.

But at church she sometimes questioned the teachings, oddly convinced that she knew something more than the minister. This conviction of "knowing more" was to recur in other spiritual and more mundane settings. I wonder, now, if it came from a deep spiritual inkling in her, a connection to truth more personal and authentic than the traditional liturgy of the Lutheran church could offer her. In later life, her absolute conviction that she was right about something (and that, by implication, others were wrong) could be immensely annoying.

On the other hand, her sense of seeing deeply into a situation and knowing what was needed often guided her in wonderfully decisive actions that benefited those around her.

Her spirituality was strongly grounded in the natural world of earth, animals, and birds. She fed the farm animals, fascinated by their behavior, and learned to love dogs. She herded the village cows, bravely enduring thunderstorms to tend them; left by herself in the meadow, she prayed when she became lonely or frightened. Immersed in nature, she imagined a broader world. On beautiful afternoons, when her chores were done, she would go into the wheat fields, where blue cornflowers nestled among the wheat stems. She would make a pathway through the grain to the center of the field. Lying down, she would look up into the sky, listen to the rustlings of the breeze in the wheat and the chatter of busy insects, and imagine the vast world beyond the confines of her Prussian village. Someday, she promised herself, she would go out to explore that world.

In the village Ruth was known as *die goldene Mitte* ("the golden center," or "happy medium") because she could play with the boys—swimming and climbing trees, joining them in their adventures—and she could get along equally well with the girls in their games. At home, she was the peacemaker. I wonder if Ruth learned to be careful and to accommodate others as a way to survive in her family, where strict discipline was often imposed from above, and self-control was required. She discovered as a small child that to get what she wanted, she had to step back, secretly plan, and manipulate others, rather than just ask for it. This training allowed her to survive difficult situations during the war and after, and later helped her navigate the sometimes choppy waters of her marriage to Henry.

Ruth's parents approached life very differently. As Ruth describes it, "My mom was a little overly on the making-business side. My father had the other side. He was a quiet and beautiful worker. He had softness." In speaking of her parents, Ruth always takes care to point out that she was close to both of them and that in the family "there was never anything absolute and constantly the same, there was a great resilience in it. And when I did wrong like with Mama and she beat or just scolded me, I would right away turn around and do something to reconcile, without saying anything. I became suddenly the good girl again, yah?

"Mutti was tough sometimes," she admits, and recalls the times when her mother would lock the door and beat all four children with a leather belt, leaving them bruised and shaken. But Ruth defends her mother, accepting the blame. "Sometimes we were very nasty, we would steal money from her and buy chocolate and things like that, and would not do our job: once were seven little gooses killed because we let them out in the rain. So it was really bad things we children did." She adds that her mother beat them with the belt on only two occasions.

Frau Schaefer's model for child raising corresponded to the form generally employed in German homes at that time. The psychologist Alice Miller discusses the pressures on a German child of Ruth's generation, noting that obedience was thought to be the preeminent quality in a child during Ruth's growing up. An early German instruction manual states: "Obedience is so important that all education is actually nothing other than learning how to obey."[2] Children were taught to view physical punishment as a necessary measure against wrongdoers, including themselves. (This pedagogy fed neatly into fascism, and as late as 1979, when fascism was being decried by Germany, two-thirds of the German population still declared themselves in favor of corporal punishment of children.) Children learned to be harsh toward themselves and to rationalize and make excuses for the harshness of their parents.

Ruth had a close and complex relationship with her mother. As the oldest daughter, she most resembled her, inheriting her mother's extraordinary energy and appetite for work, her perfectionism. She deeply loved and respected Mutti (who lived into her nineties and remained part of Ruth's life until the end). When speaking of Mutti's strictness, Ruth always hastened to describe more attractive aspects of her mother's character, like her imagination and love of fun, and to assert how hard her mother worked, sitting up all night sewing for her children.

Perhaps wanting to lighten his wife's burden, Herr Schaefer would ask her, when she was sewing clothes for the children, "Why do you do that, do you think they are worth that? Why do they have to have fancy clothes? Give them a potato sack, it would do just as well."

The upbringing Ruth describes seems fraught with contradictions. How confusing it must have been to have a mother who stayed up all night to dress her children elegantly, yet punished them so harshly for their mistakes, and a gentle, affectionate father who sometimes spoke disparagingly about his children. How does one navigate such an unpredictable environment, which says, on the one hand, "You are a precious child," and on the other, "You are bad and undeserving"? Ruth's response seems to have been to repay punishment with kindness. She was concerned to knit up the torn fabric of family life, to melt the coldness into warmth. As her mother observed, in criticism of her, Ruth was willing to give up her "pride," her proper respect for herself, her sense of her own worth, in order to maintain her closeness with others.

Ruth would continue to operate this way as she grew to womanhood, and at times this capacity to look at the larger picture, instead of demanding justice or taking revenge, may have protected her and even saved her life. And certainly it corresponded with the Buddhist perspective, which views all events as simply the result of impersonal conditions, and extends compassion to all. But what did she do with her anger at being so severely disciplined? Perhaps it came out later in the harsh directiveness that Ruth occasionally displays.

• • •

In 1929 the economy of the United States collapsed in the Great Depression. The German economy was very closely tied to that of the United States, partly because the German government had borrowed massively from Wall Street to help finance its postwar reconstruction projects and make reparations to the countries it had devastated in the

First World War. After the Great Crash of 1929, U.S. banks did not renew the loans. The recipient countries suffered and could not pay their debts, worsening worldwide depression. German unemployment rose and industry slowed. Before 1929 the United States had been producing over 40 percent of the world's manufacturing goods; when American producers cut back on their purchases of raw materials and other supplies, the effect on European countries was devastating. High U.S. tariffs hampered world trade as well.

Germany was the worst-hit European country. In 1931 the German banking system crumbled, and the next year, unemployment in Germany approached 40 percent. The government lowered the salaries of civil servants, decreased unemployment assistance, and raised taxes. Resistance to this opened the door to extremist political parties, including the National Socialists. Political instability increased, paving the way for Hitler's takeover of power. Plunged into poverty and frustration, looking for someone to blame, and goaded by their leaders, the German people began to attribute their misfortunes to the Jewish population. Ruth remembers hearing that a neighbor family had lost their farm because they were unable to make payments to the "Jewish bankers." The Jews became a convenient scapegoat—they were blamed for the downturn of the economy, for any and all social problems.

Hitler offered relief to the German workers: employment, housing, even paid vacation excursions. After he came to power in 1933, he built the autobahn, a magnificent freeway linking all of Germany. He ordered the production of the Volkswagen, a car for the *volk*, the common people. While Hitler and his National Socialist party were making such promises, they also imprisoned or murdered their critics, ensuring their own rise to dominance.

Reading about the Third Reich, I realized that all the previous accounts of that time that I had seen were produced by American historians or journalists, or by Jewish writers and filmmakers whose emphasis, understandably, was the Holocaust. What I wanted to find were histories written by Germans, from *inside* the Nazi regime, for this had been Ruth's family's experience. They were ordinary Germans of "Aryan" descent who did not espouse views opposing the government. They were trying to be good citizens of the German State, to work and raise their children and go on with their lives, just as the general population of any country is usually doing. This daily existence is what I sought to uncover, for I could imagine that during the early Nazi period, life must have gone on essentially as usual for most German people, particularly those who did not live in the major cities, where resistance to Hitler chiefly originated.

I found that the vast majority of German citizens approved of the policies of the National Socialist party. Ruth's father, learning about Hitler's social programs, witnessing how the workers' suffering was eased, joined the Nazi party. (One of the few photographs Ruth retains from her young life depicts Hermann Schaefer sporting a postage-stamp mustache like Hitler's.) The whole town of Wittenwalde, in which they lived, supported the Third Reich. Ruth's schoolteacher became, as she says, "150 percent Nazi." In the school, now, classes in religion were replaced by study of the Führer's life and ideas.

The period between the ascendance of Hitler and the beginning of war in 1939 spanned Ruth's eleventh to seventeenth years. During that time, for Ruth, in most ways, daily life went on as before. She helped her mother make flower arrangements for weddings, funerals, and other celebrations, for their own village and those nearby. In the autumn the countryside celebrated the Day of the Dead, for which the Schaefers made nearly a thousand wreaths. Ruth remembers, "While I worked, I felt connected, yah, to the dead people, the ones who would get these wreaths. I saw the funeral grounds, the graves and the tombstones."

When one of Ruth's schoolmates died, the Schaefers received an order for a wreath for her. "I helped my Mutti make the wreath, and I saw my dead schoolmate in my mind. Then I went with my brother to deliver it. We took it to her house, and I asked to see her. I wasn't afraid of death. I could stand there and breathe the cool air and the smell of death." Perhaps Ruth could be so easy with this reality because of her intimacy with the world of animals and plants, where she witnessed the continual transformations of birth, growth, maturity, and death. As a young girl, Ruth also was drawn to biographies of saints, and liked to read German Romantic poetry, which often glorified death, venerated nature, and drew upon the ancient Teutonic myths co-opted by the Nazis.

In elementary school, Ruth and the other children were indoctrinated with tales of Nazi leaders who had died for the cause. Propaganda about the childhood and youth of Adolph Hitler was taught to them: how he had studied and worked hard, how he had developed compassion for the working class. And they absorbed the vicious anti-Semitism that portrayed Jews as evil money-grabbers who forced the German farmers into slavery and plotted to conquer the world. The Nazi schoolteacher took his charges to the church on Sunday, where they stood outside during the service and loudly sang Nazi songs, drowning out the Christian hymns being sung inside. Ruth's mother—nowhere near as convinced of Nazi goodness as her husband—objected to this disrespect for religion.

Ruth herself eagerly joined the Hitler Youth group for girls. Since my early days as her student, this information had made me uncomfortable; now I wanted to know what Ruth felt as a young German girl participating in this mass movement, and what could have been her rationale for taking part in something that, from the outside, appeared patently evil.

I listened carefully to Ruth as she told me that she loved the comradeship and the healthy athleticism. "Now we didn't have religious services, but hiking and swimming and sports and dances we did." And she loved the ritual. "We brought back alive the ancient customs, we would go out and imitate them. Once we took big wooden disks to the top of the mountain at night. Probably they had swastikas painted on them. We set them on fire and rolled them down, always singing. It was very mystical for us."

Ruth's early religious beliefs now became supplanted by her Nazi rituals.

"What I had found in Christianity as a child, now I would find in the youth club called *Glauben und Schönheit,* that was my religion now, the ideology of the Third Reich. It means 'Belief and Beauty.' That group was for the fifteen- and sixteen-year-olds. It was so good, a real beautiful experience. And then 'In a beautiful body we can give birth to a beautiful mind.' But that beautiful mind was always directed to believing in the Third Reich, in the goodness of it. Well, and they did pay attention to the poor people; the feudals had to give part of their land away on which there were built now beautiful little houses with bathrooms instead of huts with little outhouses behind. That had to be done. And also for the other workers."

Her father's support of the party made sense to her. "He was helping those little groups to bring Hitler in, because it looked very good. Germany was in a depression, was really down, the land didn't belong to the farmers, all to the banks and finance magnates. And the people were enslaved under the feudal system. My father would make an advertisement to get an apprentice for the horticulture, and he would get 80 to 120 applications.

"Don't forget, it was a labor party, it wasn't just this idea of ruling. *Nationale sozialistiche Arbeiter partei* [National Socialist Workers Party]. *Arbeiter* means laborer. Hitler promised for the workers new homes. They lived twelve kids, sixteen kids in one room, being slaves. He took them out of that. There were built nice houses, like tract houses, for these people. He made a revolution with that, giving space and decent living and joy for the workers who are the base of a nation, so naturally he won. That was the big front. I don't think he was from the beginning so crazy. For us human beings they offered beautiful things. He gave us these exercises and these rituals, at summer solstice and winter solstice, and told us what the ancestors did and so on. Now we got Saturday free, and we could play in the school. We made exercises to let the mind come in, in a healthy body. It was very touching and beautiful. Can you understand that we liked it? We were nothing before."

From all accounts of those years before the war, it appears that these sentiments were widespread in Germany, where almost every young non-Jewish person belonged to the Hitler Youth. The lure of community, of sports, and of the great spectacles—the rallies and athletic events organized by the Nazis and carried out with vivid energy and dramatic flair—drew the young people and gave a sense of meaning to their lives. On the other hand, young Germans were often coerced into membership. If they did not join, they were viewed as dissenters and were ostracized. Sometimes a father was told he would lose his job if his child refused membership in the Hitler Youth.

But for those who joined willingly, participation in this movement offered many rewards. Again and again in histories and interviews, women of Ruth's age speak of having been enthralled and enlivened by the Hitler Youth.

In an account of his mother's life, Peter Handke describes her experience of the Third Reich.

"We were kind of excited," my mother told me. For the first time, people did things together. Even the daily grind took on a festive mood, "until late into the night." For once everything that was strange and incomprehensible in the world took on meaning and became part of a larger context.

All at once you had so many friends and there was so much going on that it became possible to *forget* something. She had always wanted to be proud of something, and now, because what she was doing was somehow important, she actually was proud, not of anything in particular, but in general—a state of mind, a newly attained awareness of being alive—and she was determined never to give up that vague pride.

He points out that she had no interest in politics. "What was happening before her eyes was something entirely different from politics—a masquerade, a newsreel festival, a secular church fair. . . . Pomp and ceremony on all sides."[3]

It was this spirit that swept Ruth up.[4] She describes a sports festival in a big city plaza. Each town sent a team, and Ruth—the girl who had not been able to walk when she had infantile paralysis as a little child—won third place in running. The square was festooned with flowers, the young people performed ancient dances in lines and circles. They sang the grim, stirring songs of the elite SS troops: "Morning sun, morning sun/Giving your light again/Light my way to my early death." Ruth can still sing this song. She says they had created a "sacred place, because everyone is there for the same purpose. The sacredness of your own culture you felt, you sensed your own abilities. It was just the right thing to do. It was so convincing."

Hearing about this, I can imagine the exuberance that Ruth felt, even though this youth movement formed part of the agenda of a madman who led the German people into a disastrous war of conquest and the horror of genocide. As a child Ruth had not been taught to question authority or to approach things from an inquiring, rational perspective. As she had accepted the authority of her parents and schoolmasters, she accepted the "rightness" of the Nazi philosophy.

While her Hitler Youth participation was important to Ruth, she had other, more literary and spiritual interests. By age sixteen or seventeen she loved to read the biographies of Catholic nuns. The story of the sixteenth-century Spanish Carmelite nun Teresa of Avila gripped her. "She impressed me that she was a lady of nobility, and could go down and enter the life that had such hardship and constant sacrifice. Never was *she* in the center for her concern, it was always outside of her." Ruth read the stories of Teresa's walking from convent to convent, pulling a little cart behind her with all her belongings on it, refusing help. Then Ruth found Teresa's famous *Confessions*. "This was actually indicating her progression toward her closeness or unification with God—that's the way I understood it. That intrigued me."

And she loved to read the romantic work of Friedrich Hölderlin, the eighteenth-century poet who, before slipping into insanity at age thirty-six, had produced the kind of lofty yet subjective poetry that would appeal to a spiritually inclined young woman. Hölderlin led her to be aware of what she calls the "numina." "Yah, I would take that book of poetry and go for a walk, and would read it, then I get a wider view when I look up. Then I saw the numina—that is, what is not visible in the phenomenal world. The numina is that what you see beyond the appearance. I didn't know it that way, but I felt it.

"And I also wanted to die when I was in disaccord with the family, which was very seldom. I would go into the fields where there is a kind of indentation, where nobody saw me, and I would maybe pray. I wanted either to go to a convent or to die."

Ruth laughs at the romantic young girl she had been. "You see, you make your own world."

One member of Ruth's family had not been swept up in Nazi enthusiasm. Ruth's Mutti remained cool, and in at least one instance she risked her safety to express her disapproval. All but one of the shops in the village were run by Jews, and Frau Schaefer had made friends with the shop owners. "Frau Kellerman was her ideal," Ruth reports. "And Frau Hirschfield. Well, they had good stores! And Mutti had four children, so every year we got a new set of clothes, not ready-made but she bought the material to make the clothes, and so on, in their shops. When she went in the Hirschfield shop, he would come personally and say, 'Frau Schaefer, what can I do for you?' We were good customers."

At the street market across from the shops in the square, Ruth's mother had a big stall where she sold vegetables, flowers, and wreaths. After school each day, Ruth would come on her bicycle to tend the stall for her mother and earn a quarter. One day her mother told her to "Watch the cash. I go across to Frau Kellerman," a big fabric shop.

Ruth watched her mother cross the square toward the shop, but saw her stop on the sidewalk before the door. Her way was blocked by a man brandishing a placard—DON'T BUY FROM JEWS. Ruth saw her mother meet the man's stare, lift both arms, and say so distinctly that Ruth could hear every word, *"Juden sind auch Menschen!"*—Jews are human beings too! Then she walked around the man and entered the store. When she came out later, bearing her purchases, the man with the placard took her picture. "They photographed her," Ruth explains. "They would hang now on the big board the pictures of those who are favoring something that was not approved by the Nazis. Later it could result that she goes to prison, or to the camps. But at that time they didn't do too much with her. It was before the war had started. It wasn't that strong yet.

"I argued with her. I said, 'Mutti, you don't understand, the Jews did this and that, they have taken over everything'—all what I learned in school about them. But she didn't believe me. She felt it wasn't right." There were social consequences to Frau Schaefer's action. Shortly after her visit to Frau Kellerman's store, she was asked to resign from the *Frauenverein* (Women's Association), which she had joined at the invitation of the minister's wife. "They told her she didn't belong anymore," Ruth says.

One morning after Frau Schaefer's confrontation in the village square, she arrived at her booth to find that the Jewish shops now had gentile names. When she went to investigate, she discovered that the Jewish shopkeepers and their families had disappeared. She could find out nothing about this departure, and finally speculated that the Kellermans and Hirschfields had decided to sell their shops and leave town to escape the harassment. She never found out what happened to them.

CHAPTER THREE

War Comes

When Hitler invaded Poland in 1939, Ruth was seventeen years old. She had labored so hard on the farm, working even on weekends with her mother to make the wreaths and garlands, that she decided she wanted another kind of life. She knew that the male teachers were being drafted to go off to fight on many fronts as Hitler conquered the European countries and moved into Poland and Russia. And she found out about the special classes and seminars being set up to train young girls to take over the teaching duties of the absent men. Ruth applied for the teacher training. "I wanted out," Ruth says, "and Mutti let me."

Until the end of the war, Ruth lived a life conditioned in many ways by the hostilities, yet insulated from the suffering of the victims of Nazi terror, both in other countries and her own. Her great energy and zest propelled her as she saw her opportunity and took it. In the demanding, difficult conditions of her teaching life, she worked hard and pursued her own interests, ignorant of all but the official version of her government's actions in the world. She went about her duties and pleasures with the insularity and selfishness of youth. That lack of interest in politics and world events, that exclusive focus on personal, daily life, remained Ruth's pattern for most of her life.

With her departure from home, the dispersion of the family had begun. In the next six years, caught up in the war, all four siblings and their parents would set out on chosen or forced journeys and meet with separate fates. During this first year of her escape from home, Ruth opened to a reality broader and more sophisticated than life on the farm. Besides her school experiences, she was allowed to visit her Uncle Robert, a West German city-dweller who holidayed in the Alps and "danced with elegant ladies." "I wanted that," Ruth says. "He was my model."

But by the early 1940s, Hitler was committing German troops and resources to yet more conquest, having crushed Poland, where he enslaved the population and murdered the Jews. Then he sent his troops into Russia to destroy the Russian state and subjugate the people, at great cost to the German army. In the face of this relentless grinding of war and the terrible casualties of the Russian front, the German citizens' racial pride and camaraderie began to sour. Many citizens, including Ruth's father, changed their minds about the Third Reich and passively or actively resisted the Nazi directives. Ruth herself would eventually feel betrayed by the Third Reich.

Watching the progress of the war, Ruth's father became embittered. He knew what the German soldiers were doing in Poland—crushing farmers and nobles alike, stealing land from the people—and he hated it. Because their farm was so close to the Polish border, the Schaefers saw the conquering armies on the march, and sometimes on her visits home Ruth saw them too. "When these big formations like the legions of Caesar marched by—day and night they would pass, going into Poland—he sat there and he said, 'I didn't fight for that.'"

Meanwhile Ruth had spent a year training as a teacher in Danzig, and now was sent for practicum to Grünfeld, a village in East Prussia. There she lived in the schoolhouse, teaching thirty-five to forty students in grades one through four. She liked teaching, and found she was good at it. Intrigued by the children's innocence, touched by their trust in her, she saw that she could guide and bring comfort to them. In 1942, she went back for more training and returned to the same school. But as the Russian campaign took more and more of the male teachers into the army, soon Ruth found herself alone at the school, having to teach all the grades, some of her students being boys bigger than she was. She met the challenge, and after her hard work in the schoolroom each day, still managed to have a good time fraternizing with the young officers who came to the town for training. She dated a soldier boyfriend and enjoyed her life.

Her siblings had also set out into the world. Dita, the youngest sister, had enrolled as a dental assistant in the large city of Königsburg. Chrystel had married and gone to Berlin to have her child, for reasons of safety. Heinz was drafted into the army at age seventeen, became an SS soldier, and was sent to fight on the front lines. Ruth did not see him again until after the war. She regretted her loss of contact with a brother so young. "Dahling, I went away to teacher training, far away from home. And that was now already war, don't forget. My brother was drafted in his puberty. I never saw him in uniform. He was so far away. I was teaching, and his visits home and mine were never matching."

Back in Wittenwalde, Herr Schaefer received an ultimatum. In Poland, the German soldiers had removed all the feudal owners of the estates. Now they were to be replaced by German farmers who would run the farms to feed the Third Reich. The father of one of Ruth's friends had accepted this offer and had taken his family to Poland; visiting her, Ruth got a taste of what was being offered the German farmers. "It was an estate near Warsaw, and fifty times bigger than her father's little estate in East Prussia. I visited her there because she got married to one of the high officers. That was 1943. Yah, they were in Russia fighting, and we were in Poland having this elegant, fantastic estate with carriage, four horses, we went for this wedding. And around us, everyone who had belonged to that land was pushed away or killed. We were just enjoying it, but it dawned in me that it really belonged once to the Poles."

The Agricultural Ministry ordered Ruth's father to take over and farm a similar estate in the Polish countryside, but, dismayed at the German occupation of Poland, he refused. He was blacklisted, and shortly thereafter, Herr Schaefer, at the age of fifty-five, was drafted into the German army and sent to fight at the Russian front. Given the disasters of the Russian campaign, this posting was virtually a death sentence.

Soon came the first inklings of disaster. In the early years of the war, as Ruth put it, "we were always singing and conquering." In her school-teaching job in the village of Grünfeld, she gave her best energies to her students, creating solstice celebrations and dancing with them, taking them to the forest to stage a "bird wedding." "I was schoolteacher and lived on rations but they were modest and, yah, I had my ideology, I had my lovely apartment above the schoolroom. And sometimes went back for training in the place near Danzig on the Baltic Sea. Had a beautiful time there. In the war I wasn't in the big city where they had to experience these air raids and attacks."

She could not guess the horrors of the immediate future. As the war ground on—wars actually, as the German army fought on several fronts —finally she began to have suspicions of a different reality than the official Nazi version of events. The question that inevitably arises in the case of Germans of Ruth's age is whether and what they knew of the Nazis' systematic murder of Jews. Before I asked this of Ruth, I read many answers by her contemporaries, whose discomfort sometimes led them to evade the question, contradict themselves, rationalize, and even angrily defend their own avowed ignorance.[5]

When I posed the question to Ruth, she resorted to none of these maneuvers but told me a story set in her time as a schoolteacher in the village. She had made friends with the vice mayor of the area, who was also in charge of sections of Poland. He was an intelligent man, a party member but not a wholly enthusiastic Nazi. Once he took Ruth for a holiday into Poland, to a town near Warsaw. He had a job to do there, but did not tell her what it was. He seemed distracted and troubled.

They took a walk outside the city, among big trees. The man led her through the forest to a fence, and they walked along it. Ruth describes "a big fence as high as the branches of the trees, and it was a very kind of solid wall, boarded and wire on top." As twilight crept through the trees, Ruth's friend said, "Look, Ruth, do you know what this is?" Then he told her, "Don't speak about it, it's a concentration camp." At first Ruth didn't understand, "so he explained it a little bit. But he couldn't really say much, he talked 'round about, but I knew there was something bad happening, that those were Jews inside the wall." She also knew the consequences for talking about this. "If he was speaking too loud as a *Bürgermeister* [mayor], he would be killed too, or would be on the other side of that wall."

She began, then, to be curious about events in the world, and to doubt the official Nazi version of the war. She heard about the radio station called *Freistimme,* the Free Voice. In her apartment, in the two rooms above the schoolroom, she would take her radio into bed and huddle under the blankets, because she knew it was strictly forbidden to listen. The voices on the radio reported that the German army in Russia and elsewhere was not moving forward as Nazi propaganda reported, but was being pushed back, and that defeat was inevitable.

Having read some accounts of young people in large cities who resisted the Nazis, I wondered if it might have been possible for Ruth to make efforts against the regime, and why it had not occurred to her to do so. But as I thought about it, I realized that the young resisters were living in quite different conditions. They were students who attended major universities; they were intellectuals, privileged enough socially and economically to have the aspiration and the means to take advantage of higher education. And in many cases, they were the children of parents who had rejected the Nazi ideology from its beginning. Those conditions gave them access to possibilities unknown to Ruth. She was a farmer's daughter in a small Prussian village; her father and most of the other men in the village had been ardent Nazis; her highest ambition had been to become an elementary school teacher, which required just a few years of technical training and practicum.

Yet, even within her situation, almost by instinct, and driven by kindness, she did things that brought her into conflict with the Nazi authorities and ideology. By 1943 or 1944, many Russian prisoners of war were held in small prison camps in German villages. They worked in the fields and towns to replace the Germans fighting in Russia. Such a camp existed in Grünfeld. When Ruth looked at these men, she did not see enemies but suffering human beings, and her impulse was to offer them some comfort.

"One man, it was winter and snow, his hands were cold, he was chopping the wood for my apartment above the classroom, and as he brings up the wood, I gave him a cup of hot tea and a piece of cake. But the guard must have seen me do that as he came up, because I was ordered then to come to the big supervisor. He told me *I shall not do that!* He said it was not appropriate to be friendly to the prisoners."

This is typical of the Ruth I know. She may have little reaction to an injustice done to a group of people, may be uninterested in humanizing and fleshing out the abstractions of political realities, but she responds immediately, with warmth and love, to the suffering of any person directly in front of her.

Soon German troops began to retreat over the border from the Russian front. In villages near the border, all civilians—women only, now, because the men were gone—were ordered to dig ditches in order to stop the Russian tanks that would soon appear. Russian forces were steadily pushing the German army back, and it was only a matter of time until they would come over the border.

In the little village where she was teaching, Ruth was ordered out, with the other women, handed a shovel, and told to dig. But she thought the idea that a trench could stop a tank was foolish. "I thought, it's stupid what we do, just giving us a false sense that we will succeed to defend ourselves." So she wiggled her way out of this duty. "I ran away, pretending I had done my digging. It was my inner feeling: it is stupid—we will not win!" Here is an instance in which her "knowing more" than the others, and refusing to do as she was told, could have landed her in serious trouble. But her position as schoolteacher, appreciated by the women, many of whom were mothers, may have allowed her this insubordination.

By 1944 she was convinced that Germany would lose the war. But she saw no way to resist. All around her were the signs of the desperate repression of the German populace, in which refusal to support the war brought death. "One day I saw a man hanging from a tree, and on his chest a sign saying, 'I refused to defend our Fatherland.' And when I saw how they had drafted even the old men, and the boys, I knew we were finished."

Now Ruth's insular personal world had been breached. She would soon become a refugee, running for her life, and in this new terrifying existence she would discover in herself a tremendous endurance and will to survive, no matter what it took. She would learn to scavenge, even to steal, in order to eat; she would learn to do without everything that had supported and comforted her; she would learn to go on when all seemed lost, and to persist even in the face of heartbreaking brutalities and violence. This will to survive—a flinty insistence on her presence in this life, earned at great cost—is something we recognized in Ruth as a teacher; it inspired and reassured us.

• • •

The end came soon after Ruth saw the man hanging from the tree limb. The German army had been defeated in Stalingrad in February 1943, with more than 200,000 German troops killed. The Nazis were defeated in North Africa that same year. Italy fell. Resistance groups in the occupied countries chipped away at the German forces. By early 1945, German soldiers were retreating in large numbers over the border near Grünfeld, running from the Russians. The civilians ran too, pushed by the soldiers, terrified of Polish and Russian reprisals.

In January 1945, Ruth escaped from Grünfeld, heading west in the river of travelers. As she fled she noticed the suffering all around her. "I jumped up on an open truck, military truck, and even there already people froze to death!" Ruth found herself in the middle of the great exodus westward toward Berlin. "It was a whole night and below zero, but I bit my lips and so, to stay awake. On the way we came to Elbing, where my Tante Margarete lived. My uncle and aunt had this *Speditionsgeschäft*, that means transportation business. So I packed myself onto that big chuck wagon with them. Two French prisoners were with us, from my uncle's business, we took them along."

They had killed two pigs to take with them as food. Now they entered the mob of thousands of refugees filling the crowded roads, trying to travel west. "We waited about three nights before one of the rivers to cross. There were big long lines and the military had right of way, until our turn came to cross the river with a ferry I think. It was very cold and frosty, and when you stepped upon the snow it knished [crunched], dry, frost snow. Very romantic when you have a warm room and you look out and the sunlight makes the flakes like little shining stars, hmm?

"So . . . and so . . . I walked over the river. I didn't go on the chuck wagon whilst we were transported across the river. There was a walkway for the people. And when I was there waiting for our truck to come with my uncle, my aunt—the two French prisoners they took away to help the German army—I saw my dog Rolly was hanging at the end of the car, dead. They had him tied on, and he wanted to jump out apparently, and he was on a leash. They were all sleeping, you know, and so he was dead."

In the bitter cold, it took weeks to make their way west through the Polish Corridor. But finally Ruth made it to Berlin, to the home of her mother's youngest sister, Tante Frida, who ran a bakery in the Falkensee neighborhood. Ruth's sister Chrystel was already in Berlin, but Dita, still in her teens, had disappeared. "We lost her," Ruth says. "She was lost for two years somewhere in the camps." (The Russians established work camps inside Germany for Germans.) Her brother Heinz, she would learn later, was in hiding in a dairy farm in Prussia, where the Allies never found him. Herr Schaefer, who had been fighting on the Russian front, had been captured and sent to a prison camp in Siberia. Ruth's mother had disappeared in East Prussia.

Ruth stayed in her Tante Frida's place, crammed in an upstairs room with many others, subsisting on scraps of bread from the bakery downstairs. The Allies had been bombing Berlin and other cities, and the Germans used Russian prisoners of war to attempt to clear the bombed-out buildings. Ruth has an indelible, prophetic memory from that time. With one of her aunts, a few months before the end of the war, she was riding on a streetcar through the ruined city. "We were still in the bakery, we were already refugees, and we are going in the streetcar. From its window we look down into this big mass of rubble where Russian war prisoners were there. They were sorting things out and cleaning up a little bit. I said, 'Tante Lutsi, look at it.' She was very sarcastic; she was a casino lady and had won lots of money so she dressed in a black seal fur coat. And I was so jealous of that sealskin. I would never go near a fur coat now! You see how our values change? So, Tante Lutsi sarcastically looks down at the Russian prisoners and she says, 'Look Ruth, that is us in a short while.' And I agreed. 'Yah,' I said, 'that's us. Can you imagine what we are going to do? How we will do it?' And she said, 'Better keep your mouth shut now.' You see, people knew the Russians were coming. Oh yah, at that point, yah, but still you couldn't say that."

When the Russians came close to Berlin, they were preceded by massive air strikes by the Allied Forces. The aerial bombardment of Berlin and other major cities by American and British bombers was characterized by one German historian as "nightly mass murder of civilian populations."[6] In Dresden 400,000 people, mostly women and children, were killed.[7] In Berlin the bombings and strafings became so destructive that Ruth was forced to run for her life a second time.

"That was the last three months, it was tight. Here the Russians pushed into the Polish Corridor, and they had 180 miles only to Berlin. Finally they got at the outskirt from Berlin, and that was time for us to run again. But where to run? We had two horses from East Prussia there, and we packed what was quickly to be packed from that bakery.

I got lost from my family because of the constant interruption of the deep flyers, deep, deep, airplane shooting. And they would go over the street." The roads teemed with thousands of refugees in cars, on horses, or on foot pushing carts, heading north up to Hamburg and the main road.

"What we met was I think British airplanes shooting us from above and the Russians shooting us in the back. And occupying everything. So here is the road and we ran in every direction—dispersing somewhere because the flyers came deep, *dat, dat, dat, dat*—and they shoot with automatic gun which goes *dat, dat, dat,* and then they go back and forth over the road, shooting. Again and again.

"When we saw them coming—there was no alarm, nothing—we left our belongings which we had with us, just dropped them and ran into the potato fields or into whatever fields or a little forest, whatever, and throw ourselves down to the ground. And half of us, maybe a quarter or a third did not get up anymore. So, one time, I was lying like that, and above me they come and they go very low, and then it is quiet, they have gone away and I'm going to get up now, and I realize—Am I alive? You know. I touched myself to find out, Am I alive? Where am I? That was the kind of trauma I had. And then I looked up and the others did it the same way. They greeted each other like that. They crawled out. Some were wounded, some were dead. The wounded ones stayed behind. And maybe died, I don't know what happened to them. I was here, I could get up, but my family, I didn't know where they were. I found a bicycle on the street. So I take this bicycle now and start riding. I knew where I wanted to go. I only wanted to run. North! Not back with the Russians."

The refugees scavenged for food as they went. If a horse had been killed and lay in the road, Ruth and the others would cut a piece of meat out of the dead shank and roast it on an open fire to eat. Dogs gobbled the scraps and chewed the bones. Other refugees told Ruth they had shot their pets before they fled, and she thought about how hard that must have been for them to do.

She ended up in Lübeck, and was able to connect with a cousin named Lydia. "It was a city bombed all the time. But there is where I think I learned the war is finished. 1945. I had tears in my eyes and was so naïve when it was finished. I see myself, I went down to the earth and bowed down and said, 'Oh, thank you that it is over, now we will have peace.' Hah!"

Lübeck, a city north of Hamburg on the Baltic Sea, was also a dangerous place. "For the ending of the war they celebrated by opening the prisons," Ruth explains. The prisoners—common criminals or resisters put in jail by the Nazis—flooded out of their cells bent on revenge. And another war started in the streets of Lübeck. "They burned department stores and looted them. They plundered. Germans against Germans! Indiscriminately. They opened the silos, yah, that kept butter and wine. They were underground, in the city. And the stores burned and the Nazi flags were torn down and burned."

The Russian and British occupying forces moved to restore order in Lübeck. To stop the German-on-German violence and the destruction of property, they instituted a strict curfew. "My cousin Lydia and I, we couldn't get out after eight o'clock in the evening, you couldn't go on the street anymore. Because it was plundered, you know, scavenging and going into these burning houses and doing bad things again. And in all of that you could see, in the center of the city, this so-called plaza. It had underground places and they were all opened, and out of them came the people who were finding beautiful things there. Ten-pound packages of butter, and sausage and bread, and they were loading themselves, hoarding it all. The British soldier would stop them, he said, 'Stop and drop!' and they would lose it right away.

"But Lydia and I, we got away with fifteen pounds of butter, I think, and we somehow got disappeared and no one stopped us, so we shared it with people and traded it for other food. And with all that, we could hold our room and have this safe place that wasn't destroyed. Oh, and the soldiers were drunk. When you were caught, they looked also inside your body, the soldiers. Before my eyes, Lydia was caught by a British soldier. Of course she dropped it already but he took her and raped her. I ran and escaped. Later, because of that, she could never get children."

Ruth went out into the countryside and found a small room with a straw-thatched roof. This she shared with Lydia and an old man. "That was already after the war. Yah, but it was everything so scarce, and we were stealing the apples of those who had big gardens and didn't sell them to us. I had some money and I would ask for a pound of apple and they would say, 'We can't sell you any, it's all under control.' Which we knew it wasn't true because they gave it to the black market and got much more. The farmers became rich now, hmm? And so we took a chair in the night when we knew they were sleeping, and I would climb over on the chair, over the fence. I would shake and get an apron full of apples and throw it over to Lydia. We knew it was dangerous.

"We worked in the wetland, made bricks of that black earth and then burned it and we earned our money that way. And we helped also cleaning up from the bombing. Then we went to Hamburg, sometimes, to help clean up the city, just continue working a little bit and working in the field, so."

In the summer of 1945, Ruth, aged twenty-two now, decided to go back to Berlin. She set out alone and traveled until she was stopped at the border between the British Zone and the Russian Zone, the demarcation between West and East. "The Russians were along the limit standing with guns and waiting for us civilians to come back so they could steal everything what we had. Watches and jewelry or money. I had sewn in some money into a man's jacket which I wore and they checked it all out. I think it was a thousand mark. They took it—everything. It was always like that. You could never hold onto anything. Then I came back to Berlin, back to the bakery."

During that period of flight, Ruth had learned to deal with danger and deprivation, to keep going no matter what happened. She had witnessed rape, injury, and death, and somehow managed to find ways to provide for herself and others. All these skills would be of use in the next period of her life, a time of terrible dislocation and abuse.

CHAPTER FOUR

Dark Journey

I remember first hearing of the chaotic postwar period of Ruth's life twenty years ago, during a meditation retreat at Dhamma Dena. It was a women's retreat, and I believe the subject of men arose. A woman may have expressed antimale views, which Ruth vociferously countered. "Look at me," she said, "I could be hating men. I was raped and violently handled after the war by men. But I don't charge back at them, dahling."

It was Russians, we learned, who had done it. The information fitted itself into the persona we saw before us, it became part of Ruth's lore: she had been raped by Russians after the war. On another occasion Ruth told of being held in a cage on a railroad car, being called Nazi and spat upon by Poles and Russians—another disturbing cameo to add to the legend of this intrepid character. Ruth fascinated us, with her long flowing skirts, her German accent, her combination of Prussian strictness and ebullient *joie de vivre*. She was decades older than most of her students. Her experience in the grim aftermath of the Second World War in Europe explained why she begrudged every penny spent and saved every scrap of food. It helped us understand her surprising response to the subject of sexual abuse, essentially telling those who came to her with such stories to forget it, to leave it behind, which was, we surmised, what she had had to do. We also ascribed some of the ex-

traordinary depth of her spiritual understanding to the hard training ground of war. (One of Ruth's contemporaries, Gesshin Prabhasa
Dharma roshi, a German woman who became a Zen master, told me
that war had been her spiritual training, beside which the extreme rigor
of Japanese Zen monastic training felt like kindergarten.)

In this way Ruth's students fit her war experiences into the context
of her mature, Dharma-teacher persona. Never having lived through
anything like the stories Ruth told, we were able to hold her experiences
at a distance, safely encapsulating them in the past.

But when I began interviewing Ruth for this book, the neat story
burst its boundaries and opened out in horrific immediacy. First I discovered that Ruth's period of being lost in no man's land had lasted not
a day or a month, but a year and a half, a desert of time surreal in its
cruelty. And listening to her talk about it, I felt, viscerally, the girl/
woman in her early twenties who had wandered from disaster to disaster. Not the seasoned spiritual teacher, not the mature Hollywood wife
or the sophisticated world traveler, but a young German farm-bred
woman whose greatest previous adventures had been teacher-training
school in a medium-sized city and visits to her Uncle Robert.

As Ruth described that time to me, sometimes language failed
her, she broke off in midsentence, and took another tack. She admit-
ted there was much she could not remember; the sequence of events
often escaped her. And she told me why. "I never spoke about it, after.
I didn't want to get it back." In order to live in the postwar rubble that
had been Berlin, where survival required constant struggle and vigi-
lance, Ruth put away her most painful memories. She saw individuals
around her eaten up with hatred toward the Russians, driven mad by
holding on to the outrages committed against them. Ruth wanted to
live; she locked her worst experiences away, far from her everyday mind,
and went about the task of rebuilding a life.

Now, almost sixty years later, Ruth agrees to pull up that period
of time, like an object lost on the bottom of the ocean, to drag it up
through murky water and share it with me. Isolated events appear out

of the dimness: mini-scenes brightly lit so that even tiny details can be seen. Sometimes what is not said carries more weight than spoken words, as Ruth's voice falters, and she takes refuge in a description of the surroundings—the basement room, the marshy field—or describes what the Russian soldiers ate for breakfast. Sometimes, at the cruelest parts, she laughs, chuckling at those events so long ago, keeping herself separate from the feelings she endured at the time.

The contours of this saga tend to fuzz into the outer darkness. Try as we might, Ruth and I cannot always locate events in time, cannot place them in a neat sequence. Some events float unanchored. Essentially there was no daily life as she had known it, no continuity of place and people that would allow Ruth to remember which experience came first, which followed. But the period is bracketed by distinct events: in late 1945 she left her relative safety in Berlin to go east into the Polish Corridor, to try to make her way back to a village in East Prussia. A year and a half later, she managed to get back to Berlin.

• • •

The odyssey was undertaken out of Ruth's compassion and her naïveté. An aunt had traveled from East Prussia before the war, leaving her family behind. Ruth explains, "In the summer of '44, Tante Lenchen came west to Berlin, to this bakery. She brought some butter because she owned a dairy back in East Prussia, then she supplies a little bit of the others with the butter, brought in her suitcase, two pounds or so. Then the war finished and she couldn't return. So she was now alone and was crying." Tante Lenchen had left behind a baby no more than a year old, a ten-year-old child, her husband, and the children's grandmother. Although she checked the waves of refugees daily streaming from the east into Berlin, she could not find her family among them. What could have happened to them?

Ruth, responding to her aunt's grief and worry, decided to go back into what had been East Prussia to find this family or to discover their fate. She was twenty-three years old, and even after her harrowing experiences, she was full of youthful confidence; she had no idea what she would encounter when she crossed the border into the Polish Corridor. "Tante Lenchen," she announced, "I will go and find them."

Ruth set off, carrying a little rucksack. Crossing the border, she found herself in a lawless no man's land ruled by Russian soldiers and Polish militia—a land where the trains ran but no one sold tickets, crowds simply crammed into the cars—a land where daily cruelties were committed against the devastated, demoralized population. She was soon arrested. She was German, and her passport identified her as a teacher; that was enough to arouse suspicion that she had been indoctrinating the children in Nazi beliefs. The Russians wanted to interrogate her about what she had been teaching.

Russian soldiers took her to their headquarters in a feudal estate, and questioned her. Then they put her in a cellar. She had only a pile of straw on the damp floor as a bed; a tin can of soup was shoved through the cellar window for her dinner. Later that night seven Russian soldiers came into the cellar and took her out. They transported her to a marshy area where one by one they raped her. Ruth shivered in the cold. She prayed.

"Dahling, there was nothing else to do, when you see seven guys . . ." and her voice drops off into silence.

She begins again. "I remembered my God. And myself. And that power which I always saw behind the universe, who guides the world's cosmic affair and sees everything. He is the creator and so I thought he had the power to help me."

I ask, "But weren't you disillusioned when he *didn't* help you?"

"No, I didn't connect that with him being the almighty and let that happen. I had no time for it, I was in such a stress. You are closing up under stress like that, you cannot see the whole picture."

And she adds, "In such deeper emergencies, the rational mind steps out and more universal atmosphere comes into you. It was a balance to hold me."

Even hearing her explanation, I wonder how she could not be devastated by the attack. I don't know any woman who has led such a protected life that she has not at least come close to being raped, and many I know have been victims of this crime. I have seen the damage done to them, the time and care it took to heal from the assault. In my college dating, more than once I fought my way out of a car backseat, a motel room, a back room at a fraternity party. I was physically strong, and lucky. But as Ruth described her experiences to me, often I felt in my body the helplessness, the outrage, the awful sinking awareness that there was no escape, and the physical pain inflicted. I can never know exactly what she felt, partly because when she tried to tell me her voice would often stumble, the story fall into space, and after a pause, looking stunned, she would pick up at another less traumatic point.

Ruth ponders her story, and adds a crucial dimension. She assures me that even in that dark time she understood the cause for the violence. "I saw when they raped me that they were somehow instigated by their political ideas—to believe that we Germans were all monsters. That's how they treated us. Yah, we did terrible things in their country, and this is their rage which came up. That was my ground atmosphere —and then I would take the pain."

She does not remember how that night ended, whether the Russian soldiers took her with them or left her in the swamp. "Let's say they left me there . . ." she speculates, "and in a way I was happy they left me. But then where do you go? If you go on the street, the next ones are waiting for you. But I would not go on and say, 'How terrible! I want to die!'" She chuckles. "I never said that. *I always wanted to live!*"

Ruth set out to find the railway station. But before she could resume her journey east, she was caught by Polish militiamen.

"They interrogate me, they said, 'You are now the Third Reich, *das dritte Reich*,' hmm? Sometimes they would do that, sometimes it was different and very human. Then I was finished and they said, 'Now you can go.' They would ask me where I would want to go now; they would give me a guard out of that area, or go to another questioning place. And I remember of this journey that we were finding ourselves in a little town with ruins and broken walls and only chimneys were standing, and there would be four or five soldier who took me, they raped me there in the cold, rainy weather between rubble."

She laughs. "Nice experiences."

I ask, "Didn't you feel despairing, after that?"

"No. Well, what did it help me? It made me weak. It made me cry. I did cry and thought, 'Why do we have to suffer so much?' you see, and had questions. But then I realized, 'I can't. If I do this, my last energy will go!' It doesn't move me then. I had a big power for living, and I had always hope and was always connected to my Lord. I was a devout Christian in a way. There is a saying, *Wen Gott liebt, den straft er.* Whom God is loving, he examines them, he tests them, he challenges them. And so I saw it always as a challenge. I held to that. I saw that nothing will help me. Where should I turn to?"

Going on again, Ruth largely lived on dry bread given to her by the few Germans she encountered. At one point she was put on display with a sign—GERMAN—around her neck. Polish people passing by spat at her and called her names.

Then Ruth was imprisoned in a Russian labor camp. The German women in the camp worked dismantling railroad ties to be sent back to Russia. The camp held two thousand women in hard conditions. Ruth's memory yields only a few details. "This was more in summer time, in the fall. And it was an open, open, and I don't remember...it was sleeping outside...yah, yah, we did, we had straw. We could lie down. But people got sick. And rain. They gave us always soup, cabbage and potatoes, out of a big, big...But I wasn't very long there. A person got me out."

I ask, "Some man took you?"

"Yah, but not for that purpose."

A Russian officer brought her to the house where he and his wife were living, to help his wife. By this time Ruth had realized that she should not admit having been a teacher, which linked her to the Nazi regime, so she told everyone she had been a hairdresser. She fixed the hair of the officer's wife, and did housework. The officer's house became a haven for Ruth. "Actually, you know, there were people with heart you met sometimes, who could go into the human level instead of staying on the political conditioned level. I think I was treated fine by the wife, yah, she liked it what I did. And the husband came home in the evening and they were sleeping and I had no trouble there."

In the midst of her desperate circumstances, Ruth appreciated every smallest comfort. "Every bite I got, every little gift, I was grateful. And so happy that I could have a warm room in the officer's house, that I wasn't raped. There were still moments when you could be grateful for the goodness of God."

But she could not stay there. She had to make her way back to the East Prussian village to find her Tante Lenchen's family. So one day she walked away from the safety of the Russian officer's house and made her way east. She was in daily danger as she traveled on the roads, and yet she managed to respond to beauty. "Through all these things, when I walked along with my knapsack, not knowing if in the next minute someone will catch me and rape me, or take my last piece of bread—I still would look up and see the flower and know how beautiful it is."

Finally she arrived at the village where Tante Lenchen's family had operated their dairy. Most of the German villagers had fled. The few who remained were crowded into one small house, with a straw roof. Ruth stayed there with them. "We had a little candlelight in the evening, and singing. No one, I remember, was overtly angry and hating, but more praying, quietly. I would be very touched about the togetherness of people in crisis. We were all part of the family. They were singing and chanting. Yah, Christian songs—one beautiful hymn that goes 'Take my hands now, I am yours.' I would join them singing. So I would cry but I would never be under. The crying was actually a wonderful peace.

"It is easier to carry when you are suffering with so many together. Like joy accelerates in you when you can share it with others, also the pain is easier when shared. Some were crying for their child who had gotten lost, some had suffered a great injury, wounded, or beaten, or

raped. I was touched by *their* suffering, not only for my own. I saw that
my body was still intact, that I could still think, that I believed in God,
and that I had great strength."

One night, looking through the doorway of the crowded hut at distant stars, Ruth made a commitment. "I got quiet and had a focus.
Somehow in that great big space of prayer and being connected to my
breath and to my love, my prayer was that I be saved, but behind that a
thought would go through that space—seeing how much injustice was
done and so much bad stuff that I too had participated in . . . I knew
when I get out of here I will do good and will touch life. Not a thought
exactly but a spacious, very tangible *feeling*—that I am determined to
help other people."

In the village, she could not find her aunt's family, and none of the
remaining Germans knew anything about them. Ruth set off for Grünfeld where she had taught, but at the site of her school she found only
a pile of rubble. That early life she had lived was destroyed. The happy
childhood in nature, the years of sports and dancing, the celebrations,
the challenging time as a schoolteacher—the physical vestiges of all this
had disappeared, along with the people. There was nothing else to learn
in either of these villages.

Ruth started the long trip back to Berlin. But soon she became ill,
and by the time she had crossed East Prussia and come into the Polish
Corridor, she was weak and suffering from bloody diarrhea. In Posen,
the major city in the Corridor, she was plunged once again into painful
conditions. "That was a big kind of crossroads between main Germany
and the eastern part. The trains went back and forth here, and a big
headquarters of the Russians was there. I didn't know that, I found that
out. In the night I was waiting for some kind of train, or freight train,
you know, hanging out behind these big piles of materials such as the
railway tracks dismantled by German women in labor camp, hmm? I
wanted to evade that, so here I waited. There was a place where the soldiers in the night would go into these waiting rooms and take women,

young women, take them aside and use them and then you could go back. Or, they would, well, I don't know what else they did. And then you would have to go through a real pick, a personal pick. They would, search, yah. They would even go with their fingers in your ears because women hid their diamonds there, yah, oh and in vagina. I didn't have jewels, but I had, I don't know, maybe a bottle of vodka, or had somewhere gotten some bread.

"Anyway, I got saved by a Russian medical doctor, picked me up for his use. Here he came and saw me nude with young soldiers and they brought me to him. I had diarrhea, I was depleted. And in fear. They brought me first to his clinic which was half of a train wagon. Half was his practice as a medical doctor and a little part of it was maybe his private room. He comes out and I stand there and he said to me, 'You are dirty and *schwarze wie ein Schornstein,'* in *Deutsch*—they all spoke German. *Schornstein* means chimney—black, yah. I was that dirty. So he said, 'Go in here and clean yourself and wash.' And he saw as a doctor that I needed some kind of help, so he gave, I don't know, charcoal treatments. I had to eat something like charcoal. Yah, coal, and so I stayed I don't know how long in that little compartment. He helped me with medicine, he gave me his doctor robe, you know, *kittel*, we say. Is like a doctor smock. And I had nothing else. He said, 'Throw your clothes away.' But he did not do anything with me, more, at that time yet."

Ruth stops, thinks, begins again, "Suddenly I remember. I don't know how I got to it, but in this five-room apartment, there lived two soldiers, and took care of it. And I had a bathtub there to use. I could once not make it out of the tub, I had this running diarrhea, my own blood, so to speak. In the bathtub."

I ask, "How about those soldiers who ran the place? Did they...?"

"No, the doctor told me the soldiers will behave good, and they did. They were his servants. And this was his house, his living quarter. I slept in a very big room, and you know, I've suppressed that whole thing, I think. I remember that I would sleep in the night, and he would come and be drunk. And then he would take me, I was very thin, and he would have fun. It was a parquet floor without carpets, so when you throw something, it rolls, and he did that with me."

I comment, "That sounds very sadistic."

"Yah, very." She responds matter-of-factly, and moves on to a description of the doctor. "He was tall, and spoke German. I don't know maybe he was forty-five or fifty years old. When he was drunk, then he took me in his bed and I was his flower. But when I wasn't, it had its good thing too. I was safe, I was clean. But I did fear that he takes me really to Russia, because he said, 'You, I told you, you will become my second wife in Petersburg.' That was my future. He has one wife that was old and had children, and I was young, you know, so he had a good rationale going for himself that I would be the second wife, and so. However, I got sick. I don't know whether it was the beginning of typhus—no, it couldn't be then because you cannot stop typhus. And, again, also, with the food there, I had to drink alcohol, he said, 'Drink it!' Six o'clock, five o'clock in the morning, they ate cabbage soup with fat meat. And potatoes. Hot, really like we would have dinner. It was cold outside, hmm?

"So then I got sick and he sent me to the hospital in a carriage with two horses. You know, they stole these things from all over. I had a driver who was guiding the horses. That was always in the afternoon when I had to go to the hospital for treatment. I cannot tell you what treatment I got, I was always so shrunk, and always kind of *in myself*, always I was praying, and that held me away from being overrun by fear."

Ruth retreated into a close communion with herself, and a steady awareness of God. She cultivated an inward, spiritual state of mind that would become her principal mode of being. I am reminded once again of Gesshin Prabhasa Dharma roshi who was an adolescent in postwar Germany. She said that when you saw that buildings and people could be there one day and destroyed the next, when you lived in that gray, depressed, lifeless environment, you had to reach deep inside and touch something profound in yourself, to survive.

During her slavery to the Russian doctor, Ruth looked inward and communed with God. "I had to be with my Lord, hmm? And I was always promising, if He saves me, I would be a good girl. Maybe it did go so deep into me that it has effect even with what I did later, that I got so quickly hold of the meditation practice. I always was *with me* together so when I got the Buddha teaching, it went deeper, and connected me deeper.

"But, going to the hospital. Yes, I was picked up by the carriage. This was the last time I was in the hospital—it wasn't supposed to be, but I made it the last time. Because I disappeared in the rainy, misty late afternoon. It was maybe six o'clock or so. I told the driver to stop and I disappeared, in the night. Somehow between broken houses and bombed . . . out through the ruins. And I took even on me that I would be searched again, but somehow I found my way back to the station. I knew where that was. And I think I was only one night sitting, somehow, in a little space in a pile of these parts of a railway track. They'd take the tracks and rebuild it in Moscow."

I wonder why the doctor did not come and get her. "Wouldn't he have thought you would go to the station?"

She ponders, closing her eyes to try to remember. "Well, I don't know. I don't know what happened. It was raining always and bad cold, and I was sitting in my hole in this pile and I knew the direction I wanted to go."

That night a freight train came, and as it slowed in the station Ruth was able to climb up into an open freight car. She was alone in the car. As the train gathered speed she began to be very cold, for it was winter, and the railroad wagon had no cover. Between wagons there was a little guard booth. Ruth made her way to the booth, where she was protected from the wind. The train was headed toward the Oder River, marking the Oder Line, which separated Germany proper from the eastern territories controlled by the Russians.

As dawn came and the train neared the river, a soldier jumped from wagon to wagon to check for border crossers. In the guard booth he found Ruth, huddled against the cold.

"Yah, this soldier found me and he raped me, and then the train went slow and slow and slow and somehow I must have communicated with him that I want to go to Berlin. We were approaching this flimsical bridge over the Oder, it was a repaired bridge, all the bridges were destroyed by the retreating German army. So it wobbled and wobbled very slow. You could walk with it, yah, that way the train went across the river. But this train went down south to Silesia, and I had to go straight to Berlin! The train was very slow, and he helped me to jump off in Frankfurt an Oder.

"Then I had to wait I think a day and a half until a scheduled German train came going to Berlin. I had no money, I had no food. My shoes were gone and I had burlap wrapped around my feet. In the train because I was young I was always standing, because the olders were sitting. We were in a compartment—one row here to sit and one would face and in the middle was space and there we were standing like herrings. All were Germans, and everyone was unhappy and there was swearing. I think they gave me a little crust of bread someone broke off because he saw I didn't have any.

"In those times I tell you what I experienced. When it was possible and they weren't blinded and confused by the political philosophies, then they could make a distinction: 'These are the bad Germans; these are the good ones.' Like in that train for example, like the soldier, he used me, but he helped me to get down off the train. You know, so some would be helpful, hmm?"

Earlier, in a railway-station waiting room near Warsaw, Ruth had experienced an act of even greater kindness that helped her to maintain her faith in the possibility of goodness in human beings. She sat all night among Polish women in long black dresses, waiting. Knowing how badly these Polish people had been treated by her countrymen, she could only imagine what they must feel toward her.

The station was patrolled by the Polish militia. Any German found there would be searched for valuables. People had hidden their rings and watches in their vaginas or their anuses. The Poles knew this, and they searched every orifice of the German travelers. Ruth did not have valuables with her, but feared for the bread in her rucksack, which she knew they would take from her. She also feared that the militiamen might seize the opportunity to take her outside and use her sexually. She sat among the Polish women in the dark waiting room, dreading the arrival of the guards.

"The militiamen were coming. The Polish women knew I was German, they knew what that would mean for me. The woman next to me, she put her hand over my hand and held it—for comfort. No one spoke a word. When the militiaman came to the door, suddenly she pushed me down to the floor and covered me with her long skirt, so I disappeared. And that way I was saved.

"After the men left, more waiting. I sat there and squeezed her hand to thank her. I realized that the others saw her do it, they could have exposed her and she would have suffered for that. But she did it anyway.

"You cannot just see your own perspective, you have to see the impact of your being on the outside." Clearly the bubble of Ruth's earlier youthful insularity had burst; she was now permanently part of the larger world, aware of her participation in and effect on it.

The train from Frankfurt an Oder took Ruth back to Berlin, to her Tante Frida's bakery, and her worst ordeal was over. But she had to tell her Tante Lenchen that she had failed in her mission to find out about her aunt's family in the East Prussian village. As with many East Prussian people, it would be much later that Ruth and her family would discover what had happened to the husband, children, and grandmother left behind.

Tante Frida's place in the Falkensee neighborhood of Berlin had become the destination of all the relatives fleeing East Prussia. Ruth moved back into the upstairs room, where sixteen people lived together. Soon she began to have unfamiliar physical symptoms, and was so young and naïve that she did not know she was pregnant. "I didn't know what happened in me, so I go to doctor and he tells me that and they, I don't know what, anyway, they did it. Abortion."

• • •

I stop to breathe, ponder, try to integrate and understand Ruth's reaction to her experiences. She had been severely traumatized, and yet had been able to keep her strength and sense of self through it all. She had managed not to sink into despondency or bitterness or even madness. True, she had come from a stable (though strict) family background, and she was the kind of person who could reach out to others, join with others, break through her isolation—all conditions that help one survive trauma with less damage. In her family she had learned patterns of denial and accommodation, useful tools for negotiating abuse. She describes her strong will to live, her sense of contact with a higher power, and the way she controlled her mind, not allowing herself to dwell on her victimization. Still, some of her experiences seem almost impossible to bear.

Ruth claims she had a rationale that guarded her against personalizing the rapes and brutal treatment. It is unclear to me whether that wider view really operated at the time when she was plunged into this dark period or whether it had been constructed later to explain and distance the memories. But the moment with her aunt in the Berlin streetcar, in which Tante Lutsi told Ruth that *they* would become the prisoners, the forced laborers, changing places with the Russians removing rubble on the streets—perhaps that moment opened Ruth's eyes to the view she was later to hold, placing her own personal victimization in its historical and moral context and allowing her to draw comfort from that.

"I would never cry and say, 'Why did this happen to me! I didn't do anything!' The people who said that, they got sick and crazy. No, I saw what happened to me as the legitimate punishment for what the Germans had done. I knew I was part of that. I belonged to that nation and we are wrong and have done bad things. Concentration camps and all. I saw that the Russians didn't do much better, but that was not my concern. My concern was my situation and why I suffered, yah. I saw myself being part of the society that had done wrong to the world. To the Jewish people, the Polish people, the French people, and so on. I knew we were suffering now for what we did. I paid." And she adds, with Prussian toughness, "This is my policy. Life is not cheap. You pay for everything."

Still, it seems to me that the young Ruth Schaefer paid a particularly heavy price, and I feel for the damage it must have done her, despite her strong religious faith and the philosophical perspective she is expressing. I know that, conventionally, women who have been raped need to be able to talk about their experience to sympathetic people, in order to heal, and I wonder if there was anyone in that cramped little room above the bakery who could listen to Ruth and offer comfort.

"You must have been really traumatized by the time you made it to Berlin," I prompt. And Ruth's response comes out jerky and fragmented.

"Yah, noo, I wasn't, no, yah no, I just went through that. It was never, it was always this feeling, was more, not even self-pity but it was, I am carrying that what we did. That is kind of, understanding that we did wrong, because by then we knew what the Germans all did."

I ask, "You didn't have post-traumatic stress?"

"Well, they all had, probably, yah sure."

"Nightmares and flashbacks and things?"

"Yah, well I had, I think."

Clearly, Germans in postwar Berlin were a traumatized people, each one with some loss or wound or outrage endured. The rapes suffered by one young woman may have been of little interest to people so deeply shaken themselves. It is calculated that two million German women were raped, the majority by Red Army soldiers.[8] Probably no one spoke of this, no one asked Ruth what she had suffered on her journey. During that time in the hut in East Prussia with the other Germans, Ruth had had a chance to cry for her wounds. But after she returned to Berlin, the demands of postwar survival were so great that, in order to get up each morning to forage for food, Ruth had to lock away her experience, close the door upon it, and throw away the key.

Repression exacts its own price. As a people, in order to survive, the Germans either did not or could not mourn their many losses—not the least of which was the loss of their belief in a leader who had seemed to offer all that was good. As the German psychiatrists Alexander and Margarete Mitscherlich have asserted in *The Inability to Mourn,* "Although, rationally speaking, it should have been the most burning problem in their minds, Germans have shown a minimum of psychological interest in trying to find out why they became followers of a man who led them into the greatest material and moral catastrophe in their history." Instead they sought to forget their experiences before and during the war, and plunged into the restoration of the economy. Ruth speaks of having put away her terrible experiences after the war, and she never mentions returning to them later to examine and reexperience them, in order to heal the wounds they left. As far as I know, she never sought psychotherapy to help her with this. Surely her Buddhist practice brought healing, but Buddhist practice does not directly address buried memories or past traumas, or encourage one to work with these psychological elements. And it would have been unusual if Ruth *had* sought to work on her experience of trauma, for it has only been since the advent of the second women's movement in the sixties and seventies that feminist psychologists have explored the subject of rape and its effects, and have devised methods of healing from sexual abuse. In the late forties and the fifties, there could have been little consciousness of the need to turn toward and heal sexual wounds from the past.

I wonder about the cost to Ruth of this repression. If she had been allowed to mourn the terrible outrage of her rapes, to heal herself from them, when she became a spiritual teacher she might have been able to sympathize more gently with the victims of incest and rape among her students. If she had been able to feel the full depth of the hunger and illness and abuse she had suffered, she might have softened to herself and not demanded so tireless and Spartan a response to difficulty in herself and others. When we repress, we create a blank space, a sort of caesura in our personality, and out of that space surprising and inappropriate behavior may arise.

Surely the overwhelming effect of the war on Ruth was to deepen the compassion she already felt for all beings who suffer, and to create in her a resolve to benefit them. Yet there are odd breaks in this intention of Ruth's, an occasional harshness that causes pain and sometimes even drives people away. Perhaps that is the repressed material arising— not to mention the little girl's buried response to the punishments administered by Mutti to the child Ruth, long before the war.

All this went through my mind as I listened to Ruth, and as I sought out material on the effects of extreme trauma on the personality of the victim. Unanswered and perhaps unanswerable questions emerged in my attempt to understand the full complexity of Ruth's character.

Often I wondered if I could have lived through those traumas, whether I might have given up at some point, just turned my face to the wall and wished for death. Ruth's strength seems superhuman at times. As a white person born in America, I have not been similarly tested by the experience of war and its aftermath on my own soil. Unlike certain segments of our population, the Native Americans for instance, I and my family and friends have not been conquered, bombed, strafed, starved, raped, murdered, by a victorious army. I can only imagine what that would be like.

But hearing Ruth's story, I realize that she survived because she never stopped wanting to live. She was willing to do whatever she must in order to eat, protect herself if possible, get through another day. And she was lucky not to have contracted typhus or met up with a homicidal soldier-rapist against whom no brave spirit could have prevailed. Her powerful will to live picked her up from each encounter and sent her on, able to relax into the intermittent comforts, even in the overall bleakness: the warmth of a bed, the safety of a room for a night, the taste of decent food after days of starvation. As well as her toughness, her spiritual resources guarded her from despair and bitterness, and deepened during the war into an intention to work for the benefit of others, should she survive.

• • •

In the early postwar period, in a devastated Germany, Ruth and the remnants of her family were reduced to a hand-to-mouth struggle. Food was scarce. (It is estimated that 75 percent of Berlin schoolchildren were undernourished in 1946.)[9] Ruth's family was in disarray, her beloved father still missing, her mother lost somewhere in East Prussia. Her brother Heinz, the SS officer, emerged from hiding with the German farm family who had shielded him. The overcrowded ruins of Berlin became even more congested as twelve million German-speaking people were expelled from Poland, Bohemia, Hungary, and Rumania and sent west into Germany.

The bakery, in a zone bordering on the Russian Zone, had been taken over to provide bread for the Russian Army. Ruth and her relatives huddled in the little upstairs room, surviving as best they could. And then her mother returned from the east, brought by a stranger from the train station. Elisabeth Schaefer was nearly unrecognizable, emaciated and weak, deathly ill with typhus. Ruth's Tante Frida, in helping her, contracted the disease and died, while Ruth's mother miraculously survived. Ruth's youngest sister, Dita, returned from the Russian labor camps. Chrystel lived nearby with her child.

Ruth applied to teach elementary school, for which she had to go through the denazification program conducted by British officers, to be trained away from fascist philosophy into more democratic thinking and teaching methods. When she had completed the program, she moved out of her aunt's house to go to Spandau, a section of Berlin under British occupation, and soon found a job there teaching school. One major benefit of being a schoolteacher was that she got extra food.

The British would come every lunchtime with a big wagon to distribute food for the children, serving Ruth soup also.

Then, in 1949 or 1950, Hermann Schaefer returned from the Siberian prison camp. He had contracted tuberculosis there and would remain very ill until his death, living as an invalid with Ruth's mother.

Always Ruth was occupied in the search for food for herself and others, and she would go to any lengths to acquire it. She made friends with a British captain and persuaded him to bring her wool socks from the army supply. These she unraveled and, using bicycle spokes for needles, she knitted sweaters in a Norwegian design. She would trade a sweater to the wife of a Russian officer for a bottle of vodka. "Then I could go with the vodka to the German countryside with a little pull-cart, maybe twelve miles, walking, and give the bottle of vodka to a farmer and got maybe fifty pounds of grain from that. There was a mill to grind the grain. And then we had something to eat."

At home in her little room, Ruth read the philosophy of Martin Buber and Emil Haraszti's biography of Franz Lizst; she revisited the life and spirituality of Teresa of Avila. Classical music—Beethoven, Handel, Bach—strengthened and soothed her.

Ruth and her family received CARE packages sent by U.S. citizens. One such parcel came from a schoolteacher in California, and when Ruth wrote to thank her, they began a correspondence, communicating vaguely about the possibility that Ruth might one day be able to emigrate to the United States.

In this postwar period, the West German people, led by their government, sought to make some reparations to the Jews. They gave a billion marks to Israel, and other sums to groups who had been victimized. Various German organizations and movements were created to work toward reconciliation with the Jewish people. I asked Ruth if she had heard of these organizations or participated in any similar activities. She had not. It appears that after the war she focused exclusively on work and the attempt to build a new life.

In this she was not different from the majority of Germans. While the government and some organizations sought to confront German guilt and the many catastrophic crimes and losses of the war, the general German public did not take time to acknowledge and mourn and make amends. And while I might have hoped that Ruth had done some of that, instead she—and the German nation as a whole—put aside the past and plunged into the enormous task of rebuilding a nation.

The American schoolteacher who sent CARE packages offered to help Ruth come to America. Immigrants had to have a sponsor who would provide housing and help the person find employment. Ruth's contact wrote that she had a friend whose unmarried brother in Los Angeles needed a housekeeper, and this man agreed to sponsor her. Excited by this prospect, Ruth completed the required three-year "political purification" process, and plans were made.

But she could not leave Germany as long as her father clung to life. She was living in Westphalia by then, but went on making her periodic journeys to Berlin to see him, until October 1956, when Hermann Schaefer died. It had been a little over ten years since the war ended. The events of that period had faded somewhat in Ruth's mind, merged into a relatively uneventful time of struggling to care for herself and others, particularly her father. She had been finding her feet again in teaching, then in Westphalia working at an officer's mess, slowly building a sense of normalcy as she repaired her life. Now finally she was free to leave Germany and venture into the unknown future. She filed the last papers, acquired a ticket, and after the turn of the year, she left for the United States.

PART II

The "Little Immigrant": Spiritual Training in Hollywood and Asia

CHAPTER FIVE

She Finds Her Dream

In January of 1957 Ruth spent twelve days on a ship traveling across the Atlantic from Germany to New York City. She flew from New York to Los Angeles, where she was met at the airport by the man who was to be her sponsor and housemate. As she stepped off the airplane, Ruth entered a new life that would take her in unexpected directions, provide her with unparalleled opportunities, and give her material comfort such as she had never experienced. She was thirty-four years old, a young woman who loved nature, had a deep religious faith, possessed enormous energy and good will, and looked at the world through unsentimental eyes. The scavenging skills she had developed after the war, along with the capacity to create what was needed out of unlikely or discarded materials, would stand Ruth in good stead in her new environment. Having surmounted such enormous odds during and after the war, she found no task too difficult, no challenge too daunting. As she had done then, now she would simply get to work, taking help from anyone who would give it, enduring whatever discomforts and setbacks presented themselves. She knew how to keep moving and seize her opportunities.

In the United States, her fate would be decided by her association with a powerful man, with whom she would spend the next forty years, and by her good fortune in arriving at just the right historical moment:

the period when the great sociological, psychological, political, and spiritual experimentation of the sixties had just begun. Ruth would be swept up in this movement, would expand and deepen her understanding, undergoing a prolonged spiritual training from which she would emerge as a Buddhist teacher.

But her initial months in this new world offered a rather bleak prospect. Mr. Newton, her sponsor, turned out to be a hunter, a drinker, and a contradictory fellow. He had worked for the Los Angeles public works department, and now in his sixties was planning to retire. He brought her home to his house in South Central Los Angeles.

In exchange for cleaning the house, Ruth was allowed to live in his garage, which had been "redone a little because the rooms were small. He had to go through mine to get to the bathroom. Yah, it was so dirty, so unlivable. He was a grouchy thing. He hated the black people and had guns, hmm? But every friend of him was a black person. And I couldn't put that together. I said, 'But what about so-and-so, he's black!' He said, 'Yeah, well, he's an exception.'" In typical Ruth fashion, she found things to like about her time with Mr. Newton. He was good to her, she reports. He became fond of her and called her his "little flying Dutch girl." She learned through his black friends to be at ease in the company of African Americans, and she loved his children, one of whom was a schoolteacher.

Next door lived an instructor at Pepperdine College. Ruth made friends with her and began to help in her household. "I didn't want money, I just wanted to help." The woman insisted on paying her fifty cents an hour when she saw what a good housekeeper Ruth was. She recommended Ruth to her friends, and soon Ruth was cleaning others' houses. Ruth found numerous ways to plug in. She began caring for the children of a German-Jewish refugee industrialist and his actress wife, and traveled with them to Europe as a governess several times; she worked the night shift in a downtown Los Angeles building, typing insurance policies.

Then she made a fateful connection. One of her German cousins asked her to inquire about the sociology department at the University of Southern California. When she went there she was introduced to a visiting philosophy professor from Germany, who needed help with his English. Apparently Ruth's grasp of the language was a bit better than his, or at least he thought so, for when she agreed to help him, he asked her to type his papers and aid him in other ways. "I was the accompanying lady of the professor," she says. "I helped him. When he made his lecture he had the students question him; he wrote down the questions for me, that I was the one who would dare to ask the first. I didn't understand all of it, but anyway I was interested, and he was always fascinated by my interest for these things." Ruth spent social time with the professor as well, going swimming with him and accompanying him on a trip to the Grand Canyon. He eventually asked her to marry him, but while she found this very much older man attractive as a friend, she did not want to be intimate with him. It was through the professor that she met the man who would radically change her life.

The defining event in Ruth's first years in Los Angeles was her meeting with Henry Denison. She first saw him in 1959 at a farewell party for her professor, who was returning to Germany. Thirty of the professor's philosophy students attended, and among them was a tall, aristocratic-looking man in his midforties whom Ruth immediately admired. They talked, Henry telling her he was divorced and lived alone. In the course of their conversation, Ruth mentioned that she had ordered an automobile from Germany, and that the next day she must go to the docks to pick it up. Henry offered to drive her to the ship to get her car, inviting her to his Hollywood house for breakfast beforehand.

The next morning she made her way up into the Hollywood Hills to 2796 Creston Drive. Entering the wooden gate, she found Henry working in his garden. His house perched on the hill above the Hollywood Reservoir; plate-glass doors opened onto wooden decks, looking out to peaceful views of wooded hillsides and the blue waters of the reservoir. With its large, quiet central room, his home had a contemplative feel, like a house in the mountains of Japan. Ruth immediately fell in love with Henry, with his spirit, his house, his garden. She picked up a hose and began watering the flowers and shrubs, working alongside Henry in the bright morning sun. Even on that first day with him, she claims she knew Henry was *the one*. "I had my dream, and I never left."

In the house she found a long polished wood dining table made by Henry, who was a skilled carpenter and woodworker. She learned that he had had dirt trucked in from a freeway project to create his terraced garden, and that he even cared for the trees and bushes on the sidewalk that belonged to the city. The farm girl in her, the wood sprite, knew she had found a kindred soul. "He was a nature-man," she reports.

He was also a spiritual man, having lived for seven years as a monk in the Advaita Vedanta order. Henry Denison was well known in spiritual circles in Los Angeles. In addition to being a Vedanta devotee, he studied psychology and had been psychoanalyzed by and worked with the radical psychologist Wilhelm Reich. The major figures of the burgeoning consciousness movement of the sixties had already been Henry's guests. Mystics, lamas, priests, and poets, as well as psychiatrists and professors beginning to experiment with drugs—they all gathered in Henry's living room before the fireplace, ate at his handmade table, lounged on his decks.

Henry's family had built the Santa Fe Railroad and made a fortune in insurance, but Henry had fled the family business. In 1946 he left his ranch in New Mexico, his wife, and his infant son, to make a pilgrimage to Hollywood to the Vedanta Society "to find God." Advaita Vedanta is a Hindu form of religious observance whose greatest proponent, the eighth-century teacher Sari, asserted that: "on the highest level of truth the whole phenomenal universe, including the gods themselves, [is] unreal—the world [is] *Maya*, illusion, a dream, a mirage, a figment of the imagination. Ultimately the only reality [is] *Brahman*, the impersonal World Soul . . . with which the individual soul [is] identical."[10] In Vedanta each man or woman is viewed as divine, and may manifest this divine nature. Vedanta also acknowledges all the great religions of the world and their prophets, believing that all paths lead to God. The Vedanta Society of Southern California had been founded in 1930, with a temple, convent, and monastery in Hollywood, and other centers in Santa Barbara, Trabuco Canyon, and San Diego. Its devotees included such luminaries as the author Christopher Isherwood.[11]

Sarada, a former Vedanta nun, who became a dear friend of Ruth's, recalls Henry's 1946 arrival at the Vedanta Society.

> I'm in the vestibule of Vedanta Temple, and a man walks in. I thought I saw this desperation in his eyes, he was looking toward the shrine at the end of the temple. While he was talking about books, I noticed he was extremely refined in his speech and his manners. Very attractive, sort of Gregory Peck type tall-dark-handsome look.
>
> Eventually he got involved in Vedanta, and I heard him asking Swami Prabhavananda if he could move in, as a trial monk. Henry said he would pay $250 a month as a plea to be there—at that time, that was a lot of money—so Swami reluctantly agreed, and Henry moved in. Swami probably didn't feel too attracted to Henry, there was something about Henry that bothered him. Henry served as a part-time manservant, and he really did a marvelous job of making beds and plumping pillows.

Christopher Isherwood mentioned Henry, in his diary in 1949, as one of the "new monks," and reported that "Henry [Denison], who has money of his own, is paying to have a big carpentry shed put in the garden."[12]

Henry was a spiritual seeker, intensely interested in all forms of philosophy and religion. The "desperation" Sarada had seen in his eyes reflected his great hunger to achieve "enlightenment," "liberation," "transcendence"—an appetite that was to take him (and Ruth) around the world several times, and continued unfulfilled until his death. His most important role, as it developed after he left the monastery, was to support and enable the spiritual work of others, with his money, his intelligence and openness to new ideas, his wonderful house, his skills as a host.

When Ruth met him he had been living for several years in the Hollywood house, and was ending a relationship with his second wife, Virginia, a beautiful yoga teacher and host of a television program. Ruth slipped right into Henry's life and made herself useful. She "redid" his house, neatened his closet and bedroom. "I would polish his shoes. Before that he had taken them to a shoeshine man. I heard him telling his friends, 'And you know, she *polished my shoes!*'" She cooked for his friends, large spreads of fried chicken, tomato salad, potato salad, home-baked bread. "I could cook well, and also do his house. Most appreciative was he for things that were very ordinary I did in the household—cooking, sewing, working in the garden with him, listening to classical music with him. And his friends I liked."

Henry called her his "little immigrant," and basked in her love for him. People who knew them marveled at her ability to feed many guests on very little money, and they speak of her being earthy, direct, vibrantly alive at that time.

Ruth was still living with her sponsor, still cleaning houses and working as a governess, but spending more and more of her time with Henry. While she did not formally move in with Henry until after they married in 1963, she took her place in the center of his life and his household much earlier. Gradually Henry was surrendering to Ruth's love for him. She became the hostess for his parties, where she began to meet people who intrigued her. Alan Watts, the man for whom she danced in the Shiva temple, gave his first California lectures in their living room.[13] Ruth enjoyed Watts not only for his dancing but because he was wonderfully articulate and engaging, mesmerizing his audiences. "He was a great entertainer," she says. "He was light. Always personal."

Watts loved Henry and Ruth's home, remembering his overnight stays on the deck "under a eucalyptus tree where I have slept some memorably deep sleeps. . . . In this house I have made some of my greatest friendships."[14] He appreciated Ruth as much as she him, and also was amused by her. "Rutchen," he wrote, "exhibits an imperfect mastery of English to its best possible advantage—*die schonste langwitch*— a Germanized English so utterly funny that no one wants to correct her."[15]

As Henry's partner, Ruth stepped into the center of a movement that would be dubbed the "counterculture." Many of us who had grown up in the arid, conventional fifties began to search for meaning in the sixties, challenging accepted ideas of work, relationships, society, and religion; seeking ways to break out of existential loneliness into union with all existence. Eastern religions, particularly Buddhism and Hinduism, offered spiritual paths to liberation; poetry, jazz, and folk music articulated universal yearnings; psychedelic drugs such as marijuana, peyote, mescaline, and lysergic acid (LSD) opened minds. Gestalt therapy and encounter groups gave us methods of working with our minds and bodies. And we plunged into political activism, attending demonstrations and marches for civil rights and against the war in Vietnam. Many of us saw the need for profound transformations in society and believed that explorations into altered consciousness could help to bring about a peaceful, all-inclusive world.

While flower children and young political activists reveled and demonstrated in disorderly thousands on the streets and in the parks, another group of explorers—a more sedate and decidedly more elite group—was pursuing investigations into consciousness in universities and psychiatrists' offices and elegant living rooms. Older distinguished scholars, such as the English writer Aldous Huxley, became the spokesmen and philosophers of the movement. In 1947, at the midpoint of a distinguished career as novelist, essayist, and satirist, Huxley settled in Los Angeles and began to pursue studies and spiritual practice at the Vedanta Society. He also took mescaline and wrote about his experience in *The Doors of Perception,* giving a positive account of his psychic discoveries under the influence.[16] Huxley died in 1963, but his wife Laura Archera Huxley, herself an author, remained a Hollywood neighbor and friend of Ruth and Henry.

Another of Henry and Ruth's acquaintances was Timothy Leary, the "high priest" of acid, whose exhortation to "tune in, turn on, and drop out" was taken up by a generation of hippies. John Lilly, often a guest at 2796 Creston Drive, sought to expand awareness by studying dolphin intelligence and interspecies communication. His work with dolphins led to his experimentation with LSD and his invention of the "isolation tank" or "samadhi tank," in which a person can experience total sensory deprivation, to allow subtle states of consciousness to arise. Anthropologists and psychologists studied the effects of hallucinogens and often experimented on themselves. Many who had had their minds blown by LSD or mescaline turned to Eastern religions such as Buddhism, Taoism, and Hinduism to provide a context for drug-induced insights and a way to cultivate higher states of consciousness without drugs.

All this was pursued with great zest and a belief in humanity's capacity for transformation that may seem naïve to us now. And the explorers had fun. Those who came to Henry and Ruth's home to teach and learn were well taken care of by Ruth, who cooked meals, created beautiful flower arrangements, distributed drinks and snacks and pillows, making sure everyone was comfortable. Sometimes she did this in tandem with Henry's ex-wife Virginia, with whom he maintained an amicable relationship for a period after their breakup.

"Whenever we came to Los Angeles," Alan Watts recalls,

> [Ruth] or Virginia, or both of them together, would stage far-into-the-night parties at which the guests might include Aldous and Laura Huxley, Marlon Brando, John Saxon, Lew Ayres, Anaïs Nin, Zen master Joshu Sasaki, and a fascinating cast—this is Hollywood—of

psychiatrists, physicians, artists, writers, dancers, and hippies who, in this context, somehow managed not to bore each other. Many of us would sleep on cushions on the floor and then continue the party at breakfast.[17]

Clearly Ruth had found a role among these heady intellectuals. She lived intensely in her body, attentive to food and comfort, movement and touch; she was the earth mother, who cooked and tended, bringing these celebrities into contact with the humble everyday reality of the material world. Intuitively she understood what she could offer them, and that they would value it.

Ruth loved this new life. She had found material security, a beautiful home, a partner who was an "elegant man" and a spiritual seeker, and the frequent stimulation of some of the best minds of the mid-twentieth century. But there were dark spots in all that light. Ruth discovered that Henry had some difficult traits: He could be kind, gracious, and loving, then in the next instant could withdraw into icy uncaring distance. When provoked, he resorted to anger and sarcasm. She also had to contend with his unresolved relationships with women like Virginia and Sarada.

All of this caused her pain, but she never lashed out at Henry or demanded he change his behavior. As she had in her family and her village, she restrained herself. She would even cook dinner for Henry and the woman who was visiting, then leave the house so they could enjoy the meal and the evening in private. She understood that as she and Henry were not married, she had no hold over him. "I was kind of seeing things as they are," she says. "If you are bitching about it right away, you lose it what you are doing. And you give lots of material for the other one to evaluate you in a negative way. This way I was free and I enjoyed that, being kind when I really didn't get even kindness or what I wanted. I think it is due to my time in Prussia under Soviet occupation —I have made a vow there that I would be a good girl. A good girl is not jealous and makes scenery. I rather cried alone in my pain but I wouldn't give it out."

The legacy of the Nazis now and then erupted with startling bitterness to haunt Ruth. She describes an encounter with a man at a party. "I already had my association with Henry, it was a little party somewhere and one man was so angry. He comes in this party with a picture of Anne Frank. And said, 'You killed her!' What do you say to that now? Something I may have spoken, I don't know, I wasn't provocative in any way. What he said, that is revenge, that is hate creating hate. But with me it wasn't. I always stopped it."

Physically, she was having problems, not unlike her young cousin Lydia, who had been raped by a British soldier and subsequently could not bear children. Ruth, probably due to her own repeated rapes, had suffered ovarian infections since the war. In Los Angeles she sought medical help and went into the hospital for an operation, thinking the doctors would remove her ovary. She woke up to discover that they had performed a total hysterectomy. "They hadn't asked me and I hadn't signed for it, but obviously—I was under anesthesia, they couldn't ask me—obviously it was important that they did it."

Ruth does not explore the significance to her of this surgery or say whether she had ever wanted to have children of her own. Perhaps she simply accepted this loss as she had so many others. Apparently the loss of her childbearing capacity did not affect her relationship, for Henry, who had left behind one child in New Mexico, was not interested in producing or raising another. He focused on his spiritual path, continually seeking out teachers and spokespeople. Now and then Henry took Ruth down the hill to the Vedanta Temple to attend the services. Flanked by tall trees, the temple is a small, beautiful structure whose white dome, with its gold ornament on top, glistens in the sun. Inside, in the restful atmosphere of pale green walls, Ruth and Henry sat in a pew to participate in the services. On the altar and walls hung photographs of Ramakrishna, the great Indian sage, and his wife Sarada Devi (for whom their friend Sarada had been named). Two photographs of Vivekananda, the teacher who brought Vedanta to the West, gazed from the walls. At the front of the room, a man played the organ. Ruth maintains that she did not understand the philosophy but that she "felt the atmosphere, an inner feeling . . . about surrendering . . . and being devoted." She loved the organ music, which reminded her of the Christian church.

Once again, Ruth's entire world had shifted. The first time, the war in Germany had taken away her home, dispersed and damaged her family, and plunged her into extreme personal hardship and suffering. She had survived it by entering wholeheartedly into the struggle to live, never looking back to mourn her peaceful childhood and young adulthood. Now she found herself in a new land, in an unfamiliar world of privilege and intellectual stimulation. A less resilient human being would have been intimidated, but Ruth called upon her great vitality and survival skills. She knew how to serve, please, nurture: she was more than willing to do that in order to ensure a stable place for herself in this new world.

CHAPTER SIX

The First Teacher

The explorations of the counterculture were led by men who had lived through the devastation of the Second World War, people who had seen the worst in human nature and who hoped to so transform our collective consciousness that we would never again commit the atrocities that had ravaged the Western world. Erich Fromm, a German Jewish psychotherapist, who sometimes joined Henry and Ruth at their house, was typical of these men. In his *Escape from Freedom,* he defined freedom as the realization of one's individual self, "that is, the expression of [one's] intellectual, emotional and sensuous potentialities." The seekers of the counterculture aspired to achieve this expression.

Their investigation was all about finding ways to open to an enlarged, more authentic humanity. For some that might lead to "God" or transcendence, to gaining access to deeper psychic-spiritual truths through drugs or meditation practices. Swami Vivekananda, the Advaita Vedanta seer, said that "Man is like an infinite spring, coiled up in a small box, and that spring is trying to unfold itself."[18] Henry and his friends strove to find ways to uncoil themselves and open into their seemingly infinite capacities.

Among these male proponents of transformation, one woman came to be recognized for her work in cultivating awareness. This was Charlotte Selver, founder of the Sensory Awareness method, who became Ruth's first teacher.

It made eminent sense that Selver would touch Ruth, for Ruth lived in a sensitive, nuanced relationship with her body. Since she was a child running through the grass of a meadow, spreading clothes to dry in the sunshine, sitting with the pigs and geese while they ate, reveling in the smells and textures and sights of nature, she had been attuned to the material universe, beginning with her own body and opening out to the world around her. The abuse and wounding of that body after the war had not alienated her from it; she continued to reside in its wisdom, which withstands violation, springs back from injury. She had fully experienced the attacks upon her, not splitting off or dissociating, so that, when they were over, she was able to leave them behind. In Henry's house, surrounded by men talking of the life of the mind, she had not been touched. But when Charlotte Selver arrived and began to explore the intricate complex of sensations that arise in the physical being, Ruth woke up. Charlotte spoke directly to what Ruth already knew; Ruth saw that with Charlotte's instruction she could penetrate more deeply into the experience of her life as she lived it in each moment.

Meeting Ruth Denison in 1980, I did not know that the underpinning of her work had come from Charlotte Selver. The sensitivity to body that Ruth taught us, her constant guidance to be aware of the sensations arising this very moment in us—this was a revelation to me, and a great opening and deepening. It was the very first time that someone had asked me to be aware of my standing posture, for instance—to feel the touch of my feet on the floor, to pay attention to all the subtle adjustments the body makes in order to hold itself upright. Over and over, Ruth brought us back from our thoughts, plans, fantasies to the reliable ground of our bodies. This had the profound effect on me of opening me to the reality being experienced in the present moment, that nexus where life is really taking place. That was the beginning of my understanding of and practice of Buddhism.

The Buddha identified the body as the First Foundation of Mindfulness. In Ruth's later investigations of this principle, she had a brilliant insight: she would apply the techniques of sensory awareness to the endeavor of cultivating mindfulness. She continued to practice and teach using sensory awareness as she developed as a Buddhist teacher, and some aspects of her approach have been incorporated into the teaching of many more conventional *vipassana* (insight meditation) teachers. But before Ruth had been exposed to Buddhism, she found her first guide to awareness of the body in Charlotte Selver, in her own living room.

It was indirectly, through Eric Fromm, that Selver came to Hollywood. In New York City in the mid-forties, Fromm found his way to the studio of a German Jewish woman, Charlotte Selver, who taught practices she called "Sensory Awareness." Selver, twenty years older than Ruth, based her work upon the discoveries of a German physical education teacher named Elsa Gindler. Having studied with Gindler, and later having taught Gindler's method in Germany, Selver brought the work to the United States, where she opened her New York studio in 1938.

Fromm thought that this method led to a more relaxed and alert participation in daily life, and was so impressed that he declared it "of greatest significance for the full unfolding of the personality."[19] He promoted Charlotte Selver, securing a teaching position for her at the New School for Social Research, and later inviting her to speak at the Conference on Zen Buddhism and Psychoanalysis in Mexico, where she met the great Zen scholar D. T. Suzuki. The parallels between sensory awareness and Zen soon became apparent. Selver read Alan Watts's *The Spirit of Zen* and, "amazed and fascinated," decided that on her next visit to California she would visit Watts. After meeting her, Watts attended one of her New York seminars, and immediately took to her work, saying that Selver actually *did* what he talked about. He began to lead joint workshops with her in New York City.

"She can take absolutely anything—" he said, "—the floor, a ball, a rock, a bamboo pole, a glass of water, or a piece of bread—and get you to relate to it in such a way that the harsh dualism of what you do and what happens to you is transcended. She puts you in love with the simple fact of physical existence."[20] He told Henry Denison about this exciting teacher, and Henry began to consider sponsoring Selver to teach in Los Angeles. Selver agreed to come and meet Henry at his house.

Ruth found her there one evening in 1959. "She first came as an introduction and to talk with Henry and look the situation over. I saw her elegantly German kind of style, pure silk blouse with French cuffs and cufflinks. And a nice pleated skirt. She spoke very slow and very appreciative. She was always appreciative—especially the way I had arranged the flowers. She had talked with Henry and had dinner with him. I was invited—I didn't live with Henry at that time. So I arrived now. They both were sitting and animated. She loved men, she was very animated with Henry, and Henry is such a gracious host when he plays it. They were sitting there at that long table for fourteen people to sit down, along the beautiful viewing windows.

"I came in with two dachsies. Wild, you know, and they barked, and Henry gave them his pattings. She is delighted in that whole thing. I had to catch them, and I was running after. She gets up, and says, 'How beautiful, how exciting, what a storm!' And this kind of thing. We went through the evening, and we brought her at ten o'clock to the train station to go to San Francisco. That was my first encounter with Charlotte Selver. She was excited and beautiful; she made remarks about the vibrancy there in our house—not disapproving—she *noticed*."

After that first meeting, "Henry was up for more and more connection. He was fired for it." He made arrangements to bring Charlotte out to California, and offered his home for her seminars. The living room, opening onto the outer patios, provided a setting conducive to her work. Charlotte stayed at the house, in a guestroom with a separate entrance and kitchen that Henry had built. Downstairs there was another terrace and balcony; she and her assistant (later her husband), Charles Brooks, often cooked there for themselves. Or they cooked with Ruth and Henry.

• • •

Having spent time in Ruth's Hollywood house, I can imagine the scene at the seminars. On a quiet Saturday morning in the spacious living room, the glass doors have been opened onto the decks. Cool air enters, birds call and respond. The assembled students stand on the rug before the yellow-brick fireplace. Charlotte Selver, eyes alert, brown hair straight to her shoulders, dressed in a light-colored loose smock, speaks of the full range of our potential as human beings, much of which escapes our awareness. That potential "can be brought to life," she says, "and gradually unfolded." She talks about how we often misuse our potential, not taking full advantage of our energy. She asserts that there are "no ungifted people. If we believe we are ungifted, we will find on closer examination that we are only hindered, and hindrances can gradually be shed, when we get insight into what has held us back and give ourselves new chances."[21]

She says that we react to our environment through the postures and movements she calls the "Four Dignities of Man." They are: standing, walking, sitting, lying down. Ruth and Henry, along with the other students, have removed their shoes and stand waiting for instruction.

Selver invites them to lie down on the rug. And then she asks them a question.

"Do you have enough room to lie comfortably?"

This seemingly simple question leads to a subtle exploration. Some find they are pressing their legs together, or pressing their head or back against the floor. Charlotte asks them to feel out carefully the difference between pressing and not pressing, and in the process they may find mental or emotional reasons for their tension.

The students are asked to open their legs cautiously, bring their arms away from the body, and see if they feel a new flow of sensation or energy.

"Now lift one arm away from the floor," she directs. "Stay to feel its weight, and let it return. How does the rug feel under the arm? Have we fully arrived here?"

Then the leg is lifted, held, and returned to the floor.

"Can we allow the body to rest on the floor?"

What Selver and her students are after is "not what one *knows* of one's body, or what one *thinks* about it, or believes *somebody else expects one to feel of it,* but what one *actually senses,* no matter what comes to the fore. . . . This physical self-experience is for many people entirely new, often stirringly so."[22]

In Ruth's living room, Charlotte asks her students to stand. More precisely, she asks them to "come to standing."

Charles Brooks, her assistant and husband, describes this activity. "This is an invitation to one of the commonest activities of daily living, which perhaps more than any other distinguishes man from animals, but which our culture does not recognize as an activity at all. . . . Who, in adulthood, comes to standing consciously, for its own sake, unless for the relief of 'stretching one's legs'? Indeed who, unless sick or injured, takes the trouble to feel his way to standing at all?"[24]

Throughout the session, Selver directs the students' attention by asking questions. Ruth and Henry find that there are no right or wrong answers, no preferred experiences or postures: the goal is each student's discovery of his or her own experience. Ruth, her face intent, her body alert, participates with all of her sensitivity and concentration.

The whole morning may be spent lying down, or walking. In the afternoon, objects such as stones and wooden poles are brought into play for further exploration. Selver works to awaken the student to "the ever-changing relationships within [him/herself] and . . . between that 'inner' and the 'outer world.' "[24] She cultivates awareness of the mind and body together, "one rich, unified organization, functioning as a complex reality."

• • •

Ruth, so awake to her own body, immediately resonated to Charlotte's work. She knew something crucial was being offered to her, and she enthusiastically agreed with Henry to invite Selver back. There began a yearly schedule in which Charlotte Selver and Charles Brooks would come to Hollywood each winter, stay with Ruth and Henry, and conduct their workshops in the living room. They became family to Ruth. "I learned it while she was in our house—four-hour sessions—I would have attended two half hours because I was busy arranging things. But I also enjoyed it. And it wasn't just because of the people there—a contact high you get—but because I *felt* it, it was getting me. When I was standing there, I thought God yes, *I can feel it*. Charlotte said, 'You can do it when you hang your clothes.' And she would point me out sometimes as an example that I do everything so nice."

Ruth acknowledges the gift she received from Selver. In the days, weeks, and years that followed, Ruth would often fall back on the sensory awareness exercises, and later would take them further, into the realm of spirituality, where Selver never ventured.

In the Hollywood house, Ruth utilized Charlotte's teachings to help young pregnant women. Henry was volunteering in a clinic for unwed mothers, as a psychologist, and he brought the women home to Ruth. "He'd say, 'They need something, dahling, to ground them, like they could maybe do ironing or the laundry.' So I did that with them. I saw that sensory awareness might help them—where the mind is directed—without directing it, hmm?—to the slow lifting of your arm. Now you transfer that to your weeding in the garden: there is also the lifting of the arm. I could connect that. So that's what I taught the pregnant young women, with ironing. 'You take the iron, and instead of thinking, you feel your arm as it moves. Leaving thought behind.' "

She resorted to Selver's teaching in trying to help Henry, and the sensory awareness entered into their intimate life. "Henry did praise Charlotte, and he brought this all about and worked on it, that people came, and he did also attend the sessions. But sometimes he would just go into his studio and stay away. The real time when I helped him was when we were alone, in our intimacy. Henry could not sleep without a sleeping pill. He would wake up in the night and take another one. I said, 'Dahling, maybe instead of another sleeping pill, maybe I give you a little massage—that is body feelings—and you can go to sleep while I massage you.' So there was one period of our bedroom life that we would lie down and notice that he was not going to sleep, so I said 'Maybe you slide down a little and let the feet be open and I will do your feet.' I did it for a long time, almost every evening. Massage his feet, and then say something like Charlotte said, 'Feel the space,' and then he said, 'Don't talk, just let me feel it.' And he would fall asleep under my hands. And gradually the midnight or four o'clock in the morning pill did go away. He slept more relaxed.

"Also [because of Charlotte's teaching] our very sexual intimacy was more emphasized on touch and cuddling. In the sexual act itself we realized that that striving toward a climax is not natural, or not so good. There was a book he had that described the withdrawal of the climax and just allowing it to come while you are more in touch with your body. We explored that. Sometimes in the morning we were leisurely. You know, he didn't work, and so we had the mornings in this house, it was just paradise."

• • •

Soon Ruth would find that Charlotte's teachings came to her aid in a spiritual setting, and she would begin her life's work of exploring the sensations of the body to ground herself strongly in the present moment—the base from which to access the great truths of the universe.

By the time I encountered Ruth Denison, when she had become a mature Buddhist teacher, she had developed numerous ways to apply sensory awareness to the teaching of mindfulness. She would lead us in slow stretching exercises, reaching an arm to the side, pausing to be aware of all the sensations of weight and muscle tension involved in that action. She would have us lie on the floor and feel our bodies sinking as our spines relaxed. She would take us out into the desert and guide us in moving mindfully in a circle, lifting one leg, swiveling the torso, setting the foot down again with full sensitivity to the touch of foot on sandy soil. Whimsically, she had us dance in full awareness of our skeletons, shaking our bones. All this served as an invitation to me and the other students to enter into the complex subtle reality of lived existence, to be present for the actual moments of our experience.

Ruth has so thoroughly welcomed and integrated her early work with Charlotte Selver into her life and Buddhist practice that it comes out in myriad obvious and sometimes very subtle ways while Ruth teaches. Nowadays, there is no way to separate her understanding of Buddhist principles and practices from her ability to penetrate the sensations of the body, but it is a sure thing that Ruth's extraordinary physical sensitivity and her ability to awaken her students to this were nurtured, first and foremost, by Charlotte Selver.

CHAPTER SEVEN

Pilgrimage—to the Second Teacher

In the early sixties, Henry, who had never traveled outside the United States, proposed to Ruth that they go to Asia to study with spiritual teachers in Japan and Burma. They would first fly to Japan to join Alan Watts in Kyoto. Watts, in love with Zen, had begun teaching groups of Westerners in a Japanese setting. Ruth already knew a bit about Zen, as the Japanese Zen teacher Joshu Sasaki had become a friend of Ruth and Henry in Los Angeles. Ruth had attended some of the sittings he led in a garage; Sasaki and his German female student Gesshin[25] sometimes stayed the night in Ruth and Henry's house. So Ruth felt comfortable exploring more about Zen.

Henry's plan to go to Burma had been suggested by his reading. Ever in search of spiritual liberation, Henry had found a book by a retired British naval officer, *An Experiment in Mindfulness,* published in 1960. In it Rear Admiral E. H. Shattock described his experience in a Burmese Buddhist monastery. Shattock had gone to Rangoon to the Thathana Yeiktha Monastery to pursue a course in meditation with the renowned monk and meditation master Mahasi Sayadaw. Intrigued, Henry decided he too must go and learn this new meditation practice.

Shattock's book reveals a lot about Henry Denison. The two men even look alike—as evidenced by Shattock's photograph on the book jacket—with their high, broad foreheads, long cheeks, and thin-lipped mouths. I would bet Shattock, like Henry, stood more than six feet tall. He peers out of the photograph with the clear, intelligent gaze of a fellow who knows his own mind, certainly not one to be swayed by mystical folderol. His dark suit jacket, tie, and neatly brushed-back hair proclaim his identity as a proper British gentleman—not a beatnik, hippie, or bohemian. Henry also gave that impression, no matter how exotic his explorations in consciousness. Alan Watts called him an aristocrat, "tall, gentle, courteous, urbane, and literate, but entirely relaxed in acceptance of his wondrously crazy friends."[26]

One could imagine Denison and Shattock (who did not in reality know each other) comfortably ensconced in the easy chairs before Henry's yellow-brick fireplace, long legs extended, brandies in hand, discussing the issues raised in Shattock's book. I am looking at Henry's copy of that book right now, and it is revelatory to see his underlinings on the pages, the vertical lines he penciled in the margins to highlight specific sections. In chapters on karma, the workings of the mind, the phenomena of dimensions and of time, Shattock seeks to draw parallels with the discoveries made in science; he speaks practically and, sometimes, psychologically. Henry was obviously intrigued, marking the most compelling arguments. Shattock's description of the meditation practice and regime he followed in Burma is delivered matter-of-factly, claiming no more than what he can recount from his own experience for the edification of others.

Henry announced to Ruth that after their sojourn in Japan they would go to Burma, in search of Mahasi Sayadaw.

And Ruth was terrified. Thathana Yeiktha was a monastery, Mahasi Sayadaw a monk! Having spent seven years as a monk in the Vedanta tradition, Henry showed distinct proclivities for the monastic life. What if he decided to take robes with Mahasi Sayadaw and live as a monk in Burma! She and Henry were not married yet. Ruth had no binding claims on him. She might lose him! They set off on their trip. After their stay in Japan, and visits to other Asian countries, finally Henry and Ruth arrived in Burma—a country of green rice paddies, thatch huts and oxen, its people brown-skinned and gaceful in patterned sarongs—in search of Mahasi Sayadaw.

Burma had for many years been a British colony. It was devastated by Japanese invaders during the Second World War, and since then had been racked by civil disorder and political intrigue. It is also a Buddhist country, in the Theravada Buddhist tradition.[27] In the 1960s there were some two or three hundred meditation centers in Burma, most run by brown-robed Theravada monks with shaved heads.

At Mahasi Sayadaw's monastery, Ruth and Henry stayed only a few weeks because Ruth was suffering severe back pain. The accommodations included a wooden platform with thin straw mat for bed, a curved piece of wood for pillow, and only a mosquito net for protection. After spending a few nights on this bed, Ruth could not get up in the morning. She was in excruciating pain. Her back problem had begun earlier in Hollywood when she and Henry had been doing some repair work on his house. They were patching a leak in the roof, covering it with tar. In the process, he asked her to help carry a piece of heavy equipment, with disastrous consequences: "I sunk into my knees, and from there on. . . ." Before this she had been exceptionally flexible, able to easily do a complete backbend. Now she found herself rigid with pain.

Henry was kind and accommodating, inquiring about other meditation centers that might offer more comforts. He contacted the International Meditation Center in a Rangoon suburb, and came to reassure Ruth, "Darling, we can change—and they've promised to provide you with a special bed." They traveled across the bustling city of Rangoon to a quiet neighborhood, where, built on a little knoll, there stood a pagoda-like structure about thirty feet high. This was the meditation center run not by a monk but by a layman, Thray Sithu Sayagyi U Ba Khin, otherwise known as U Ba Khin or Gurugyi. Here Ruth found the mentor whose teachings were to guide her for the rest of her life, and who gave her the authority to teach and take her place in his ancient lineage as his Dharma heir.

The bed at the International Meditation Center was made of ropes, a little more yielding than hard wood, and Ruth's back pain began to lessen. "Henry stayed in another quarter. We could eat together—there was a little table in front of the window. He came to luncheon, and we ate together there. We didn't go where everyone ate. I had an attendant and we got the food carried in."

U Ba Khin was living nearby. "I go a little walkway past his pond. Then here was my little *kuti* [cottage], and the window, cement floor and a little water disperser you turned on with a string, so you could have a cold shower. Then this part was here a bed and here a cot. Henry sat on it sometimes. A little table, a window, here a chair and here we would sit, and I would write my memoirs, just saying what I experienced.[28] Here was another pond, and everywhere papaya trees with papayas hanging, and the big parrots in the trees were talking. U Ba Khin would talk back to them."

In the eight tiny meditation cells in the temple, Ruth, Henry, and a man named Robert Hover were the only foreigners. Robert Hover was destined to become another of U Ba Khin's Dharma heirs. U Ba Khin, a powerfully built man in his early sixties, wearing a plaid sarong and white jacket, led the three Westerners in vowing to uphold the precepts, then briefly instructed them in *anapana sati* (mindfulness of breathing) and sent them to their cells to meditate. The precepts are to refrain from killing, stealing, lying, taking intoxicants, and engaging in sexual misconduct. U Ba Khin had the students concentrate on the breath, in order to build *samadhi* (concentration). From the fourth day through the tenth, he instructed them in vipassana and led them in a "sweep" of the body, whereby the consciousness explores every part of the physical/mental being, to awaken *panna* (wisdom).

All this was an arduous endeavor for someone whose only experience of meditation had been a few Zen sittings. But Ruth soon discovered that her work with Charlotte Selver had given her a strong foundation for this type of meditation: Selver had taught her to be aware of her body and mind, which was what U Ba Khin was asking her to do. Ruth thought she already knew how to do what U Ba Khin was teaching. Besides, she had not chosen to come there, and she was still fearful that Henry would be stolen from her. So for most of that initial ten days she resisted U Ba Khin.

Still, as her back stopped hurting, she followed the rigorous schedule, which began with wake-up at 4:30 a.m. and went on long into the evening. "We had to sit all the time in our little coops. I was standing on my head, yah, to relax a little more, and that kind of loosened me through the whole body, and I could somehow realize there is a *body* to this focus. Then, dahling, I was okay. But then I realized, *that is what I already did*—that's Charlotte Selver sensory awareness practice!"

Ruth did not yet tell U Ba Khin about her private reservations, but the Burmese master held individual interviews with the Westerners, and also visited them in their cells, so he began to notice that Ruth was very seriously meditating and had achieved good concentration. He began to take a special interest in her, although initially it had not been Ruth who interested him, but Henry. U Ba Khin's "greatest passion and lust, he said, was to bring the teaching to the West." But the political situation in Burma made it impossible for U Ba Khin to leave the country to teach in the West, because he would not have been allowed to return. He was looking for Westerners to carry the teachings as his agents, and Henry seemed an excellent candidate. "Henry came to U Ba Khin as a golden angel," Ruth explains, "a psychologist, into which U Ba Khin had put a lot of hope to be a carrier of the Dharma for the West. He thought Henry would be his agent."

But Henry was having problems concentrating. He spent hours of each day talking to Robert Hover, the other American, who was a scientist and shared Henry's intellectual interest in meditation. U Ba Khin, who emphasized the practical rather than the theoretical approach to Dharma, was not pleased. One day as she sat in meditation, Ruth heard him shouting at Henry, his voice echoing throughout the center—"You are caught in your evil forces!" Ruth interprets, "Caught by his hindrances probably, hmm? [The hindrances in Buddhism are lust, ill-will, torpor and languor, restlessness and worry, skeptical doubt.] That Henry is obsessed and doesn't let go, and things like that. U Ba Khin did the same to me for nine days, but to me it was in a different way, for me it was the beginning. I resisted for about a week—inwardly resenting.

"I resisted mainly because I had touch to myself already. When I realized he was asking me to feel my sensations, I thought, 'That is what I did already with Charlotte Selver!' So I said, 'I didn't come for that, I want enlightenment!' In myself I said that, I didn't tell U Ba Khin that. But I thought, what he's giving me, it isn't so much: why are we here? And he could feel that. I was kind of pouting probably, hmm? So then he criticized me and said, 'I'm not talking to *you* now, I'm talking to your evil forces!' He didn't say resistance, or hindrances, but he said the evil forces were there. I was angry probably. I didn't want to be there. I was seeing that it wasn't what I had thought it would be. It was feeling my body and my sensations, that was what I already did in Sensory Awareness with Charlotte. I said to Henry, 'Look, dahling, what's new about it? We already did that!'—then I got *Henry's* anger.

"But when my teacher faced me with my resistance, I somehow got a grip on myself. I got away from these images coming from heaven and seeing a picture of myself being enlightened. And I saw also on the tip of my nose some light coming.[29] Then I had nice visions, of myself or somebody coming down from the clouds in a long gown, peaceful. I did meditate with these images but they were actually already an indication of going away from thoughts and resistance. You now shifted your mind with images, and they were nice. And the next there was, I became very absorbed, and I began to touch what I could feel and learn, I deepened now what Charlotte had taught me.

"Then U Ba Khin initiated me for the next stage. It was after the third day of *anapana sati,* and I go for an interview. U Ba Khin and I, we sit here and he says, 'Now I will guide you into vipassana.' He said, 'Bring your attention *here,* and hold your attention *here* [leading her through her body], and feel the *anicca* [impermanence] *here.*' I could feel the energy, the movement. And I said, 'But I did that already. I already feel that.' He said, 'Well, that is no wonder because why shouldn't you? You have it all the time there. I initiate you now to see that more deeply. Some people don't have that expansion, you see. So now you go deeper into that.'"

Ruth's resistance began to dissolve, as she understood that U Ba Khin had something to teach her. Then, in one of the rooms of the center, she found a page torn from a book describing the Buddha's "eight-fold noble path," the road map he had given his disciples for living a pure life and cultivating awareness. Even this isolated scrap of doctrine gave Ruth an inkling of the larger goal of this practice.

She surrendered to U Ba Khin's teachings, and he began to direct his attention to her. It was the beginning of a deep and long-lasting relationship. "I let myself be led through the body, and he would come around and say, 'Sensation, sensation'—that was sometimes his chant —'Feeling sensations, anicca.' Now you had to recognize anicca."

U Ba Khin himself describes the process:

> When the student has reached a certain level of *samadhi* [concentration] . . . the course of training is changed to vipassana or insight. This requires the use of the powerful lens of *samadhi* already developed and involves an examination of the inherent tendencies of all that exists within one's own self. He is taught to become sensitive to the ongoing processes of his own organism, which in other words are atomic reactions ever taking place in all living beings. When the student becomes engrossed with such sensations, which are the products of nature, he comes to the realization, physically and mentally, of the truth that his whole physical being is after all a changing mass. This is the fundamental concept of anicca in Buddhism—the nature of change that is ever taking place in everything, whether animate or inanimate, that exists in this universe.[30]

Ruth says, "I took what U Ba Khin did, I took this modality of mindfulness to body as a practice, as a primary practice, because it is tangible right away, it makes sense, it is giving a bridge to physics, to modern science, and it gives you a personal touch with yourself. It is all spiritual and enlightenment. So it was not something to believe in or to bow to, you didn't need to pray to it. It brought me into daily life, where I know that everything is having this impermanence.

"Then I made good progress. I really went to that.

"I would tell him that I felt strong vibrancy here, in my cheeks or in my mouth. I would also report that when I breathe in and feel a deeper breath and allow that, then I felt the relationship between the breath energy and the body energy. The breath moves into the body and changes the sensations, that aliveness, and it is recharged with the in-breath. And then it goes out and comes again. I also discovered that when I am allowing more deeper the breathing, that I have deeper access to the body sensations, because I can witness or feel that every part of the body is now in my attention, like it is enlivened with the breath. It's always so, but now because of my attention I could experience that directly. So it was not anymore anything I have to worship or ask how to understand. I just thought *'Aha, this is this!'*

"Then I could also go into deep absorption. I remember that once U Ba Khin came in to my cell with Henry, and I heard them a little bit. I didn't react to them or turn. I think he had said, 'If I visit you sometimes don't turn around, I just want to see if you are sitting.' I had a great delight in deepening my concentrated mind, my attention to the body sensations, and that changed the consciousness so I wasn't frightened about losing Henry anymore. I wanted to become a nun, even, at one point. And saw also that many of the things we do in life, like intimacy, are a little bit, on one level, a compensation for this deeper experience.

"So U Ba Khin came in the cell with Henry and I didn't move. U Ba Khin said, 'She is sitting in a deep absorption. I just wanted you to see.' I think he wanted to demonstrate to Henry that she sits and you talk. He knew that Mr. Hover and Henry were talking a lot together. Mr. Hover had good comprehension, but Henry had been a monk himself, you see, and he talked with U Ba Khin probably about his practice with Vedanta, and he had a lot of questions. Then U Ba Khin would tell Henry about how well I was doing. And when I told U Ba Khin my experiences in meditation he would say, Fine, Nice, and make a little comment. He would always nod and smile. He was very jolly.

"Then, after, I practiced always with body sensations as a focus. He would give occasionally support with guided meditations again, and sometimes with me alone. Other people came and went, we stayed longer. We stayed there two months."

Through her own hard practice and U Ba Khin's instruction, Ruth achieved a further level of awareness "where the mind, it has something to do with absorption, where the mind holds itself in the concentration, you don't concentrate anymore, and there is this knowing faculty coming in, so the mind knows itself where it is concentrated, where it is focused, and even that loses itself, it is more a spaciousness where you however know that you are the conduit for it, and you stay in that. For some time, twenty minutes or so, he would guide me to that. And then he saw a big capacity in me. Then I had to tell him what I feel about my experience and how it related to what he is teaching—the elements, and impermanence."

I ask, "Would you call that an enlightenment experience?"

She looks displeased at the question. "Well, I don't know. I never used that word. What is enlightenment? You see? I had a deep experience in which I could see anicca, I being a conduit, that is revolutionary. Now it's natural to me. But at that time, it is the first entry into the great stream. . . . But then you lose it too. It's one touch. The Zen people call it *kensho*. You see, I had the Zen and I had Charlotte, so I was well equipped for this kind of thing. I knew how to get to that deep experience, and I had support enough from Charlotte's practice. Later when I came to teaching, I was able to give a good grounding to the students from that place."

Perhaps it is not surprising that a layman like U Ba Khin would become Ruth's root teacher, as she herself has long been committed to lay life and practice. He was an eminently practical man, who had briefly been a monk but lived most of his life as a householder and public servant. After the British had left, he became accountant general of Burma, and taught meditation to his employees. In 1952 he built the International Meditation Center. After his retirement he continued to labor in government, heading four different departments. When Ruth was there, he was still going to his office every morning. Before leaving he would walk around the outside of the octagonal temple where the meditators sat in their little cells, and would chant in a deep resonant voice, to encourage them.

When he returned from the office each day, he either gave interviews to his individual students, or received groups of Burmese in the central room of the temple. Rocking back and forth in a rocking chair, he would give his teachings. Sometimes Ruth would find him at work in the garden. "He has a pond with lotus flowers and some little fish. One evening I came out of my cell and he was standing there and trying to save a rat out of it. She was eating the roots of the lotus, and maybe the fish too." Although he had a wife and children and a home, U Ba Khin slept at the temple, on a mat on the floor.

In the Burmese religious community he was criticized, not only because he was a layman who dared to teach the Dharma—which had been a function almost exclusively of monks—but also because he had devised a ten-day course to teach vipassana, which was thought to be too short a time for people to establish themselves in the practice. But U Ba Khin wanted to give the method to as many people as possible, and he maintained that ten days was long enough to learn the technique of vipassana meditation. (His Indian student S. N. Goenka imported this ten-day-retreat model to India and the United States, keeping the strict form, with great success.)

Ruth's relationship with U Ba Khin would deepen and last for the rest of his life and after his death. She took on the practice of vipassana as her spiritual path, and incorporated it into every other spiritual training she found herself in. Wherever she was in the world, she knew what time it was in Rangoon and when her teacher would be meditating, and she timed her meditations to coordinate with his. She wrote to him about her practice and went back to Burma whenever she could, to continue her training with him (not an easy thing to accomplish, as the Burmese political situation worsened and restrictions on foreign tourists grew more strict).

In her continued practice she managed to integrate the austere formal lineage of U Ba Khin with the modern practices of Charlotte Selver—the two modalities combining to carry her forward on an authentic, profound spiritual path. Without ambition for official validation, Ruth nonetheless established herself in a lineage and received her teacher's authorization. Her motivation was to learn, to explore, to make her way in this endeavor, and that is what she has continued to do.

CHAPTER EIGHT

Marriage and Millbrook

Back in Hollywood with Henry, Ruth felt great happiness. She had achieved her dream. Henry belonged to the "Great World," the world of beautiful houses and important, fascinating people that she had longed to know when she lay dreaming in the fields near her childhood home. He was like her father's brother whom she had so admired, Uncle Robert, who was not a farmer but lived in the city and went off to the Alps to ski and dance with sophisticated women. Yet Henry loved the earth too, and knew how to nurture life and how to build; he was older than she, with a restrained, dignified mien. In all these ways he fit her ideal. Now also she had found her spiritual teacher and embarked upon a spiritual path.

Photographs from her early days with Henry express her delight. A young woman in a short nightie cavorts in the garden above the shining expanse of reservoir; she dances on the deck, flinging her arms high, and laughs with audacious joy into the camera. She looks like a nature sprite, a wild thing that has just pranced in from the woods. Another shot finds her in long skirt and bright patterned shawl, stooping to leave food for the coyotes who roamed the hill below the house.

Ruth made her way by serving others. "I couldn't do what many of these people did who were Henry's friends, this kind of philosophizing and so on. But I did what I could do well and what I enjoyed and where my heart was, and that gave to all of them always great comfort and cheerfulness—*Gemütlichkeit*—with coziness, with real caring. Because I rejoiced in their joy about it. So I would cook and bake and sew everything for them. Like the wife of my neighbor, she says, 'Ruth I have to reimburse for what you cooked...where's the bill?' I said, 'I didn't shop, everything was in your refrigerator, I just reconstructed it.' She appreciated it. Also the way I cooked. Potatoes with peels. And home-baked bread. Brought it to the neighbors and that's the way I got my way in.

"Henry saw something in me. He would say, 'What she does is with a full heart and with a full presence,' and I was so amazed that what I naturally did he appreciated so much, that it was suddenly so valuable. Giving nice meal for friends. They got into ecstasy and appreciated me. That was a new world for me. I hadn't before much opportunity to do that."

One can imagine that Henry, such a contained man, was fascinated by Ruth's raw joyful energy, her uninhibited expressiveness. And clearly he basked in all her attention to him and his friends. He deeply loved nature, and was grateful that Ruth gardened with him, and camped out with him in the desert and the mountains. "He delighted in my earthiness in my being with him," she says, "going camping and making the home. I flowered in that very much. I experienced myself, experienced his joy, and became more and more—what do you say—inspired. Inspired by my own delight, being in it and seeing I enjoyed it."

In 1963, just one day after the assassination of John F. Kennedy, Ruth and Henry were married. On November 23, they had a wedding in Guadalajara, Mexico, presided over by a shaman woman. High in the mountains with her, they took peyote and participated in a ceremony to join their lives together. And Ruth later suffered the consequences. "I got double-side pneumonia as a result of this wedding in a hut through which the wind blew, and the old lady gave us a blessing and gave us mushrooms to eat, as a sacrament. I was gotten sick from it. You know those magic mushrooms. Henry took them. I was so hostile to it, but then I was the bride and so I had to. She dressed me nicely with the handmade tunics they have in Mexico.

"Then we went down from that hill. It was a spiritual sacred area. We lived in a hotel and then we did our wedding after that. It was legal—as we came from signing, from city hall, we came back for the lunch for celebrating. Henry forgot the rings. I said, 'Dahling, it is not necessary.' As long as I have his signature whether I have a ring or not doesn't matter. He wanted to rush out to buy them. We were on a roof garden there ready to have our luncheon. We had invited two boys, maybe twelve years old, wonderful boys in the street, to come with us and have good fun. We had the whole garden. We wanted to have some guests and they were available.

"Henry wanted to rush to get the rings; he said, 'You have entertainment with the boys till I come back.' I said, 'Okay, dahling, but don't bother with rings, bring me something which is very ephemeral. Very anicca. So he comes back with a big bunch of colorful balloons. Then we had them tied up in the center of our table, and the boys said what they wanted to eat, and the waiters knew what we were doing, they were serenading us. It was a very simple wedding. I never got a ring."

The wedding picture was taken on a brick walkway in the Mexican sun. Henry stands tall in a dark suit, white shirt, and gray tie, wearing a short, already-gray beard, his high forehead shining in the sunlight as he gazes seriously out of the picture. Ruth, clasped to his side, looks small and sturdy and utterly adoring as she lifts her face to Henry. She wears a pale lavender jumper, a white blouse, and white high-heeled pumps. Her straight hair falls in yellow bangs over her forehead and down to her shoulders.

"Then we came home—that was the death of Kennedy, we learned about it on the airplane—and I came down with a terrible pneumonia. We had a wedding reception on Alan Watts's boat in Sausalito planned, and we had to postpone it till I healed."

In 1961 Watts and his partner Mary Jane, called Jano, had moved onto the houseboat *Vallejo,* moored on the Sausalito waterfront just across the bay from San Francisco. They lived in half the boat; on the other side lived Jean Varda, a Greek painter notorious for his wild parties. The *Vallejo* became the site of Watts's seminars and lecture series, and of the visits of Asian spiritual teachers, including Krishnamurti and Lama Govinda. Sometimes Watts and Varda combined to host celebrations where wine and various psychedelic substances facilitated the jollity of the guests.

"On his boat Alan made it known that he marries Jano, and he called Henry and asked, 'Why don't you come and do the same?' Then one stroke killed a lot of flies. So he gave us the blessing, and to himself, and we had glasses of champagne, and as it was finished the fire was burning in the fireplace, we threw glass and champagne into the fire."

· · ·

Settled once again in Hollywood, where now she formally moved into Henry's house, Ruth continued the vipassana meditation she had learned from U Ba Khin. She experienced the fruits of this practice, saying that clear sight or wisdom-energy came to her through meditation. Ruth went looking for a vipassana teacher in Los Angeles, so that she could deepen her understanding. No such creature existed in the early sixties. So she turned to Zen. She and Henry became serious Zen students, with Sasaki roshi, whom they had known before, and another Japanese Zen master, Maezumi roshi.

Among the people who came to Ruth and Henry's house in the early sixties were psychologists and philosophers experimenting with psychedelics. Henry began to be interested in this kind of exploration. Ruth comments, "There were some big philosophers in that direction. Don't forget, I met Henry in a philosophical society, with professors of philosophy and explorers on the spiritual level or awakening level who had a new paradigm—a different direction in philosophy, as well as in religion. And Henry had been a monk, dahling, he was known. He also was a psychologist, and Leary and Alpert, these two psychologists, were dismissed from the university in Cambridge for exploring. So he was alert for that." Soon Henry would meet Leary, and he and Ruth would spend time at Leary's center in New York.

A professor at Harvard, Timothy Leary had begun to listen to the voices of the counterculture, and had taken LSD. He became friends with Alan Watts and other seekers, and he began to give the drug to his Harvard students in a series of experiments. Richard Alpert (later to be known as Ram Dass), a junior colleague, enthusiastically participated in Leary's experiments, and the two became notorious for leading students on LSD trips. In 1963 Leary and Alpert were fired from Harvard.

That same year, relatives of Alfred Hitchcock, the film director, offered Leary their estate in Millbrook, New York, as a place in which to continue his explorations in expanding consciousness. Leary describes the estate, a two-hour drive up the Hudson River from Manhattan. "It was a magical location, twice five miles of fertile ground with an imposing gatehouse complete with sallyport and huge portcullis."[31] From the gatehouse a mile-long drive under rows of maple trees led to the mansion, four stories high with two towers. In this elegant setting, Leary stated his intention to "go low-profile and, in secluded isolation, continue our research into altered states."[32]

Millbrook, where Ruth and Henry spent six weeks, constituted a grand experiment. Leary and his supporters thought of the place as a "space colony" lost in the dark ages of the 1960s. Leary and his space travelers imagined themselves as visitors from the future, who had landed at Millbrook and, through intellectual and chemical explorations, sought to create "a new paganism and a new dedication to life as art."[33] Through reading and writing about expanded consciousness, regular programmed LSD sessions, and study of spiritual masters, Leary and colleagues created a lifestyle aimed at liberating the true potential of the human mind, body, and psyche. "At Millbrook," Leary wrote, "a veritable earthy [sic] paradise was in full-scale operation.... It was a non-stop festival of life with ceremonies, seminars, music, fertility rites, star gazing, moon watching, [and] forest glade revels."[34] Well-known psychologists and philosophers, spiritual teachers, poets, musicians, and artists came to visit Millbrook and sometimes stayed to join the community for weeks or months.

Millbrook became an important environment for Ruth in several ways. She arrived there in defiance of Henry and generally operated independently during their stay, marking a new chapter in their relationship. No longer the all-suffering, compliant helpmeet, Ruth established her own identity in this highly unusual setting, and was recognized for her powers. Because she was versed in both sensory awareness and vipassana techniques of mindfulness, Ruth became the one who was called upon when someone had a bad trip. She found she could work with the disoriented person to return him or her to sanity. This was the beginning of her understanding of herself as a healer who could help the lost, the insane, the terrified—a capacity that she has continued to develop throughout her life. She also guided groups of people in meditation, her first formal teaching experience. And she was given the opportunity at Millbrook to further experiment with LSD, note its effects on her, and come to her own conclusions about the drug.

Ruth got there not by invitation but by devious means. Leary had sent out invitations for a special seminar: a week of philosophizing and LSD sessions, culminating in the performance of a play based on Hermann Hesse's novel *Magister Ludi (The Glass-Bead Game)*. Dignitaries from a number of fields were invited, and Henry Denison managed to be among them. Ruth was delighted at the thought of going with him, but Henry told her she would not be welcome, that he would go by himself.

"There were dignitaries so to speak from the Christian religions. Bishops and psychologists . . . and Henry was invited to it, or he found out, and he got in. I wanted to go with, but he did not take me.

"So this was the event, maybe in 1966 or so. Henry already had taken LSD, and I too, and I knew what it does to me because I had vipassana, I felt my body transforming and I paid attention to it and I had wonderful experiences. I had explored that. So then he did go to Millbrook."

Ruth was not happy at home while Henry enjoyed himself at Leary's grand festivity. With her friend Sarada, who was living there, she was left to take care of Henry's son, who had been wounded in Vietnam, and had come to visit his father.

She talked on the phone with Henry, and told him she wanted to join him in New York. Henry said no. But Ruth was determined to go. She made her preparations by sewing a special dress for herself. "I knew that the Saturday night it's a finishing of that whole training, hmm? And they all would take LSD. Henry tells me that on the phone very happily, and I was glad to have the information.

"So I take a ticket to New York, I didn't know where I was, I took a taxi, went to Millbrook with a small train. I hadn't been there before and it was evening. I had my dress, it was silk, straight, loose, and this was the basis and then was veil-like material over. So when I would go in I could take it over my head, like a chiffon thing over my face, and I could look through. They couldn't see me, hmm? So I was veiled. I thought I will appear in that party when they all have LSD, I think at least sixty people if not more.

"I arrived. The taxi driver lets me out at the gate and I knew inside that park is the Millbrook estate, where the whole thing was. I didn't know where to go, so I listened. Sometimes I heard flutes and music and I followed. Oh, it was dark, and I had nothing, no guide, nothing. Suddenly I see, coming through the woodsy park, there is a big fountain and the fountain had different colored waters—they must have put some dye in. And it was in front of a beautiful villa, long. The villa had a kind of a porch with a fence around.... Then here came the big walls with stained-glass windows and elegant doors and high ceilings and so on. It was a summer evening and they were all gathered there."

The interior of the mansion featured handcarved woodwork, tapestry-covered walls, and wood-paneled ceilings. Leary had furnished the house "harem-style, featuring low couches, acres of cushions and silken pillows."[35] As befits a harem, on that night a number of women moved throughout the room, attending the male guests. Henry's reasons for excluding Ruth soon became apparent.

"I saw them floating, the ladies in long dresses and it was all elf-like, you know? I knew they are all under LSD, and I could act it out like they did because I knew what LSD does to you.

"So I floated in like I was just coming from the other side of the house, and [there was] this beautiful music and they were a little bit dazy in the heads and looking at everything. Henry is there in the middle part of this party on that porch and he is in an elegant rocking chair, back and forth, happy, really, and ladies at his feet all around, and he had wonderful things to say about no-self and nonattachment and so on. His Vedanta teaching, hmm? He was high.

"I moved into that, dancing. Some just floated. I didn't see Tim Leary, he was somewhere else. I floated in and danced a little bit and stood and did these movements. So I come to sit in Henry's group and then sometimes the ladies came a little closer and went away and kissed him, and so did I. I kissed him nicely. Not too familiar, hmm, on the cheek. And so he said 'Who are you?' and then I floated back. Then he would meet me. He would walk around and he would see me again. 'Who are you?' and I would do this or that and was gone. I was not recognized. The women looked also. I watched it under my veil, I had it always over. I had to make sure that no one could take that veil quickly off.

"Then the bell rang and suddenly they all gather and Tim Leary appeared there. He organized it and said now we are going the *Perlenspiel* [the performance of *Magister Ludi*] and that will be in the bowling alley. We had now to do our procession and everyone got a candle, in the hand with a base, and then they were chanting. Ohm ah Ohm. . . . and a little dancing. We had to go through different pathways through the park and around the fountain. So we are going through the park and humming and somebody was playing a flute and so on. Suddenly we are before the building, going into the bowling alley.

"Henry kept a little bit always looking. When there was a star, someone he felt was mystical or somehow mysterious, he would always investigate. He probably knew them all. I wasn't investigated yet, hmm? So then somehow we enter this big hall, the bowling alley. Beautiful. It was a group following Henry, he was also the leader. Then on the opposite was Tim Leary with his followers, and I was next to Henry. So I was standing with him in the center, and Tim Leary comes and says, 'Henry, who is she? I saw her already a few times.' Henry said, 'I haven't discovered it yet.' Then somehow, Tim Leary takes my veil off—and then Henry had *his wife*! He was so disappointed."

Ruth laughs mischievously. "Can you imagine that for him? It was a down for him. However he played the loving husband, he embraced me and said, 'Rutchen.' And everyone clapped, they realized now who I am. So he delighted in everybody's delight, but then the kind of clarification came later when I was offered the bedroom with him. They gave us the main bedroom on the second floor, which was looking out into what I described as the fountain place.

"He was not really angry. He said, 'How did you get here, dahling? Don't you know our agreement?' I said, 'I must have fallen out of it, I was only loving you and I wanted to see you.' At that time we reconciled, and it was good. And then he delighted in my influence there."

• • •

When the guests had left, the community shrank to twenty or twenty-five, and settled back into its routine. Ruth took over several tasks— baking bread for the community, cleaning up the cat boxes and dirt which the inhabitants, bent upon more lofty pursuits, generally ignored. She liked Timothy Leary, finding him "very soft. He was a kind of walking friendliness and tenderness, very, yes. And such a beautiful face he had. Dahling for me that was a world dream how I got into it. They always accepted me because I had this naturalness. And I didn't philosophize. Wherever I came, like even where he lived, I was at home in the kitchen. They wanted to get food brought in, and before they thought and had planned it, I had it done. So I was always the kind of homemaker, making home, wherever we were. And Henry loved it and was proud of me, that 'you cannot fool around with Rutchen,' he said, 'she just goes down to the essential' and so on."

Ruth began to occupy a special role at the estate as "earth mother," the one who maintained and restored order, the healer who could attend to those having bad reactions to LSD and bring them back to ordinary consciousness. When Leary's daughter dissociated under LSD, Ruth had her put in a bathtub full of warm water. Then she sat with the young woman, moving her hand in the water, helping her gradually to connect with the sensations of her body, until she had returned to sanity. She also attended to Leary's son. "He was seriously freaked out, he had taken maybe 5,000 grams—sat in the middle of the meadow with a knife in the hand and said, 'Nobody gets near me!' So they called me." Ruth was able to calm the young man.

In this healing, she drew from her vipassana experience and also her explorations with LSD, from which she learned an important distinction. "I knew what LSD can do to you when you are not attentive to your sensations. I was having some LSD. I lie in Millbrook under a tree, looking up, but a little bit always connected to the body, because I knew if I don't then I would go out into what I see there. I saw suddenly the leaves—beautiful like bodhi tree leaves—and in each leaf was a golden eye. Gold! Then the little sound of the critters in the background and the light sounds of the birds. It was suddenly like they were all orchestrated into cosmic sound. It looked like the sound came through the golden eyes. I was fascinated by it. But I knew that isn't the reality. Then I closed my eyes and rubbed myself, or I stood up and walked. But I could very much see what happened to them when they got so crazy. *I* could have been in that and suddenly realized, Where am I? That's why I could help them."

Ruth came to the conclusion that LSD did not lead to true insight. This conviction led her to attempt a radical rearrangement of the Millbrook scene. At Millbrook, meditation was maintained around the clock, each person taking his or her turn in the gazebo to meditate and take LSD for a twenty-four-hour period, from noon to noon. In the morning the other community members would come to listen while the meditator described her/his experiences. Ruth did her meditation duty, like the others. In the little gazebo where the lone meditator sat all night, there was a statue of the Buddha. "One night when I was sitting at Millbrook, first I meditated until twelve o'clock. Then for the second twelve hours I took this stuff [LSD]. And at five o'clock in the morning I was seeing something. I knew something was not quite right. So I took the Buddha out of the little meditation hall. I said, 'He doesn't belong here!'"

Ruth was on her way up to the third floor of the main house to wake up Timothy Leary and deliver the statue, along with her revelation, when she was intercepted by Henry, who returned the Buddha to the meditation hall and convinced her to come back downstairs in silence.

"But they all loved me," she says, "because they put me in the position there to make babysitting of them and helping them along. You had to go back to feeling your body, that's all I knew, and feeling your breath, and you know that you do it. I learned how to lead the groups. When I said to Henry, 'How shall I guide them and do meditation?' he said 'Why do you say that? You had the most beautiful training. No one has it here. You can do it.' And I did. So I guided them. Yes, small groups when they had LSD, seven or eight, and sometimes with me together, I would also take a little bit. Then I would hold them in their experience when the drug started working and they didn't know what to do and were afraid what happens now to the body. I called their attention to body sensations. In the manner I had learned with my teacher, I led them to see what is changing and carefully observe the sensations. And of course I had support also from Charlotte Selver's touch.

"Ram Dass was gone at that time; he apparently was very good-rooted, he stayed more on earth.[36] Tim was more out there, hmm? Even he spooked out, and they called me. I had a good concentration, and just by looking at his eyes and seeing the kind of fear which was there and the confusion, I knew what to do. I called to the body and to the sensations and that balanced again, brought the mind from the images and fears and projections and so on, or the experiences from the past—I could always bring them to the present moment. It was beautiful.

"Then I would dance with them like elves around the fountain. I would take it with six or seven women only. I would make beautiful dresses for them and we'd play the goddesses. Yes.

"So that was Millbrook."

CHAPTER NINE

Stepping over the Edge

During the sixties, Ruth and Henry always returned from explorations such as their Millbrook sojourn to their Zen practice in their home town. Their first Zen teacher in Los Angeles, Joshu Sasaki roshi, was a fierce, powerful Rinzai Zen master. He had just arrived in Los Angeles in 1962, and was teaching in a garage in the South Central part of the city. It was there that Ruth and Henry came to practice. Later Sasaki founded the Rinzai-ji Zen Center, housed in a beautiful Spanish-style converted church, of stucco and red tile. It sits in a flagstone courtyard within a high wall, like a monastic cloister, in a mostly African-American neighborhood. Sasaki, in his nineties, still teaches.

Their other Zen teacher was Hakuyu Taizan Maezumi roshi, who was a Soto Zen master. Handsome and cultivated (he was a connoisseur of Asian art, and had earned official recognition in more than one Zen lineage), Maezumi roshi founded the Zen Center of Los Angeles. It was housed in several shingle and frame houses arranged around a courtyard/lawn in a Korean and Hispanic neighborhood.

Henry and Ruth helped both roshis establish their centers, giving fundraising dinners for them, inviting friends to participate in a tea ceremony led by Maezumi roshi, and practicing faithfully with them. So now Ruth was led from the strict Theravada perspective of her Burmese teacher, U Ba Khin, into the wider view of Mahayana Buddhism, where the figure of the *bodhisattva*—the one who lives to benefit all beings —is emulated. "I saw always the things that related to me. The bodhisattva, well, when I heard about it, I thought, I want to be that. I imitated it. I fed the coyotes in the hillside of Los Angeles, I did bring flowers from my garden and supported the Zen Center, four o'clock in the morning I would go every day to the zendo [meditation hall], to prepare with Maezumi roshi. I gave my house for tea ceremonies, and for Alan Watts's seminars. I would invite Maezumi to the ballet or the theater." She chanted the Four Great Vows of a bodhisattva, promising to practice diligently in order to save all sentient beings.[37]

Ruth participated in the *sesshins* (meditation retreats) held regularly at both centers; she was enthusiastic and wholehearted in her Zen practice, sitting long hours, following instructions precisely. This ardor pushed her beyond her mental limits, and she experienced a breakdown. The account of this break and the long period of recovery that followed has become one of Ruth's classic stories, told often in the meditation hall before a rapt audience of sitters. It illustrates the immense value of vipassana practice in an emergency and explains in part Ruth's uncanny ability to stabilize people who are experiencing mental disorientation and terror. As to the roots of her dissociative episode, certainly the austere, physically demanding Zen practice provided the trigger, but Ruth was also living within the contradictions of her relationship with Henry, who at that time swung from extreme to extreme, offering love one minute and withdrawing it the next. And one could speculate that the traumatic experiences of the postwar years in the Polish Corridor, which Ruth had shut away so efficiently, rose up to intensify the disorientation and fear that overtook her.

It all began during a *rohatsu* sesshin at Sasaki roshi's Rinzai-ji temple. The rohatsu is an extremely strict seven-day winter meditation session. The students got up at 2:00 or 3:00 a.m. and sat until nightfall. They had to go see Sasaki roshi three times a day, to be questioned about their practice. There was very little relief or rest in this Zen pressure-cooker. At the breaks the students were not allowed to sit down, but had to stand leaning against the wall. "Everything had to be very fast," Ruth explains, "fast walking, fast eating, fast run to the toilet, fast working in the work period."

The goal of a Zen sesshin is to eliminate all the opportunities for distraction and relaxation, to increase the pressure until the student breaks through her usual ways of being and seeing, into the spacious wisdom-mind that Ruth had achieved through vipassana. The image is of a snake put in a bamboo tube, who must wiggle through, hardly able to move, its frustration building, until it bursts out the other end into freedom.

It was during a period of walking meditation at this sesshin that Ruth realized something had changed inside her. Her way of checking on her state of being—of getting to her calmness and inner settled-ness—was to connect with body sensations, as she had learned from Charlotte Selver and U Ba Khin. Suddenly she realized she was disconnected from her body and mind.

"When I started walking, it was so airy in me, and so unconnected. I felt that I was actually without a mind. It was so airy that it felt almost like I don't belong to here, I'm dead, hmm? And then I realized that it felt like the mind was going away, it was on the fence, and went behind the trees. Then I took a deep breath, I noticed energy coming in. I could pull it back, but I couldn't hold it, it went right out. Then I acted badly and insecurely and Sasaki Roshi said, 'Oh, you are just tired.' But I wasn't tired, I was so awake, so alert.

"I tried to explain this what I experienced, and he tells me 'You are only tired, you should rest.' But he didn't tell me to go and sleep also. And then he said, 'We'll go back to *zazen,* hmm?' [*Zazen* is Zen seated meditation.] But I couldn't meditate then because I was sitting like an empty vessel, empty! And I had no breath either. When I wanted air, several times I had to initiate this action of pulling the air in like huff, huff, and still it got here stopped in my chest. Then I let go and I was so exhausted of it."

Ruth tried the methods of breathing she had learned, but this only exacerbated her condition. "I had to do this kind of deep breathing, this Rinzai way of breathing really forceful. And I breathed out the fine energy and connecting. That was really the sign where I realized something very bad is wrong. Because I had no breath, no normal breath. Something happened there. I probably got the minimum supply of oxygen and almost zero *prana,* that finer, more primal energy, hmm?[38] Which comes with oxygen. But the oxygen was so little. Anyway I was in terror, breathing and not being able to feel in any way alive from that breath. So then they called Henry."

Henry was also sitting at the rohatsu. He interrupted his practice to drive her home and take her into the house, telling her to rest, as Sasaki roshi had recommended. Then, he left her and went back to the sesshin.

Luckily Sarada and another friend were living at the house with Ruth and Henry. Sarada put Ruth to bed, where she began hallucinating and could not connect with her breath. Even in this condition, Ruth took charge. "Sarada said, 'Rutchen, I don't know what to do with you.' I said 'You don't need to know, I will tell you. I feel like I'm dying. I don't have any breath. I haven't any connection. I don't know whether you understand what I mean by it. And my mind feels away from me, actually now, more away from me than before, in the zendo.' Everything was loud around me. You know, in Hollywood we had a dead end there, sometimes a car got lost, they came up and they made a turn, and the motor I would hear and then it would stop my breath because that little breath I had and connection would go into that motor.

"It came evening and I struggled. I would walk. I would do all kinds of things and it didn't come back to me. I was exhausted and at midnight I say, 'Sarada, I don't think I can continue living, I exhaust myself in getting what I need.'"

Ruth had Sarada call Sasaki roshi, who was leading the sesshin. When Sarada came back from the phone, she was upset, and said, "Rutchen, I cannot tell you what he said." Ruth insisted, "You tell me. I am ready for everything." Sarada then told her, "He said if you feel you're dying, please die peacefully."

Far from being shocked by that response, Ruth thought it made sense. But she wasn't ready to follow his advice. She tried looking out the plate-glass windows in the bedroom, out through the branches of the pine tree, over the reservoir, and felt her energy deserting her and going down behind the opposite hill. "That was so exhausting. I knew, this is my life force, if I don't get it back, I will have to die. It made sense to me what he said, 'Die peacefully.' But I couldn't quite accept it."

Next, she asked Sarada to call Maezumi roshi. Maezumi came to Ruth's house, sat on her bed, and listened to her description of what was happening to her. He said, "There is no need to fight. Let go." Ruth recalls, "That means he implied then you give up. And I was at that time so exhausted that I wanted to do that. He took my hands, he looked at me and he sat a little while there. And then he left."

Sarada remembers that night. "Ruth was desperately trying to connect. She was reaching out her hand to touch someone else's hand, to get back. She had sort of lost it somewhere. I called Henry at the Zen center. I said, 'You've got to get here, Rutchen is really in a bad way!' He said, 'I will finish the retreat and then come.' It was, 'I'll be there in due time.'"

Sarada continues, "Two of the roshis did come, but they seemed totally at a loss in what they were telling her. They were unable to help her. I don't remember them saying she just ought to die. But I remember she was talking about dying—she lay on the floor and we put candles in front of her head and in back. I didn't think she was dying, but she did. She was in this confused state."

Ruth recalls it in more detail, from the inside. "Sarada was still there. So that was my beginning. I said, 'Sarada, please go in my garden,'—it was spring—'and bring me flowers.' The amaryllis, I had these pinkies, like big lilies, hmm? At least ten or so she brought. Our bedroom, remember, it was a master bedroom and here was the glass, all like this, here was the fireplace. Here was his desk, kind of a round, half-circular desk. She put the vase with the flowers there and I sat up in my bed, said, 'Sarada, I will go now. Be very quiet, sit there and don't talk, I want to concentrate and go with that flower energy.'"

Ruth gazed at the flower and began to realize that there was a subtle energy in the amaryllis that might help her. "Then I was still and almost not breathing, and concentrated into the form of the amaryllis. I was not pulling the air, yah, but kind of having my attention there with the flowers and then bringing the attention across to me. I could do that for a minute, and I noticed that was a good, wonderful, satisfying feeling. Safe. And so I thought I will go like this, together with the flower. But this feeling increased. I began to notice more energy in me. In my hands and in my chest. Not by pulling but by being open and terribly concentrated into the energy of the flowers and into the energies of my body and breath. The flowers were so beautiful! They looked so like they were the carrier of very refined energy. I concentrated and comprehended it. It isn't just the breaths—everything somehow gets it. I noticed that I might be able to bring it back.

"So after two or three hours doing that, I said, 'Sarada, I cannot even die' or, 'I don't need to die' or something. I think I fell asleep by then. But sleeping was also not possible for me. I was so falsely awake, so the connection left me, of course. But I knew I can probably do it again.

"In the morning I walked out in my nightgown to the pine tree and looked into the branches and I could do it the same way. For a little while, and then I could walk and realize a little bit there is a possibility. It left me maybe two times, two seconds, but I could only do it because I have vipassana. If I didn't have that, I wouldn't know what to do. Look, the roshi didn't know! So, so then as soon as I got a little connected, I had not enough skill to hold it, it would also leave. Any outside thing, anyone talking to me, would take the energy."

When Henry returned from the sesshin the next morning, he drove Ruth to see a doctor. The doctor could see that Ruth was dissociated, so he gave her "an injection for relaxing." She believes it was Thorazine.

With the drug, she was able to rest a bit. "I was so stiff and so tense and so fearful, so that at least I could let go. And then I realized a little bit more life in me, but still terribly separated.

"Then began my real work of connecting the energies which were far away with the energy of my body and breath. I knew now I can do it. I have to relax; I have to be very quiet. And I have to stay away from interaction with people and with events. I couldn't even drive the car. And I couldn't ride as a passenger because the motor energy—it's all energy, dahling, strong energy—took my mind in. I was rolling in the motor. Oh, I tell you, it was fearful!"

Ruth was so hypersensitive and frightened that she lived in the basement for several weeks, avoiding contact with everyone. "When visitors came I would go down. I had a lounge chair there and I said, 'Henry, you know I cannot be here.' I did begin to have some connection, but it didn't want to stay, it would leave me. Any kind of connection, even if I felt some breathing energy, it was always makeshift and I couldn't rely on it. And so I would now begin my world with day-to-day life. I would wash dishes and I would say 'washing' and check whether I really knew it."

• • •

This was the beginning of a process in which Ruth focused her attention on simple tasks such as sweeping, cleaning, doing the dishes. Standing in front of the sink, if she could not feel the plate in her fingers in the warm water, she brought her attention to her body. "I would stand and just let go everything and would relax and do this movement, shifting weight, to one side and to the other side. This is all energy and you shift, it's a different feeling inside, hmm? And that I could feel, but still not enough, not really alive. Don't forget, I had vipassana. I had a sense of the healthy wholeness of life, so I knew that this wasn't enough. I needed more steady paying attention in a witnessing, mindful way. In all these efforts to reestablish mindfulness I felt I was knitting myself back together."

Sarada remembers Ruth's extreme vulnerability after her breakdown. "After that she was never quite as robust physically. She was sensitive, easily influenced. She said to me, if she could just sweep a floor, if she could just put her feet on the ground. She would go out in the yard and lie there under the pine tree. There were times she couldn't be too close to the people in front of her. It was a sensitivity that took a while to get over. . . . Now of course she's stable as a rock again. But it took a while!"

Ruth describes her period of knitting herself back together. "I did things in the house. Henry helped me. Dahling, Henry was really most beautiful in that time. He always supported me. And protected me. I couldn't even listen much to music. But I lived actually most, in the beginning of my practice, in the garden under the pine tree. I would sleep there in the night. Yah, and concentrate into the green, into the aliveness of a branch or of the whole tree. But better to a flower which was close, and it had to be in the earth. I would sit there and look and breathe. Or with my dachsie. I had a baby dachsie at that time. And I would take it on my chest when I sleep and watch him moving. And then I would tune into that rhythm, also I didn't feel any much, just the gesture when the breath in that little body expanded I tuned in to that movement, and when that body went down I went down too. So I got inadvertently a little concentration to the energy. Somehow I would always get a little touch, hmm? But it had to be alive."

Through this dedicated practice of closely observing the simplest actions in daily life, she not only healed herself but also learned a great deal about psychological problems and how to bring a confused person back to balance. In the succeeding years she has had many occasions to practice this skill, with students in meditation retreats who have temporarily lost their bearings, and with disturbed people whom she agrees to house and care for. Sometimes when mentally unstable people put themselves in the silent and demanding atmosphere of a meditation retreat, they will experience anxiety, perhaps suffer traumatic memories, or may dissociate. While this does not happen often, it is understood to be a risk of meditation practice. Skilled teachers can recognize people who may be vulnerable and protect them.

Ruth is known among Buddhist teachers and students as one of the few teachers who will allow avowedly troubled people to attend her retreats, where she works individually with them, devising simple physical activities to calm them and help them connect to themselves. At Dhamma Dena there is often a disturbed person living in one of the dormitory rooms or a cabin or trailer, brought there by concerned relatives who have heard that Ruth can provide safety and a kind of attention that will help the person regain his or her faculties. Most of these people have longstanding mental illness not connected to meditation. Ruth, a wounded healer herself, takes these people under her wing, just as she rescues abandoned animals and feeds starving wild creatures; she monitors them, comforts them, teaches them, encourages them.

CHAPTER TEN

Travel and Transmission

Ruth and Henry had agreed that every three years or so they would set out again on an extensive journey. Over the fifteen years from Ruth's meeting Henry until she began teaching and living a somewhat separate life, they took several long trips, and, in between, one or the other of them might go alone to Asia or Europe. Ruth went four or five times to Burma to be with U Ba Khin. (Joan Buffington, an old friend, reports that when the political situation in Burma had created a closed society hostile to foreigners, Ruth was still able to slip into the country to be with her beloved teacher. Perhaps she was calling upon some of the skills she had developed in postwar Germany, allowing her to evade notice and negotiate official checkpoints.) Henry sometimes went alone to Asia to study with Japanese or Indian or Burmese teachers.

Over the years, some details of these trips have merged in Ruth's mind so that in particular instances it is difficult to know which trip, during which year, is being referred to. But one of the journeys is happily fixed in time, for Ruth wrote a series of postcards and letters home. She wrote up her experience, and then sent copies of the same letter to people such as Alan Watts and her old friend Hope Winthrope. The letters to Watts achieved a certain fame, as he would read them aloud to his guests on the houseboat *Vallejo,* who found them hilarious in their original use of the English language, and wonderfully evocative of an innocent pilgrim's perspective.

I was able to acquire a copy of the assembled letters from Hope Winthrope, who now lives in a cabin owned by Ruth, in the desert near Dhamma Dena. Some were typed by Ruth herself, and some were typed by a Marjorie King, who scribbled a note saying she knew that Ruth would have wanted her to correct the spelling, "but there is something so beautifully 'Ruth' about the way she writes that I can't bring myself to."

When I sat down to read the thick sheaf of letters, which begins in January of 1967 in midvoyage and ends in May 1968, still in midvoyage, I bowed low to that typist for her perspicacity, and to Hope for keeping this document. I could see why Watts and his friends had been so hugely entertained. Ruth's travel letters convey a tremendous joyful curiosity about everything: history, buildings, churches, mosques, people, and animals. In the most revelatory passages, she does not just bounce along on the top of an experience (or a camel) but enters intimately into the moment, observing with precision and originality. The letters reveal her profound gift for enjoying herself and for connecting to other beings. And they also offer a glimpse into her spiritual awareness at that time. At age forty-five, when some women of her generation would have been settling into staid middle age, Ruth set out with high heart to know the whole world.

The letters begin in Cairo, Egypt, move to Venice, Italy, and then to the Algerian Sahara, to Egypt again, to Beirut, Lebanon, to Jordan, Syria, and Jerusalem. After Venice again, Athens, a period in Baden Baden, Germany, at the spa, and a meeting with Ruth's brother and mother in East Berlin, the letters move to Spain, where Ruth hates the bullfights but loves El Greco, on to Paris with its churches, then to Florence, Italy, where she has a spiritual opening in the San Miniato Church. Then she is alone in Istanbul for five days. Later she travels with Henry in other parts of Turkey. The final postcards find them in

Japan, where they lived for a year to meditate in Zen temples, and
Henry stayed for a second year while Ruth came home.

Often Henry would rest and read in their hotel room while Ruth
went out to explore. On one such day in Cairo (January 23, 1967), she
took a camel ride.

*It is not so easy to ride a camel for any length of time, the camels gait
puts quite a strain on the spine and back muscels (I could hardly walk
next day—so sore were my muscels) I followed the old riders example,
curved the right leg around the sattle point and the camels neck—and
than gradually tuned myself into his body rhythm. How beautiful a
camel's head looks seen from its own back. His eyes are dark big shiny
globes, protected by long bushi brows, which look alertly with acceptance and dignity to either side. He holds never his nose down, he rocks
it back and forth on his long curved neck, like a boat through the
waves, he ploughs with his big feet through the deep sands of the desert.
I learned the arabic terms to guide him properly, to stop and to lower
this improbable creature—and toward the end of the 3 hour practice
ride, I was swinging high up on his back, with camel line and whip
in my hands, like an old Sahara king.*

*On our return, we passed through the narrow alleys of Mena
village. It is quite an experience to observe arabic village life from such
a height. Everything possible happens outside, right in the middle of
the narrow dirt town-roads. Here goats and sheeps have their meals
and rests whilst next to them women are sitting in the same dust to
nurse their babies or wash their hair or laundry. Here tailors sew on
old sewing machines and women make their homespuns from the
sheep's wool. The butcher is killing his animal right next to the veg-
etable donkey cart, hangs it simply on a spike and cuts from the cadaver,
as the customers come along. Even arguing and desputes are carried
out freely and openly in those alleys, simply phantastic to plough
through this jungle of animals and people, who also seemed to be*

*puzzled in reverse with that blond "crazy creature" on top of the camel
in the middle of their privacy. Some must have thought a wild affaire,
they yelled and screamed and run with me or away from me, with joy
or with fear or with wonder, I could never find out. The elder water-
pipe smoking ones I easily won with a smile and the arabic Mahs-
Salaam greeting, they seemed to be pleased with the occasion. And
so was I—turned on and tuned in to this strange arabic village life
around me.*

*When I gallopped into the camel drivers "Terminal" camp, I was
no longer a tourist, whom one can "take for what he is worth." I was
accepted as a friend, sat down with them next to the resting camels,
and had tea.*

A touching reunion with Ruth's mother and brother Heinz took
place at a spa in Germany. On July 5, 1967, Ruth writes:

*My mother from the Russian Zone visited us here in Baden-Baden.
Besides those inevitagle Mama-daughter disagreements, I enjoyed her
present and often sneaked out of my bed to jump into hers. She loved to
pet her "Moseschild" (as she named me in L.A. at her Christmas visit)
and sometimes we argued and chatted until dawn. Last weekend I flew
with her back to Berlin—to say hello to my brother, who was allowed
to meet me at a military guarded control-point of that big "Iron Curtain Wall", that separates the city into two political opposed halves.
Despite this sad affaire, I was glad to find my brother and his family
in good cheer and health. The harshness of life in East Germany lays
in the political pressures and not economically. However nothing much
else is moving there, everything is so dead serious and absolute, there-
fore depressing.*

In Florence, Italy, at Easter, Ruth went alone to the San Miniato
Church, where she had a powerful experience. She attended services
with the monks and many worshippers doing the stations of the cross.

During the services throughout the day, Ruth meditated, achieving a deep absorption, and when night came and the last service ended, she found herself trapped. In her July 5, 1967, letter, she says:

I was locked in that church, then discovered by a monk, and brought before the father Superior. All monks had gathered too—it was true what they all felt, something of a revelation (in the Catholic sense) had taken place in me, for the first time I was genuinely beyond doubt, the Outside was me and the me was the outside. It was moving in me. . . . What strange or lovely things one encounters—life simply is phantastic and rich everywhere, the "Flow" even can move on within rigid heavy walls of an old traditional Catholic Order.

Always in her travels she is sensitive to the animal world that exists alongside the human, and she makes efforts to alleviate the suffering she finds there. At the end of a long communication from Istanbul on September 8, 1967, she writes:

Before I close now this letter I like to give you the last act of tonights show around me. It is the drama here of every night, i.e. the time when "Dogging" begins; when all those hundreds of starving dogs are leaving their day-sleep-holes. They take off in little herds, jauling and hauling in search for foodmorsels, they are terribly afraid and flee when they see humans approaching them. Well I am not (yet)? detached enough from form to feel such suffering without identifying with it, my pookel-love also simply overruns me and so I find myself feeding them, wherever I see them—believe me, my handbag looks inside more like an old food-morsel pouch. Sometimes I make a special trip down into the narrow harbor streets, where there are plenty of dogs and cats, some already know me, they wiggle their tails when they see me coming since they learned I throw breads or meaty bones instead of stones. Something like a lause or flie I must have received last night from them as thanks in return, I was scratching on some untraceable bites quite a few times.

On their boat passage to Cyprus (August, 1967), Ruth tunes in to the silence at the center of the universe, and urges herself to make a more consistent effort on her spiritual path.

> *The good old turkish "Urdo" ploughed through the Agaen Sea 24 hours, one could see the mountainous shores all the time and in moonlight play with the imagination of mysterious coves, barren mountain peeks, little islands, or lonely sandy beaches. I camped out both nights, next to our car in the stern . . . and "grooved" with the waves, with the stary heaven and the ships' engine.*
>
> *Even the monotone sound and beat of an engine can become a vehicle for a journey into the Unknown—and I am sure, everything really in this univers is fit for it. The secret is only one's own attention and openness for letting the Tune-In occur. The more I give to it, the more I feel my heart filing with a humility for more and more listening into that wonderful vast Silence, which lays in the unity of my within and that what gets touched by it on the "without." Just do it more, Ruth—shake your boundaries, brake through this skin of yours, let It come in and let It flow out so that you can experience the world around completely without separation . . . . and then what richness of Knowing, what fountain of Wisdom, what intelligent, natural Understanding!!! But do it!!*

In Kamakura, Japan, Henry rented two apartments, one for himself and Ruth, and one to house their guests. Ruth began what she calls a "leisurely Zen training," with sittings and retreats in several cities, with Yasutani roshi and Yamada roshi, two of the Zen masters who had the most influence on Western Zen students, and with Soen roshi at Ryutakuji Monastery. Or she would do a self-retreat with her U Ba Khin practices.

She and Henry did ten-day sesshins with Yasutani Roshi, to good effect. "With Yasutani Roshi I got very deep, good concentration, I learned to consciously, awarely, perceive the space of humbleness, to see sometimes what have we to do as human beings in order to get what we basically want. I had to sit three hours to listen to a Japanese discourse, I didn't understand a word. We had hard, hard training there." (So much for leisurely.)

Her back was bothering her to such an extent that she had to take opium. At home for the night, she was given the drug by Henry, who carefully controlled the dosage. In the meditation hall, she had to be lifted up from her seat by the monks, and she walked very slowly with a cane.

After a year in Japan, Ruth's back pain became so insupportable that she returned to California to get treatment. It was decided that she should have surgery. But the operation revealed a condition more serious than expected, perhaps engendered by her childhood infantile paralysis, in which the nerves intertwined with the muscles in such a way that certain movements squeezed them and produced pain. She was left with back problems that still plague her. Although, years later, a second surgery was recommended, Ruth chose instead to work with her pain through meditation and exercise. When a back episode assails her, she is able to quiet the pain and return into balance.

Henry stayed in Japan for another year, studying the Japanese language, flower arranging, and the tea ceremony, sitting *zazen*, and hosting a salon for Westerners interested in Zen.

• • •

Having returned to Hollywood in spring, 1969, leaving Henry in Japan, Ruth lived with Sarada and with Henry's son in the house on the hill. While recovering from back surgery, and continuing her meditation practice, she resumed her support of the Los Angeles Zen centers of Sasaki roshi and Maezumi roshi, presenting a temple bell from Japan to the Zen Center of Los Angeles. She hosted fundraising events in her living room, inviting the cousin of Ravi Shankar to play the tabla; joined the Women's Democratic Club (of which she remembers nothing but the social aspect); played tennis, and studied piano. She also began learning to do the kind of glass mosaic work she had so admired in the churches of Florence and other Italian cities.

In the meditation hall at Dhamma Dena, a mosaic mandala, five feet in diameter, hangs behind the altar, gleaming with jewel-like colors; in the dining hall two similar mosaics have been used as tabletops by retreatants for years. We would hear Ruth tell how this craft had brought her great comfort during difficult times, especially in her marriage—how the meticulous cutting and fitting of the glass pieces in their beautiful circular patterns had calmed and soothed her. But the first table, she says, was done out of "sheer delight, because I suddenly discovered this craft, hmm? I was fascinated with Venetian glass, I was becoming aware of the beauty of these when I was in Italy, always admiring these beautiful mosaics in the churches, murals, San Miniato in Florence.

"The first one I did, the big one, was my own exploration coming from the journey. I enrolled in a little city class and learned cutting and colors and so on. I wanted to make a mandala. Then Charlotte Selver was so enchanted by it that she wanted one. So I made one, and she didn't like it. She said, 'It's not the same as the first.' She was right, the first one was more earthy, and the next one I colored up. The one I made for Charlotte Selver is now behind the Buddha in the zendo. I kept it. And I think I made her another one. I made many.

"So, for years after that, I had this hobby. I needed something to do when I was sad—having some kind of bad mood or being unhappy—but also with Henry when he was cold and too arrogant, or had flirted with one too much. So, instead of arguing, I would go in my basement. The color and the fitting of the glass pieces took my mind into that, and I purified. After that, I could say, 'Dahling it is all right.' Without being resentful or carrying this or pouting."

In the years before Ruth began to be asked to teach in formal situations, she had started to teach informally, gathering friends to meditate in the Hollywood house. And she was always pursuing her own vipassana practice. Then in 1971, before his death that same year,

U Ba Khin gave her the teaching mantle. "I got the permission to teach just before he died, in a letter. U Ba Khin would openly state that he has only one passion, and that is to bring the Dharma to the West. And he had only a few people who he knew he could trust, maybe they had enough—whether he called it enlightenment experience or . . . the first entry . . . *sotapana* or something like that. In that stage I was." (U Ba Khin specified the stages of enlightenment from *sotapatti magga,* "the first path of sanctity" to the culminating stage of *arahat,* or liberated being. Ruth emphasizes that these are Burmese Buddhist categories, not useful to Westerners, and in her own teaching she avoids the use of such markers.) The "transmission" of the authority to teach carries crucial weight in traditional Buddhism, in which the connection between teacher and student goes back in an unbroken line all the way to the Buddha. Ruth felt the gravity of this authorization from her beloved meditation master, but she was too modest to step out into the world as a Buddhist teacher. She barely registered his injunction, no doubt reflecting a traditional Asian Buddhist view, that she teach only women. For the next few years she went on with her usual life.

But that life, without her choosing the goal, was carrying her forward toward her inevitable path as a Buddhist teacher. Ruth was on fire with interest, devouring all aspects of her existence and deepening her practice. After Henry returned from his year alone in Japan, he and Ruth went on hosting teachers and savants in their home. They traveled to Asia again, and then to Hawaii to study with Robert Aitken roshi, one of the foremost Western Zen teachers.

Ruth and Henry, or Ruth by herself, often came up to the San Francisco Bay area to the *Vallejo,* the houseboat in Sausalito where Alan Watts had performed a second wedding ceremony for them. One of the reasons Henry Denison visited there so often was that he was a founder and financial supporter of Watts's Society for Comparative Philosophy. Henry was on its board of directors along with Alan and his wife, Jano, the poet Elsa Gidlow, and others. Seminars and courses in philosophy were held on the old ferry boat, and Watts talked wonderfully in a rich,

British-accented voice, in polished cadences: "You are not, as parents and teachers are wont to imply, a mere stranger on probation in the scheme of things; you are rather a sort of nerve-ending through which the universe is taking a peek at itself."[39]

Ruth traveled north to the *Vallejo* to attend Watts's seminars, and those of Lama Govinda. Lama Govinda, the German-born founder of the Buddhist order called Arya Maitreya Mandala, came often to the *Vallejo* with his wife, Li Gotami. He became an important teacher for Ruth and Henry, who would travel to the Himalayas in India later to study with him, and would host him in their home. On the *Vallejo* Ruth also heard the teachings of Tibetan master Chogyam Trungpa Rinpoche, as well as Krishnamurti. Most of the teachers hosted on the *Vallejo* spoke from a high philosophical or mystical perspective about spiritual life. Ruth, the eminently practical woman, claims to have admired these men, but also often admits to not understanding what they were talking about—and as her practice developed, she increasingly began to disagree with some of them. She was the woman moving noiselessly through the room, filling glasses, offering snacks, plumping pillows, the "angel in the house," semi-ignored by these luminaries, who directed their attention to Henry, an intellectual male like themselves.

But as she became more grounded in her practice, Ruth did not hesitate to challenge them, and sometimes a sort of "Dharma-combat" would ensue.[40] U. G. Krishnamurti, a more austere and obscure guru than the celebrated teacher of the same name, came often to Ruth and Henry's house; later Henry rented a chalet in Switzerland for U. G. to give teachings. Ruth describes U. G. Krishnamurti as very strict. "He's absolute, he's Advaita. He lived like a nobody, with two sweaters, with two shirts, two pants, and that was it. He was only drinking hot water, he was eating totally vegetarian. He was absolute in his teaching. He didn't say he was a teacher, he said 'I'm natural, I'm not awake, whatever they say.' He said 'This is a natural state of being.'"

U. G., as Ruth refers to him, came of a high-caste Brahmin family and was deeply schooled as a child and young man in the Advaita philosophy. This involved a denial of all aspects of ordinary reality: an attitude that everything was *neti, neti,* meaning "not this, not that," in the search for God. In later life he suffered a "death" experience, amounting to a shedding of his conditioned energies, that left him profoundly altered. After that he no longer identified as a Brahmin but asserted that he existed in a "natural state."

"When he talked he made sense but I always challenged him in that," Ruth says. "I said, 'U. G., it's wonderful, yes, but when people hear you they don't know what you're talking about. There must be some practice.' Then when I had a little bit more practice I would tell him what I had done with U Ba Khin. 'Yes,' he said, 'that's for the lower classes' or something. He said 'You cannot get anywhere that way, it will just come.' It happened naturally to him—the absolute balance of the energies—and suddenly he was somewhere else; he was in an awakened state.

"So he will say, 'You can go to that chap [the other, more famous Krishnamurti] for a long time and it will not happen.' I said, 'U. G., you are evil sometimes, you take away anything which we can hold on as un-enlightened people. You take the rugs under our feet, you tell us it's natural, yes, but we are not natural, we have to have a practice to start. If you be mindful and you practice and do this, like you once did, then. . . .' Well, he said, 'That was all for the birds, that would have happened anyway [without any practice]!' We had a beautiful relationship, but he was a little bit too radical for me. Henry was 150% for him, because it fitted Henry, he himself was Advaita once. So anyway I had a good time always with U. G. That was two or three summers we went there to Switzerland." As well, Henry sponsored U. G. Krishnamurti to come to the United States, where he stayed and taught in their home.

Without knowing it, Ruth was in training for her teaching life. When she was not challenging them, she soaked in the wisdom of some of the foremost spiritual teachers and visionary thinkers of the twentieth century. It was an amazingly broad spectrum of teachings that she came into contact with.

"Yes, Hindu teachers, lama teachers, Zen teachers. But mainly I was in the background and let Henry be first, and Alan Watts, but I was always being the hostess and I enjoyed that very much because I was on both levels. Once there was Chinmayananda [Swami Chinmayananda Saraswati, world-renowned teacher of Vedanta, and Hindu religious leader, who established numerous ashrams and schools in India and the United States]. He was very attractive to me from all the Hindus because he talked about the mind training. He had a beautiful system for it and he put me to tears. Henry was very much moved."

When he came to the United States, Swami Chinmayananda lived in Ruth and Henry's house. During one visit, as Ruth drove the swami down the hill to the Vedanta Center where he was to give a lecture, he commented on her good karma. "You are very blessed, Ruth," he said, and when Ruth asked why he thought that, he responded, "You have the great fortune to be in your spiritual practice together with good support on the physical level."

Chinmayananda spoke the truth. Because of Henry's wealth, and his serious quest for spiritual development, Ruth could be introduced to mentors and metaphysical thinkers throughout the world. Her life with Henry was one of immense privilege, and she used that privilege to develop her capacities for spiritual awakening.

For fifteen years, with Japanese Zen masters and Hindu gurus, radical explorers into the realms of altered consciousness and traditional Theravada Buddhist teachers, innovators in bodywork and psychology, Ruth listened, experimented, and pushed herself to go deeply into the practices she was offered. She tested their value, kept that which made sense to her and got results, and left behind what was not useful to her. And the organizing theme, like the backbone of a living animal, was the practice taught her by U Ba Khin in Burma, supported by her work with Charlotte Selver. Ruth entered each new situation armed with techniques of vipassana meditation and sensory awareness. In her life with Henry she practiced offering service to others, and at Millbrook she learned to work with people who had dissociated. Caught in the throes of her own mental breakdown, she developed and deepened her understanding as she painstakingly brought herself back to balance. By the time U Ba Khin gave her the authority to teach, she was matured in her practice and sophisticated in her awareness of the spiritual path.

PART III

The Teacher:
The Ripening Years

CHAPTER ELEVEN

Beginnings

While Ruth had been leading afternoon meditation sessions for her friends for years, in 1974 she began to be asked to conduct formal meditation retreats, first in Europe and then in the United States. This came about because of Robert Hover, the man she had met in Burma ten years before at U Ba Khin's International Meditation Center.

Hover was an unlikely candidate for Asian spiritual seeking. Two years older than Ruth, he worked as an aeronautics engineer at Lockheed Aircraft and, later, at North American Aviation, in Southern California. Having found transcendental meditation in the late fifties, he journeyed to Rangoon, Burma, for a thirty-day course in vipassana with U Ba Khin, in which he was the only student. A few years later he went again to Burma to study with U Ba Khin, the sojourn in which he had long fascinating discussions with Henry Denison, and met Ruth.

In our phone conversation, Mr. Hover related that, in 1969, U Ba Khin commissioned one Indian and five Westerners to become Theravada lay-teachers: S. N. Goenka of India, John Coleman of England, a man named Armsfort in Amsterdam, and three Americans—Hover, Ruth Denison, and Leon Wright.[41] Hover plunged into teaching, offering ten-day courses like U Ba Khin's, in Europe as well as the United States. He was enthusiastic in connecting with his fellow vipassana practitioners, establishing communication vehicles that included the *Vipassana Newsletter* in 1974 in La Mirada, California, and the Sayagyi U Ba Khin Memorial Nonprofit Corporation.

In the early seventies, Zen Buddhism was established in the United States and Europe, but vipassana was only just beginning to be heard of. This newly introduced method of meditation began to attract lively interest, and Robert Hover found himself much in demand to conduct his ten-day courses. Leading a course in Hannover, Germany, in August 1974, Hover saw the woman he had met in Burma, sitting in the back of the room, and he knew that she too had been given authorization to teach. Ruth explains, "I was with Henry on a holiday in Switzerland. They telegraphed me [about Hover's retreat in Germany]. That was for me wonderful because U Ba Khin had said that once a year you had to make a retreat. For ten days. You could do it anywhere. So I thought, fine, I'll go, and I was also curious."

The retreat was held in a small villa, with living rooms on the ground floor, and upstairs a large room that the owner had arranged as a meditation hall. Ruth was pleased to be at the retreat, and to see Robert Hover leading it. "I sat very obediently in the audience of twelve people, facing Mr. Hover, and he looks at me and said, 'You belong, from now on, *here* [up at the front, with him].'

"Then he asked me to talk, and listened at me talking enthusiastic about my ideas, my spirituality and my insight. They knew that I had the transmission received from U Ba Khin. I had forgotten about it. I didn't know what to do with it. It was Dr. Friedgardt Lotter Moser who invited me to that retreat. Friedgardt was highly informed. She had connections always with Burma and she knew I had these teachings received. She was a wonderful support for me because she knew fabulously the teachings of the Buddha."

Mr. Hover says of that first retreat, "That was where we were going through Ruth's fledgling steps. She was sitting up front with me then, and of course in both that one and the one in France we were working together. The next one was at Toulon sur Arroux. Then she went ahead and you might say launched on her own on another course that was following that."

After her foray with Mr. Hover, Ruth was invited back to the Hannover house to lead her first retreat alone. She felt insecure about her abilities and her training. "They were Dhiravamsa[42] students having a seminar in that little house. There had been working Professor Frau So-and-So with breath work and Dhiravamsa, and I kind of crumbled when I heard that—I didn't want to start there. I thought, How can I match that? There was in me a kind of little pride. I wanted to be equal and I in myself didn't have that confidence. Because my Dharma was developed at home. I must say, Henry helped me to move forward. I said, 'I don't have enough training.' He said, 'What, you don't have enough training?! You have Charlotte Selver, you have gone to all the great masters! Yamada roshi, Yasutani roshi, Soen roshi, the swamis. And you were able to handle psychedelics—you did so well at Millbrook—you could guide them.' "

During that first retreat in Hannover, she could teach in German, but in subsequent retreats where she would have to teach in English, she felt insecure. Her friend Joan Buffington recalled, "She was nervous about her English then. She isn't anymore, though it's always been the same. German-English words would fly in there, and French. But it was totally understandable."

Her strongest support in those first retreats turned out to be her training with Charlotte Selver. "I knew I could do it because even if I wasn't able to teach anything, I could let them stand, and I hear Charlotte saying, 'Please come to standing.' That was the attitude of listening, and Vipassana mind. I could teach what U Ba Khin stressed —body sensations, sensations, sensations. Mindfulness. Conscious attention. That I could do."

The house in Hannover was owned by a photographer named Anneliese Bushbaum, who had her own unique way of teaching mindfulness. She made regular trips to the Sahara desert to photograph. Then she projected the images for groups of people "to teach them the silence through the movement of the sand." Ruth elaborates, "She speaks Dharma through the sand movement of the Sahara, so to speak. They leave and they don't know they got their Buddhadharma teaching. With the Dharma you can do this because it relates directly, without any agent, to your blood cells, to your touch of life, and to touch of death, which is touch of life, and to your intellect and intelligence. Through calming the mind so deeply, in the experience of body touch, you have pure energy in your mind and you begin to see clearly. Intellect becomes wisdom, then."

While Mr. Hover says that Ruth went next to France, she remembers her next retreat, immediately after Hannover, in England. "I was the first one in England who gave organized retreats in vipassana, in a formal little estate house, was the Oak Tree House. I had in that Oak Tree House I think two retreats, one after Christmas that was in January 1975. It was cold there in that house, an old kind of elegant rich people, everything crystal and carved and tiled. With a beautiful little park. These people paid the rent. They were hippies. It was sometimes sloppy and a little bit out of joint but basically they had all been in India, they all had maybe sat with Goenka or something. Some came from rebirthing and some came from yoga and some from Maharishi and I kind of grounded them in vipassana, and united them with my skill. That I could do. I felt my body, I taught them that. Bending down, and reaching out and moving and how to serve and how to be the witness."

As for theory, she taught the "Four Noble Truths," the Buddha's core message, and focused most strongly on the first—*Dukkha* or "suffering"—about which she could rightfully claim to know a great deal. The Buddha himself, when asked what he taught, answered, "I teach suffering and the end of suffering."

Not everyone responded well to Ruth's early teachings. "I remember one I had in Austria early and one professor from Münster complained to Dr. Friedgardt (she was always defending me). He had one leg only. He was a critic on me, hmm? I was not always clear what I said, so he said, 'I can't make here all sense.' The woman, his wife, was good. She loved it. But he was angry with his body—one leg not there—he couldn't sit rightly. He couldn't comprehend that the pain was a sensation to look at, he was hostile and transferred it to me. So he goes to Friedgardt, 'You organized this retreat, how can you take her in here?' She said 'Yes, it's true, perhaps, that she's in the beginning but she can hold us together, don't forget. She unifies everybody with a basic of the practice.' She tells me that. That gave me such a beautiful confidence.

"I had no model, dahling. No model. I had no history, I had no authority really. I didn't bring the big history of an Asian country and culture with me. On top of it, I come from the Nazi country. I mean I was so in space without any support on that. I had no one to consult. Mr. Hover was busy at that time.

"My god, that wasn't easy. But I had Charlotte's practice and that was the ground for me for vipassana. The way it was taught to me by U Ba Khin, I don't think I would have had that depth because of the short time I was able to spend with him, but the teaching when I began, it was just falling like the water out of the spring back into the pool. Very natural. U Ba Khin had actually said to me, 'Don't worry, you are a natural.'"

Ruth was not being overly modest when she said that she did not have sufficient training. Most Buddhist teachers have spent years of intensive practice and study with a master before ever being allowed to teach, while Ruth was able to practice only a few months with U Ba Khin, and sporadically with the Zen masters and Hindu swamis. Without an extended training to guide her, she had to cobble together the practices she had picked up in various traditions and unite them by the strength of her personality and her insight. She had been a teacher all her life, in East Prussia and Berlin; she had been called *die goldene Mitte* who inspired others, and U Ba Khin had recognized her innate capacities—so she had a foundation on which to begin. And she had experienced deep levels of insight. But the lack of thorough formal training and the sometimes negative response to her unconventional methods planted a seed of insecurity in her that even now sometimes causes her to extol her own strengths or to ask for reassurance.

Ruth was one of the first Western teachers to bring vipassana to Europe, meeting the needs of the hippies who were returning from Asia.

"The flower children, they came with ponchos and beads. The globe-trotters came from India from Aurobindo,[43] came from Himalayas from practice with Lama Govinda, some from Burma from U Ba Khin's center. They came to Europe and looked for a place to practice, and I was one of the few who were teaching.

"In Holland, in a stable where the cows were outside, fresh straw, we were sleeping there. In the day we went out in the meadow with the cows and had a retreat. Or we sat in the stable. In Germany, a more educated and refined group had a Buddhist Society, called *Stillehaus,* and also in private homes. In Sweden and England. In France, in a castle in Provence. Then somewhere north of Marseilles in a winery—an Indian teacher was teaching yoga and I teaching vipassana, and we were very happy with each other. Switzerland, Austria, Italy—all these places I taught."

•••

In California Ruth visited the Dharma Vihara (an early vipassana center) in Felton. Julie Wester, now a teacher at Spirit Rock Meditation Center, who had taken the job of cook at Dharma Vihara, remembers seeing Ruth there in 1974, and gives a picture. "The first time I saw her she had on stretch pants and a poofy hairdo . . . a Hollywood housewife who would talk about her dogs and her Karmann Ghia and playing tennis. That was my first impression."

In 1976 Joseph Goldstein, Sharon Salzberg, Jack Kornfield, Robert Hover, Eric Lerner,[44] and others started the Insight Meditation Society in Barre, Massachusetts, in a large dignified building that had housed a Catholic monastery. They invited Ruth to help begin the schedule of courses that continues to this day. (The Insight Meditation Society became the principal venue for vipassana meditation in the

United States for fifteen years, now balanced by Spirit Rock Meditation Center on the West Coast.)

Given Ruth's initial tentativeness and insecurity about teaching, it is surprising to realize that she allowed herself to be so innovative and eccentric right from the start. Not only did she use movement and sensing exercises to teach mindfulness, but she arrived at the Insight Meditation Society toting a small dog whom everyone remembers. Mr. Muffin was a Lhasa apso, a Tibetan breed with long straight hair and a tail curling up over the back. The drama coach Stella Adler, teacher of Marlon Brando and other movie stars, had been his former owner. She had stayed in Henry and Ruth's house during one of their round-the-world trips, and had left Mr. Muffin behind. Ruth, naturally, had adopted him.

"Yes, in the winter of '76, three consecutive retreats I had at Insight Meditation Society, and I brought Mr. Muffin with me. Snow was outside that high, and the kettle which gives the fire, for the central heating, broke and we had no heating. It was below zero zero zero and we hovered all together in that little small room. I did from January till February three or four consecutive retreats. Ten days long, each, with two or three days in-between."

Julie Wester, who was a self-described "Dharma bum" at that time, going from retreat center to retreat center, and studying always with male teachers, had come to the Insight Meditation Society to join the staff as a cook. Just twenty-five years old, she was more than impressed with this fifty-four-year-old absolutely unique woman teacher.

> Ruth taught the first retreat, and I was her attendant. I was also a cook but I would bring Ruth a tray of tea, walk her dog, and I was just completely ga-ga. She was covered with lace and velvet. And long swishy skirts. Her dog would walk in the hall with her, and sit by her, her Lhasa apso—he would come tippy-toeing into the meditation hall.
>
> She was just so elegant. There she was always on her best behav-

ior, the most elegant version of Ruth. She would do things like being late to sittings but at that point there was no form, nobody was stuck on the form—the walking, sitting, be-quiet form—so nobody knew she was unusual.

Ruth would take the students down into the basement to a room she called "the romper room." There she would lead the movement sessions. She was apparently not quite bold enough yet to do this in the main meditation hall. Some of her students were dignified M.D.s or Ph.D.s —whom she would encourage to dance about like butterflies in the basement. And she would take the group out onto the lawn at night, to do slow mindful movement in the dark. Julie Wester was delighted. "To me it was a breath of fresh air. She was so alive and so female that I thought I had gone to heaven, because after all these guys, it was like, Oh my gosh!"

Sharon Salzberg, guiding teacher at I.M.S. and author, was also captivated by Ruth. "I thought she was dazzling. We used to call her the Zsa Zsa Gabor of the Dharma. She had Muffin in those days, that really ugly little dog. She used to go into the meditation hall and after her you'd hear this tap-tap-tap-tap as Muffin would follow her in, and would sit on a cushion beside her up at the front of the room. She was such an eccentric, and so delightful. This was before I knew the circumstances of her life, like in the war. She was so outrageous, I thought it was wonderful."

But as the Insight Meditation Society became more organized and settled into an established mode of teaching, there began to be problems with Ruth's unusual approach. Ruth herself never set out to challenge tradition or conventional practice. In many ways she still remains a quite traditional teacher. But she understood that the sensory awareness practices were a powerful tool to awaken and cultivate mindfulness—this was her most profound gift—and so she employed them. As well, her natural energy and zest for life led her to invent practices on the spot. She respected tradition without allowing it to limit her creativity, and some students did not understand this.

Many of the young people had sat with S. N. Goenka in India, or had been taught by Goenka's students. Goenka specified a strict form, taken literally from his teacher (also Ruth's teacher) U Ba Khin, and this form brooked no variation. In this version of meditation practice, there was to be no walking meditation, and certainly no other kind of movement. Goenka's version, some students believed, was the proper and only way to practice meditation; they loved him and were strongly focused in his method. So when Ruth asked them to walk, and led them in often whimsical and challenging movement sessions, some reacted with confusion and resistance.

Jacqueline Mandell (then Schwartz), one of the original teachers at I.M.S., describes the situation:

> Ruth's doing what she was doing became controversial to those who had been told "not to walk." So there was a lot of conversation about that, after she started teaching. It was a major controversy. Some were saying, "Oh she's not part of the tradition."
>
> I believe that they really wanted to follow U Ba Khin's teachings to the word. And it's a very strong practice. One becomes very focused, very one-pointed. So if somebody says, "Oh this will detract from the practice," then you don't want to do that. So Ruth bringing in movement, and walking—that became hard. I can remember there being lots of conversations. And there was less information about meditation at that time. [Many people did not know about the traditional form that included walking.] It was actually difficult. You have a teacher you love saying one thing, and then you have somebody else who you know isn't doing anything wrong but is asking you to. . . .
>
> There was a tremendous amount of aversion from the Goenka teachers and students against Ruth at that time. It was not good. Very hard.

Ruth's strength and uniqueness seem exceptional. She must have known the prevailing philosophy at the Insight Meditation Society, yet she carried over her sensory awareness work into her teaching of mindfulness. Her conviction that these practices would benefit her students overrode any discomfort she experienced. But she felt the disapproval of many. "At I.M.S. I was a bit looked down upon. Jack and Joseph were always very kind to me, but their students were used to a rigid pattern. Three-fourth hour sitting, and not a minute earlier or later. I would move from three-fourth hour to an hour and a quarter. And I did other things unusual.

"They had to make a big raised platform for me, not for one seat, but for the doggie too, and when I went away for an interview Mr. Muffin would sit there, like a temple dog. Everyone had fun. I introduced the *zabutons* there, the meditation mats, and the round pillows and I let the women sit and sew the zabutons whilst we were in the retreat. Before that they had only socks, pillows, coats wrapped up, whatever—to sit on, or little carpets. I unified that and from there on they did more."

She began to wear a particular costume for teaching. "It's a Zen skirt, called *hakama*. When Zen monks are in session they put that on. It's exactly that design. Then I decided to cover my head because everyone came and wanted to make a hairdo for me. Yes, it was easier. All black I would go and my black little hat and I liked it, also. I had hair till down here always and it was too bothersome. My little hat made me feel better."

Her teaching style was as unconventional as her clothes. "I started doing my sensory awareness. In a side room I'd have a meeting and say, 'Now here is a rock—you take it. And now notice your taking it and how you are holding it. Do you understand that? Do you know it?' They thought I was a little off. I said, 'Now I take each a rock and I give it to you . . . they give it to the next one. That was to bring them into the connection with their body sensations, which was the main issue for vipassana. But to do that with the rock, carrying that, didn't work yet: they were numb to their bodies. So one got up. Everyone was on the floor. One got up and walked fast to the door, opened the door of the meditation hall and said *'Enough of this hanky panky!'* Loud. And left. Not one word was spoken after. I did not respond to that at all. I said, 'Would you please now put down your hand and let your rock go and give it to the next one?' And it was finished."

Finished for Ruth, perhaps, but not for the man who had stormed out. Many years later, at a fundraising party for Spirit Rock, Ruth was approached by a stranger. He said, "Hello, Ruth, do you know who I am?" She said she did not. He explained, "I am the one who slammed the door and spoke about your work in a most unappreciative way." Then he told Ruth that at least partly due to that very sensitivity training that he had rejected, he had changed his occupation. "You know my profession was killing the animals which I catch in my traps," he told her. "I began to hear myself, what I said to you, and also what you taught me, and it freed me from my traps, I no longer do that." Ruth explains, "It's wrong in him and he realized the insensitivity, he can feel something in what I did, and when he does that to the animals he realizes they feel it, too. That's my idea, my feeling. He did relate to the bad things he did and he stopped."

Despite the difficulties that arose over the years, the I.M.S. teachers accepted Ruth. Jack Kornfield became her principal ally, and Sharon Salzberg recounts, "I think everybody pretty well appreciated her. There were other moments much later which stand out in my mind, when seeing her sweep down the grand staircase at Sharpham Abbey in England during a teacher meeting, you know—settings that kind of suited her—or hearing her saying something very pithy. Once people also understood her background, and heard how much she had been through, it was very clear that this was hard-bought wisdom. The wisdom, and the emptiness side of things, were very clear in her. She expressed all that very, very well."

And Sharon adds, "Ruth has her adoring devotees, and people who are not—well it isn't their style. It's very distinctive, you know—there's a lot of hands-on instruction, there's a lot of personal confrontation in a way. It's not for everybody. Some people come to Insight Meditation Society really for a classical sense of solitude and serenity, and to be crawling over the front lawn, you know, things like that, is a little much for them. But other people of course really love it."

Ruth had never been a purist. She tells this story about an encounter with Robert Hover when he was leading an early retreat in California, before she had begun teaching. "When I came in he said, 'Come and sit with me.' So he had a little raised platform and he said, 'Here is Ruth, she is my colleague.' He said to the students, 'Now you have an opportunity to hear a different view about the issue we are all struggling with.' And the issue was, Shall we just follow one pattern impeccably and don't even listen to the others and screen ourselves off and isolate? He said, 'Now you will hear Ruth.' I gave the global view. I said. 'Since we're all on a spiritual path and we all have one motive which brings us to it, which is our suffering, our dissatisfaction with the present situation, or our not knowing where to go, I think in a culture as we are living we cannot afford to restrict ourselves. U Ba Khin and the Buddha himself says you have to integrate into the culture and work with those.'

"They loved me for it. Then I introduced walking meditation and then they wrote a letter for the *Vipassana Newsletter* and said, 'Ruth Denison brings new aspects to the Vipassana meditation.'"

When friends in Los Angeles learned that Ruth had begun formally teaching, they began to organize retreats for her. James Tuggle, a lawyer friend, set up a retreat in the hills of Santa Barbara. Ruth says 103 people attended, and she was somewhat intimidated by the large crowd. "How could I do that—get them together? But I had confidence, from my Zen training, discipline. Zen helped with the outer aspects. So I said, 'We do *kinhin* [Zen walking], and then we have interview and I will ring the bell for each person, like they do in Zen.' And with Charlotte's training."

By the late seventies, Ruth was traveling steadily to lead retreats in the United States and Europe, and she had begun to bring people to Copper Mountain Mesa near Joshua Tree, to the little house that would develop into Dhamma Dena Desert Vipassana Center. Her schedule in 1979 listed eighteen retreats, including two sets back to back at the Insight Meditation Society. That year Ruth added the women's retreat at Dhamma Dena and retreats in several other venues, and she was now inviting people to come to stay at the center for self-retreats.

I spent a day in the office at Dhamma Dena looking through the albums and notebooks and file folders casually collected and stored on shelves, to find as many as possible of the course schedules. Ruth was leading sixteen to eighteen retreats a year—in places as disparate as Switzerland, Hawaii, and Massachusetts, with the necessary travel involved—retreats from five days to ten days to three weeks long, with only short periods between for rest. This is a staggeringly heavy schedule, testament to Ruth's enormous energy and her eagerness to respond to any invitation to teach the Dharma. She was to keep this up for twenty years.

Ruth's life had been transformed. Now she traveled and taught for most of each year, developing her skills and her confidence. This new competence and her frequent absences from home threatened Henry, who struggled to encourage her while resenting her newfound recognition. At the same time he was pursuing yet another spiritual guru in ways that almost destroyed their marriage.

Ruth's grasp of Dharma, which was deeper than tradition or dependence on outer forms, allowed her to respond to the actual situation in which she found herself teaching, and adapt her practices to fit it. One early retreat exemplifies this flexibility and also expresses her female nature. "I had babies there . . . six toddlers we had, and a different person had each hour to be with the babies. I was one of the babysitters, too. While I would be doing my babysitting duty, someone else would sit in the front. That is very important. And all of that was not accepted as vipassana. But I had enough confidence in me in the beginning because I had been exposed to so many masters and I knew their weakness, and I knew what is right and what is wrong, even if it's misinterpreted. If they would have said I'm not doing vipassana, because I have the babies, I would have just smiled. You see? That was *practice,* being with the babies."

CHAPTER TWELVE

Conflict and Clarity

It was the controversial spiritual teacher Da Free John who almost cost Ruth her home and her marriage. Born Franklin Jones, this young American journeyed to India in 1970, where he had an "enlightenment" experience and acquired the name Bubba Free John, which later became Da Free John (Da being a title of respect). Returning to the United States he began to teach soon after, and styled himself a "crazy adept," claiming to transmit "crazy wisdom"; among his teachings was "sex as transcendent communion." Encouraging devotion to himself as God incarnate, Da Free John gathered numerous devotees. (By the mid-eighties, according to the *San Francisco Examiner,* his 1,100 followers were concentrated in Marin County and Lake County in California, at a retreat center in Hawaii, and on an 1,800-acre Fijian island.)[45]

Henry encountered Da Free John in the late seventies and decided to join the community forming in Marin around this charismatic spiritual teacher. But there were conditions to meet. First, he was encouraged to sell his beautiful Hollywood house and give the proceeds to Da Free John. Second, the community members were required to be in one-to-one relationships. As Ruth was busy teaching and not willing to follow Henry to join Da Free John, Henry filed for divorce in order to be free to mate with one of the women in the community.

Appalled, Ruth went into divorce court to fight for her marriage.

Throughout her life, after each setback, she had managed to land on her feet; now, threatened by Henry, she was not about to give up. When the judge asked her, "Isn't there a way of reconciliation, Mrs. Denison?" she answered, "Yes, I never wanted this divorce!" and convinced him to issue a legal separation instead. Henry accepted the separation, they celebrated their parting, and Henry went to northern California to connect with the Da Free John community, having instructed Ruth to sell the house and send the money to Da Free John. Instead, she hired a lawyer to draw up a paper giving her half the value of the house, and then she stopped the sale.

Six months later, when she got off a plane from Germany, where she had led a course, she was startled to see her tall, dignified husband awaiting her in the airport, holding a bouquet of yellow roses. Da Free John, it turns out, had not been the answer for Henry. Henry moved back into his Hollywood house, no doubt grateful to Ruth for having saved it for him.

• • •

Ruth talks about how radically her life changed when she began to teach. "When Dhamma[46] came, everything left. My mosaic, my piano I sold, my tennis playing. Actually I neglected Henry, and so we had difficulties. And the household. I was always gone. So I really sacrificed my private life gradually. And later I chose even to stay out there in the desert. So I became a renunciate, actually."

Henry always took her to the airport and picked her up, to support her in her teaching role. But he opposed some of her plans. "I was looking for a place, I wanted to have a center, and Henry didn't like that, you see. Also he was engaged strongly with Baba Free John and so on. Ayya Khema[47] came in our house, and Henry and she argued. He defended Baba Free John and she, Buddha. Ayya thought Henry was off. Well, he *was* a little, maybe at that time at least. Oh, what I'm gone through! It was enorme [enormous] what went on. It was hard for Henry to carry that, and I also lost what I had had, the intimate relationship. I wasn't so willing anymore."

Ruth began to establish her center at the desert cabin near Joshua Tree, which she had purchased with her lawyer friend Jim Tuggle. The house cost $17,000. Henry gave Ruth money for a down payment, and later she would buy out Tuggle's share of the property. While she was developing Dhamma Dena, Ruth and Henry tried various living arrangements, with Ruth living down the street on Creston Drive in Hollywood for a while, then inhabiting a separate apartment that Henry had built into his house. She would stay out at Dhamma Dena during retreats, but always returned to some closeness with Henry. It was not until the mid-eighties that she began spending most of her time in the desert. But she always maintained her legal and emotional bond with Henry and returned regularly to Hollywood to help him with house finances and chores.

At her property in the desert, at first "there was only the garage and the little house in the center. Cunningham also lived there. Michael Cunningham. I met him that first Christmas I taught in Europe. He is English, and he followed me from England. He was very quiet and contemplative, a very nice man. And Martin from New York, who later died here. We were sitting at a retreat in Santa Barbara, and some of them wanted to continue. So I said, 'Kids, you can continue, I have a little weekend house there.'" Five people followed her to the desert, and converted the garage into a bunkhouse/meditation hall. The following weekend, more people came from Los Angeles, including Jim Gillon and Jim Tuggle.

The young men worked along with Ruth to create the bare essentials of a meditation center. And Ruth connected with her neighbors. "They had five foster children and Stevie was the mom and he was working at the marine base." The neighbors participated in various early events, prompting Ruth to comment, "How could I separate men and women here [referring to U Ba Khin's requirement that she teach only women]? It was just impossible. So when we ate outside someone put up the cauldron full of beans and peppers and cheese layers; it was the most beautiful meal I ever ate. And someone stood up and said, 'Ruth and sangha [Buddhist community] friends, we have a new center now!' It was very touching."

At the same time, the teachers from the Insight Meditation Society had begun to journey west to the desert to lead retreats at Mentalphysics, a retreat center on Highway 62, east of Joshua Tree. They would invite Ruth to lead movement sessions for their retreatants, and their Asian guests would visit Dhamma Dena as well. The Indian teacher Anagarika Shri Munindra, who greatly influenced Joseph Goldstein, visited Dhamma Dena. Another such visitor was the Venerable Mahasi Sayadaw, the learned Burmese monk to whom Henry and Ruth had initially gone before settling with U Ba Khin. Mahasi Sayadaw was tremendously accomplished, having written sixty-seven volumes on Burmese Buddhism and established meditation centers throughout Burma, as well as in Thailand, Sri Lanka, Cambodia, and India.

• • •

Ruth was developing her teaching skill and her understanding of the relationship between theory and practice. "When you really know a little bit of theory and you do now the practice, you can relate, and at one point the practice will make you understand the theory. The theory originally comes from the experience, yah? What is true, the mind when it is clear and calm, hooks into it. The spark is transferring. And you get right view. At least that much, and that is enough.

"I was engaged in retreats and the students were all kind of more bewildered than I was. I was only a little bit ahead of them. I heard Mr. Hover saying to me, 'You know I wished I was a little bit more ahead than my students.' Yes, that little margin he had between him and the students, but enough to guide them."

She was learning to let go of striving for a goal, as she settled into the mode of consciousness that would sustain her. "I never occupied my mind with that goal [of enlightenment]. I enjoyed the whole atmo-sphere that happened inside me and also around me, when I have good harmony with myself, whether I am at I.M.S. teaching or in Germany or here in the desert making livable the bunkhouse. You don't strive to cut through, you just sustain mindfulness, the presence of your con-scious awareness, and will fall everything into place. If you can sustain the quality of the witnessing mind, then everything that comes up has no influence anymore. It is not fed, it's not attracted by our mind, and it's not pushed away. It becomes neutralized energy—yah, like an un-invited guest who will leave and go back to where it came from. It was so clear to me, I could give instruction that way."

• • •

People who need help or direction have always been drawn to Ruth. They arrive and offer themselves, surrendering to her, and she takes them in. Susanna was one of these. A brilliant woman who had worked for the federal government, been a radical feminist, and then shed shoes and possessions to walk barefoot across the country as part of a religious cult, Susanna found her way to a Ruth Denison retreat at the Insight Meditation Society in 1978. Later that year she came to Hollywood to move in with Ruth. Susanna lived with Ruth in a house at 2726 Cres-ton Drive, down the street from Henry's house, that Ruth had moved into some time after the Da Free John escapade. Later she moved with Ruth back into Henry's house, where he had built a separate wing for her.

Susanna recalls, "Ruth saw me as her challenge—that I needed to learn to cook and sew and clean—to still my mind, first and foremost. She taught me to meditate and I tried very hard. She was very delicate about asking me to clean. Either she picked up that I was a radical fem-inist and would resist being seen as a servant—or if it was just her prin-ciples—but we decided that I was her 'personal assistant.' She said, 'You must have a title. If you're not going to be a meditator, then, well....'" Susanna would go out to the developing desert retreat center to clean and fix things up and get ready for retreats. Then she and Ruth would return to Hollywood where they lived together with Henry. Although Susanna left Dhamma Dena and Ruth some years later, she still expresses great gratitude for the teachings she received while living and working with Ruth.

• • •

In 1979, Ruth attended a meditation retreat in Santa Cruz, where she was to acquire the name for her desert center. The retreat was led by the Venerable Taungpulu Sayadaw, an aged Burmese monk considered in his homeland to be a saint. Taungpulu, at first a great teacher, later became a forest monk, meditating in seclusion, and after that the head of a temple and a missionary to other countries. He came to San Francisco at the request of Dr. Rina Sircar, a Burmese-born woman who holds the World Peace Buddhist chair at the California Institute of Integral Studies. Later the Taungpulu Kaba-Aye Monastery was established near Santa Cruz, with the help of Dr. Sircar.

Ruth relates, "In Santa Cruz in a seminar we were playing forest monks and nuns. Together with Rina Sircar, I had to sleep outside the villa in which Taungpulu with his entourage was residing. [As Theravada monks are not allowed to sleep under the same roof as a woman, women visiting a monastery must find somewhere else to sleep.] There's where I got the name Dhamma Dena, from Taungpulu. Because I told him that my teacher died and I have no way to connect and I felt he was my teacher at that time. He accepted me too. Then when I came to him at two o'clock in the morning—he made interviews then—he said I had to learn the Burmese language and to introduce myself in Burmese, 'I am Dhamma Dena, I am asking permission to be taught by you, the Dharma,' and then I had to bow again. That was his formality."

The name that the Venerable Taungpulu Sayadaw gave her was *Dhammadinna*. Dhammadinna had been an "almswoman" or nun, during the Buddha's lifetime 2,500 years ago, foremost among the enlightened women who could preach. Her eloquence caused many women and men to join the mendicant order established by the Buddha. The famous story of Dhammadinna's extraordinary grasp of the Dharma recounts how she answered the questions of her former husband "on many and various of the tenets." When the man went to the Buddha to check Dhammadinna's answers, the Buddha said, "Learning and great wisdom dwell in Dhammadinna. Had you asked me, I should have made answer exactly as she did. Her answer was correct and you should treasure it up accordingly."[48]

Learning and great wisdom were just what Ruth felt she did not possess. So rather than take on the name herself, she gave it to the little house and garage/bunkhouse in the desert that was fast becoming a rustic meditation center, and with characteristic nonchalance she bent the spelling of the name, coming up with Dhamma Dena.

•••

While Ruth's teaching of body awareness in the Dharma, and her unique inventiveness, were drawing more and more students to her retreats, the conventional vipassana community tended to disparage her. As one old student put it, "She was considered not serious. If you were a serious vipassana student, you did not sit with Ruth." Letters were being written, conversations ensued. The letter that had been sent by Robert Hover's students to the *Vipassana Newsletter* describing Ruth's innovations to practice struck a sour note with traditional teachers and students. When Ruth, teaching in Germany, called to arrange a visit with S. N. Goenka, the Indian Dharma heir of U Ba Khin who was also teaching there, he refused to see her. "He said to me, 'Ruth, I hear you are teaching Zen together with vipassana and you do seem to go on a different track. Maybe this is not the right time that we are meeting now.'"[49] People began to question Ruth's credentials: was she really qualified to teach vipassana?

In the context of this insidious undertow, the British meditator Michael Cunningham wrote a letter to a concerned student, beautifully delineating Ruth's legitimacy and power as a teacher. Cunningham's letter of July 5, 1978, described how John Coleman, the British Dharma heir of U Ba Khin, had found it necessary to invent new methods for teaching Westerners, rather than sticking with the framework of the ten-day retreat developed by U Ba Khin. Western students, Coleman had pointed out, were too rigid, prone to grasping, clinging, and striving. Mrs. Denison had encountered the same problems, Cunningham wrote, and had also found that "Western students were very distracted, often without any subtle awareness, or unable to sustain it." So Ruth applied her intuition, "arising from a deep understanding of Dhamma, to the teaching situations in which she found herself."

He goes on to assert that Ruth attained the *Nibbanic,* or enlightened, state during her stay with U Ba Khin, but for her to teach in the way originally demonstrated to her by her teacher would not be appropriate to her Western environment and students. Cunningham went on to praise her.

I can testify to the relevance of the way she does teach. When I first sat with Mrs. Denison a year ago, I had been practising for 4½ years, including 110 days with Goenka, and thought that I had learned a great deal. In working with Ruth, the depths of my ignorance became clearer: many barriers were confronted and overcome. I found no contradictions with what Goenka taught, but gained a much more real connection with it. My respect for Mrs. Denison's qualities as a teacher continues to increase. She is much admired by other teachers—for example Ajahn Sumedho[50] said that his teacher Ajahn Chah was the only teacher in Thailand who had Mrs. Denison's rare ability to trip people up and press the specific buttons needed for them to see clearly at that specific time—much more difficult than following a set pattern in a formal context.

U Ba Khin asked Mrs. Denison to teach women. She says that this was for her own protection. When she was with U Ba Khin twenty years ago she was in her mid-thirties, and was described by Alan Watts as "sexy." Now she is in her mid-fifties and has been a celibate for twelve years, that protection is less relevant. She does not feel that it would be possible to work with that restriction in the West, and she is certainly a fine teacher of men.

The controversy reached all the way to Burma, to U Ba Khin's successor, Sayama, and her husband U Chit Tin. Not only Ruth, but all of the other Western Dharma heirs of U Ba Khin were viewed with disapproval by Sayama. Even Goenka, who purports to teach exactly as U Ba Khin taught, ultimately came into conflict with Sayama.

Finally, in early 1980, Ruth received an ultimatum from Burma. It was contained in a letter that reached her in a retreat center in Mendocino where she was engaged in leading a retreat for thirty-five or forty people. Nearby in the forest, crews were busy clear-cutting trees. Ruth and her retreatants, hearing the saws, felt the pain of this devastation. In the disturbance of the forest, animal life was disrupted, driven from its environment, and injured, and some creatures found their way into the retreat house.

"An injured owl flew into the room. I tried to save it, but it flew off and died," Ruth remembers. "A coyote came in, looked around, and walked off. Later we found his body."

That night in her little teacher's cabin in the woods, Ruth opened the letter from the International Meditation Center in Rangoon. Sayama spelled out her requirements. "She said, 'If you don't give up walking meditation, give up your body movement that we hear you are doing, your mixing Zen practice in, then you are not belonging to our lineage.'" And Sayama also cited Ruth's teaching both men and women, which she had been forbidden to do.

Ruth understood the gravity of these demands, and her responsibility to herself and her students in responding to them. Truly there was no way she could accede to Sayama's directions, but then how was she to continue teaching, when her legitimacy had been based on

U Ba Khin's inducting her into his lineage? Ruth stayed up all night in the log cabin with the dark forest outside. She lit a candle and placed a photograph of U Ba Khin before it. And she began to meditate on her predicament.

"I went into myself to see how strong I was. Through the night I saw myself in a dream, going upstairs to a big stupa [shrine]. After the first third of the stairs I stopped. I looked up and there was, higher, U Ba Khin, looking down to me, and on top was the Buddha. I felt like I awoke and I was going with that dream, and took it into my meditation. That was very deep for me. It gave me the message: Continue walking. I saw clearly. My teacher and the Buddha gave me courage. Also I think it wasn't just a dream—it was confirming because I knew I can give the Dharma on a deep, genuine level, through the sensations. I was well established in this. Then I felt my teacher was close."

Telling the story, Ruth reflects on her teacher's views. "U Ba Khin was enticed by his great passion to bring the Dharma to the West. Yah, and the Buddha said that you have to consider the conditions you find in the new culture where the Dharma you are introducing. In their native language it should be taught, in alignment with their customs, and not bringing so much new but allowing more to emerge and then to integrate it. The Dharma it is so universal, not for one culture only. It is global and beyond. My teacher always said this."

She meditated through the night, and came to her decision. "It didn't hurt me in my heart. I decided to continue. I thought, What can they do? The affirmation, I have. I'm able to teach. In fact I don't even need to be afraid that I am not scholarly versed about the teachings and the philosophical aspect of the Dharma. U Ba Khin said to me, 'You are a natural. Whatever is in your heart you will feel what to communicate.'"

The next morning she went to the meditation hall to speak with her students, and told them about the letter from Burma. "I said, 'I got this letter and there is the perception that the way I'm teaching you is not totally in line with what Sayama thinks. True that I do give some other aspects, but they are basically tied in to the elementary practice, the Four Foundations of Mindfulness. You know it is difficult, and if you feel I have misled you in my additional modes of meditation, if you think it is not helpful, well then you have to go to some other teacher. Because I have not slept all night, and I was communicating somehow with my teacher and with my inner energy, and I know I will continue teaching, if there is only one student, or two, or fifty. You can decide for yourself whether through this retreat you will go with me or not.' I told them if they all left I then finish the retreat alone. Nobody left!

"It was a very beautiful experience."

Of course, despite being officially ousted from the lineage, in her heart she remained U Ba Khin's loving student and knew that external rejection could not change that. In the meditation hall at Dhamma Dena hangs an oil painting of U Ba Khin in brown monk's robes; in every retreat Ruth acknowledges him as her teacher. But at that time, in the vipassana world of Asian and Western teachers and students, soon many people knew that she had been expelled from the lineage of U Ba Khin. So, in some true way, she was on her own, without the support or protection of official credentials.

Every one of the other four Western Dharma heirs of U Ba Khin was similarly excommunicated for behavior that Sayama judged wrong and inappropriate. Even the scrupulously traditional Goenka clashed with Sayama and U Chit Tin and was expunged from the lineage.

Seen from a wider or deeper perspective, this casting out from the nest, while it seemed unfortunate at the time, in fact expressed an inevitable truth about Ruth Denison. Certainly she learned from Charlotte Selver and U Ba Khin principally, and she teaches within the Theravada or Vipassana tradition, but the real truth is that Ruth exists outside any lineage. She has followed her own instincts so loyally, honoring her deepest knowledge of how to survive and heal, how to grow and teach others to open to their larger selves, that she spills out over the boundaries of denominations and conventionally defined spiritual paths. Watching her, one thinks sometimes of an ancient priestess, a wild shaman woman whose whole being is dedicated to bringing the earth into balance. This insistence on the truth of what she sees puts her at odds with the established forms, and challenges those people who come to learn from her.

CHAPTER THIRTEEN

Finding Ruth

It was shortly after this crucial juncture in Ruth's teaching career that I entered her story, attending my first retreat with her and making the connection that has developed over the twenty-three years since. I had come from a period of intense commitment to the women's and anti-nuclear movements, and I found myself tired out and needing internal nourishment to balance the constant output required by political activism. I was open to some kind of spiritual practice, some comfort in the wilderness.

So, in March 1980, riding with several young women in a van that suffered a flat tire en route, and arriving after midnight, I came to Dhamma Dena to stay for five days of the women's retreat. My journal records glimpses of my beginning sitting practice:

> Hard to sit. Right leg going to sleep. Upper back between shoulder blades tight and burning. Concentration on the breath, on feelings in nostrils, throat, diaphragm.
>
> Ruth rang the bell, and we got up to go out into the desert for walking meditation. Almost always I did it barefoot. Slowly lift the foot, glide forward, set it down. Weight on foot, sharp stones and thistles pressing into bottom of foot. Mindful of this motion, all the sensations in it. Be in it totally. Cold wind on face. Sun warm on head and

hands. Slow step after slow step. The mountains out there in the distance. Snow on their tops.

After half an hour or so, the bell rang. We came slowly back to the zendo to sit again.

Second day. After breakfast I ran in the desert, leaping over bushes, exhausting myself, working out the frustration. Then shouted into the wind.

Came back tired and sweating, body tingling, feeling half crazy.

In that sitting meditation, I let myself be there. Then I said in my mind "I can't do this," felt very sorry for myself and was present in that.

In the walking meditation, I began to cry. Feeling a great compassion for myself, feeling how distractions generally enter between me and myself, and feeling sorry about that. A wonderful, deep time, this walking—so deeply alive in myself.

After the morning session, we went out into the desert for a short while, before lunch. I felt in a very unusual state—centered, yielding, tremendously, deeply alive. Sat before a green bush and looked down at a crooked stick on the ground. And all of existence was there. I lacked nothing. I was in perfect balance and filled with satisfaction.

A tiny glimpse behind the veil.

Looking back at that very first encounter with Ruth and the experience of meditation, I am shocked by how much of the essential teachings I took in, writing them in my journal. Now after a quarter of a century I know how many long years of effort it takes to bring those insights from their clarity in the thinking mind down into one's physical, psychological, emotional being; how excruciatingly difficult it is to put these insights into practice in one's life, how hard to maintain awareness, even for an hour, of the true nature of existence.

This is what I wrote:

The breath is the bridge between mind and body. If you are able to reside there, you unify the two. Breath is the bridge between life and death.

And breath is part of that experience **before expression**.

Before expression. That is, before talking to myself, before making a story, before lashing out. How hard it is to interrupt the programmed behavior of my continual mental and emotional commentary on every moment of my life—how hard just to be present in my body/mind.

And Ruth's teaching on Dukkha, or "suffering," struck deep. In this I saw my living in reaction to discomfort. In the microcosm of sitting still on a cushion, experiencing discomfort and desiring change, I saw the pattern of my whole life so far—how my decisions and major actions had come from suffering, not from freedom. And I felt trapped.

Most of our actions are attempts to relieve our own suffering. This they do, for a short while. Then more, different suffering arises. We act to relieve that. For a short while we are content. Then . . .

In reaction to suffering, I act. My action causes something to happen in the world that I must then react to. So I act to change it. Again my action causes a situation that affects me. I suffer again, so I must act again. Thus I am involved in a chain of activity that goes on forever, lifetime after lifetime.

•••

In that retreat, besides these powerful teachings, there were aspects of Ruth's behavior that troubled or annoyed me. She seemed exceedingly bossy and controlling, sometimes chastising wrongdoers and shaming them before the whole group. Another problem for me was her Dharma talks. At times during the day Ruth would speak with piercing insight, expressing a deep wise apprehension of life and the Buddhist teachings, but her formal Dharma talks in the evening often rambled in a disor-

ganized jumble of ideas and stories and went on so long that half of her
listeners would be tilting into sleep. Loving the English language as I
did, and appreciating literary form, I sometimes was tortured by Ruth's
mangling of language and disregard for grace and economy of deliv-
ery. In English-major high dudgeon, I would rant internally in protest.

She seemed never to end a session on time, but would keep talking
to us long after the gong had rung for lunch or dinner. None of this, at
first, posed a serious impediment to my enthusiastic first awakenings
to the Dharma, but over the years to come, I would struggle with my
reactions to these behaviors, sometimes retreating into sullenness, or
stoking anger and blame, only occasionally seeing the humor in my ex-
pending so much energy disapproving of Ruth while she went blithely
on her way. There was a period of whole years in which, when Ruth
opened her mouth to begin an evening Dharma talk, I fell asleep on
my cushion, and only awoke hours later when she finished. I did not
approve of this behavior of mine, not only because it was rude to be so
publicly unconscious while Ruth spoke, but because I missed whatever
insight might be buried in the river of her words. So I decided to keep
myself awake by taking notes, and proceeded to write down everything
she said in a tiny notebook. Later, looking over my notes, I often found
an important piece of Dharma information given or a beautiful connection made, and was glad I had forced myself to stay awake.

There was one period of my association with Ruth in which all my
judgment of her fell away. I was struggling to survive major surgery and
long-term chemotherapy for cancer, when I went down to Dhamma
Dena to attend the women's retreat. Seeing me trying to sit upright
in the meditation hall, Ruth immediately recognized my condition,
and she reacted with tender solicitude. She had me lie down among the
other sitters, positioned a pillow under my head, and tucked a shawl
around me. During the retreat, she watched over me, excusing me from
activities that were too strenuous, encouraging me to go back to the
dormitory to sleep when fatigue overtook me. And in the following
months, throughout my difficult course of treatment, I was sustained

and strengthened by the practices Ruth Denison had taught me and the state of mind she had helped me cultivate.

But at the time of that very first retreat in 1980, I was a beginner to meditation and brand-new to the wisdom teachings of the Buddha. After the retreat, in my apartment in Oakland, I created a small altar; on it I placed a candle and a vase with a single flower. Almost every morning I sat before it for half an hour or more to attempt to reproduce the experiences of body awareness and investigation of the mind begun at Dhamma Dena. As well, my lover and I began to attend the Sunday afternoon chanting sessions at the Nyingma Institute, a Tibetan-Buddhist center in Berkeley. And soon we would enroll in a class there on the Abhidharma, the codified teachings of the Buddha. So, inspired by that first retreat with Ruth, I had embarked on a program of meditation and study that was to continue to the present.

CHAPTER FOURTEEN

Inviting Women
to the Dharma

Ruth Denison's impact on American Buddhism has been wide-ranging. She initiated the practice of conducting all-women retreats, which were unheard-of in the early days and now are routinely offered in most centers. Additionally, her incorporation of movement and bodywork into the traditional practices, which was considered so very radical in the mid-seventies and drew such harsh criticism, has now become accepted in many Buddhist centers, which offer some component of yoga, stretches, or movement along with conventional sitting and walking meditation, to cultivate mindfulness.

In many ways Ruth introduced a feminine perspective and energy in her teaching. She was body-based, intuitive, flexible, creative, and innovative. While conventional teachers taught in rigidly prescribed blocks of time, Ruth flowed from one activity to the next, taking her cue from the students, inventing as she went along. As Julie Wester noted, Ruth provided a breath of fresh air to women stifled in traditional Buddhist environments. Like all world religions, Buddhism has been conditioned by the patriarchy for thousands of years. It began with strong female practitioners as well as male during the Buddha's lifetime in India, 2,500 years ago, but after his death the men gained increasing power and prominence. They fell back into the mores of ancient Asian society, which relegated women to the kitchen and the birth chamber, and they even asserted that before a woman could be fully enlightened she would have to transform herself into, or be reborn as, a male (contradicting the Buddha, who had declared women as competent as men to achieve full liberation, and who had recognized the enlightenment of numerous women).

Although the nuns' order lasted for a thousand years in Southeast Asia, and the female lineage still exists in North Asia, male scholars and monks essentially took ownership of Buddhism, demonizing women or forgetting them altogether, and proceeded to codify and interpret the teachings through a masculinist lens. This was the Buddhism that arrived on American shores. Theravada or vipassana Buddhism was not brought here by Asian masters, but the young Westerners who returned with it from Asia had all studied with Asian male teachers. Despite themselves, they brought the male-supremacist attitudes that lay behind the practices along with the techniques themselves.

Women like me (I had spent ten years cultivating a feminist perspective and struggling for women's equality) yearned for a spiritual practice and could see the value of Buddhist meditation and study. But we found it difficult to tolerate the usual Buddhist-center arrangement: a hierarchical setting that situated dominant males on top and women in lesser roles, where they often gave of their reverence and their labor to support the physical plant and provide emotional support to the men. In the early eighties, also, some of the most prominent Buddhist masters were exposed as power abusers who secretly had sexual relations with female students; a few were also abusing alcohol and misusing funds. Some women, disillusioned and wounded by this behavior, left the Buddhist centers and set out to find female teachers. Others stayed and worked within their institutions to transform structures and demand ethical standards. Additionally, there were the women who had been sexually abused or battered as children, by their fathers or other male relatives, and who felt vulnerable in any situation where a male authority figure held power.

In the women's movement, we had experienced the freedom of

working exclusively with women, bypassing the conditioned societal values that favored men—and our own internalized sexism that led us to defer to men even when it was not in our interest to do so. I for one, having had a dominant father and having been heterosexually married for ten years—much of which I spent listening to and supporting my husband and other men—felt by the end of the seventies that I had "done my time" in the patriarchy, as I used to put it, and now wished to give my best energy to women.

So we were looking for women spiritual teachers, but they would have to have some consciousness of themselves as women, would have to approach the practice in a quintessentially female way. It is ironic that Ruth, who did not consider herself a feminist or even understand the basic principles of feminism, should become the first female teacher to lead an all-women Buddhist meditation retreat and institute a schedule of two women's retreats a year, which continues to this day. But, seen from another perspective, she was a natural, in tune with the world of living beings and the outdoors, loving all creatures in a genuine hands-on way; she was wonderfully sensitive to her own body and could lead her students into intense awareness of physical sensations; she loved to dance, to celebrate, to stretch and move; she acted and taught not so much from her head as from her heart and her senses; she was a mature woman, grounded in the physical world, having wide life-experience. In all these ways Ruth was one who could open the door of the Dharma to women, particularly to feminists and lesbians and defiant women, who responded happily to her outrageous and eccentric personality.

Ruth herself, however, despite U Ba Khin's dictate that she teach only women, would never have thought to offer a women's retreat. She was invited to do so by a young lesbian-feminist in the late seventies, and she said yes, without understanding the significance of the event. This was the beginning of the creation of the community of women who came down from Oregon, northern California, and the San Francisco Bay Area to regular women's retreats at Dhamma Dena, from 1980 until the mid-nineties. A student named Carol Newhouse generated this phenomenon.

Carol had helped found a women's country residence and retreat center in 1974. Begun in an old farmhouse in the woods near Grants Pass, Oregon, Womanshare had quickly developed into a thriving community of residents and women from surrounding areas who came to the workshops and classes. The founders of Womanshare identified as part of "Lesbian Nation," a subgroup of the women's movement in the United States, made up of young lesbians who had set out to create a minisociety separate from the dominant heterosexual culture.[51] Women's spirituality, an eclectic blend of goddess worship and witchcraft, constituted Carol's spiritual explorations as she and her friends repaired the old house and offered their skills to the community. Womanshare was structured as a collective, with all resources and duties shared. Carol and the other members of the collective wrote a book called *Country Lesbians* chronicling their struggles and discoveries.

Then, on a trip to the East Coast, and on the lookout for a spiritual path presented by a woman teacher, she signed up for a retreat at the Insight Meditation Society with Ruth Denison. Carol was searching for a practice that would "alter my consciousness and my awareness in a deep and ongoing way." She found this in Buddhism as taught by Ruth. And she found her teacher. "I liked Ruth. Her presence, how she looked, how she could get up in front of all those people—those are very big retreats there. She was a role model at that point. She had her big blouse and long flowing skirt. She was restrained and dignified. She was impressive to me. Here was an age-old practice that seemed to have good roots. It worked on me. And it was taught by a woman, a woman about twenty years older than me, which was just right."

Carol remembers an early conversation with Ruth about teaching women. "She said, 'My teacher said I should teach women.' I wanted to say, 'Yeah, that's right, you should!' But she said, 'I think I should teach men too, I'm a good teacher and I shouldn't just teach women!'

So I said, 'Well, I agree, I think that you can teach men and women but teaching women is very special. U Ba Khin must have meant something by that: maybe he meant you should teach women separately.'"

Carol began to ponder some way to integrate the two distinct parts of her life: her iconoclastic feminist-dyke persona, in jeans and flannel shirt, and her newfound meditator self. She decided to ask Ruth to come to Womanshare to lead a retreat. There was a risk, she realized, because "this was my chosen family, my friendship group, my foundation in the community, and I might be seen as bringing an eccentric German old lady up to Lesbian Nation! But I had to do it, to see if it would work."

Ruth accepted Carol's invitation, and plans were made for an autumn 1978 retreat at Womanshare. Carol corralled the Womanshare collective to participate, and then called her other friends, persuading about twenty women in all to come to a long weekend with Ruth. And "it worked fabulously. The reason was Ruth. I didn't know it, but she was in her element. I didn't know that she had grown up in the country; I didn't know she liked cooking and food and gardens just like we did.

"She slept in a chicken coop. That was where I was sleeping, so I gave my place to her. She didn't flinch. You can imagine. Especially in those days when Dhamma Dena was not much more developed than Womanshare."

At first some of the women found it hard to accept Ruth. They had never experienced a silent retreat, or the discipline of vipassana meditation. As lesbians and country women they were natural rebels, who did not respond obediently to authority. The women were meditating in the house, going outside at mealtimes to eat at a makeshift table of planks laid on the grass, sleeping wherever they could find a nook; but sometimes they sneaked off to walk in the woods and grouse about Ruth.

Carol recalls a crucial encounter through which Ruth won the trust of the group. One woman sat leaning against the wall. On the second day, Ruth told her that she must move away from the wall. The woman resisted, claiming she had a bad back and could not sit without support. Ruth told her it was not good for her back to lean against a wall, and the woman began to cry. As everyone watched this struggle of wills, Carol Newhouse cringed, wondering if her friends would understand what Ruth was doing. But Ruth came back to where the woman was sitting, arranged pillows, physically helped her move and rearrange herself to sit up straight, and said to her encouragingly, "You see? You are stronger than that, dahling. You can sit up!" For the rest of the retreat the woman sat without support on her cushion.

Carol saw this incident as a turning point, "when people started to take Ruth as an authority. Up to then it was just another workshop. Because of that moment of asserting her authority in a good way, I guess, people accepted her."

Ruth does not remember the "turning point" at that first Womanshare retreat, as described by Carol Newhouse. But although she had only been teaching for a few years, she felt she could trust her intuition. She remembers, "I wasn't that wise at that time, but I had a good sense for how people's makeup was on the mental level. If I hadn't had that sense I wouldn't have done that. From my inner contact with them, I thought, I can do it. And it worked."

• • •

When Ruth realized that the women at the retreat were lesbians, she asked to see the book *Country Lesbians,* and stayed up all night reading it. She remembered that she had once had a friend who had loved women. The next morning she discussed the book with Carol, asking questions about the lesbian lifestyle and the women's work together at Womanshare. Carol found this reassuring, for Ruth was genuinely interested and utterly nonjudgmental in her questioning. The whole retreat felt healing to Carol, as she witnessed Ruth's entering a challenging situation and making it her own, and as she watched her friends open up to Ruth.

"She saw something in us," Carol says. "She saw community. I now know that she saw *sangha*. She saw the power, the strength of women, and she saw our belligerence and our limitations and distrust too."

Ruth did not realize the revolutionary significance of that first retreat at Womanshare, nor could she foresee the future, when an extensive network of women Buddhist practitioners would develop. But then, as her own center at Dhamma Dena was developing, she said to the women, "I have come to you. Now you come down to the desert next year."

So in early February 1979, Ruth held the first women's retreat at Dhamma Dena. It was attended by women from the Womanshare community and others from Oregon, northern California, and the San Francisco Bay Area, who drove down to the desert. Thus began a long and fruitful association for Ruth with a challenging group of students. (She agreed to come north to Womanshare again in October of 1979, but told the women that from then on they had to come down to Dhamma Dena.)

I was not present at the first Dhamma Dena women's retreat, but found my way to the second one, which took place from March 15 to 30, 1980. That retreat was my very first encounter with the Buddha-dharma, my introduction to Ruth, and my first stay at Ruth's rustic retreat center on Copper Mountain Mesa.

The women's retreats became a staple at Dhamma Dena, and soon there was a women's retreat in the fall and one in the spring. Attendees were not limited to lesbians; there was always a mixture, but the core group was lesbian. (Ruth's third Dhamma Dena retreat each year is the holiday retreat that runs through Christmas and New Year's and is open to men and women.) Certainly for me, and probably for most of the women who attended those retreats, Ruth was the only one who could invite us to the Dharma. Because she was a woman, and because she was so grounded in her environment and daily life—asking us to work with her to create something, and being totally honest with us about her own life, her background, her relationship with Henry—we could trust her.

Her work with the body, teaching mindfulness of physical sensations to lead us to an experience of impermanence, gave us a powerful, transformative tool. And her spontaneity, her creativity in guiding us to pay attention to every aspect of life, her great *joie de vivre,* charmed us and helped soften and sweeten the hard times of resistance and anger, helped us forgive her transgressions and ultimately open our hearts to the profound liberating message of Buddhism.

• • •

Rituals both individual and shared began to gather around the retreats. At Dhamma Dena I would get up each morning just at dawn and go running east in the cool air toward the horizon, my tennis shoes thudding on the sandy road, my eyes greeting the pale light that gathered like liquid behind distant hills, grew and brightened, and then flooded up to fill the sky with waves of pink and mauve against most delicate blue. We sat to meditate in a very small zendo, knee to knee, sharing each other's colds and sniffles. Ruth had acquired the hunter's cabin near the main house the year before we came, and had transformed it into a meditation hall. Often Ruth took us outside into the desert to move in a circle, lifting arms to the sky, bending to the earth, twirling slowly, mindfully, to honor our animal siblings and our own precious beings. Sometimes in the afternoon, to counteract our lethargy, she took us outside to stand facing the open desert, raising our eyes in a "seeing" meditation, in which we received the environment as "form and color, dahling" and learned to let our minds and bodies relax to experience the act of seeing. Or she might lead us in a mindful conga line just at dusk, down the road to Dukkha House and back, barking at us to be aware of the touch of foot on earth, the movement of muscles and joints.

In the zendo, she guided us in deep exploration of our body sensations, with great penetration and subtlety, directing us to explore our throats, where tension is held, to experience the aspects of the head where so much sensitivity is concentrated. She took us through the entire body so deeply that we apprehended the bones of our own skeletons. It was hard work to direct attention in this way. Ruth's voice came softly, resolutely, in the textured silence of the room. I did my best to go to the place in my body that she indicated, to penetrate with my consciousness into the physical, energetic reality of my flesh. Sometimes I succeeded, and came to experience the flux of this body, the movement of energy, the reality of bones and tendons, and with this apprehension came the awareness that this body would one day cease to be animated, that it would die, decay, even the bones crumbling finally to dust.

Emerging from a meditation like this, I would experience a great wash of tenderness for myself and all the other beings in the room. We shared the same elements, we partook of the same impermanence. This knowledge held me in a heightened, spacious consciousness.

This, for me, was the heart of Ruth's teaching.

Then, in the afternoon sessions, sometimes she would have us sit on the floor and move knees and feet, shoulders, buttocks, sometimes walking on our "sitz bones," sometimes lying down and wiggling snake-like across the rug. I had no idea at that time that Ruth had learned the basis of these maneuvers from Charlotte Selver in her living room twenty years before. Amid stifled laughter and sotto voce rebellious mutterings, Ruth invited us to stay with each moment of our lived reality, not to escape into memory or future projection but to attend to the experience of this moment—scratchy carpet under nose, stiff knees not wanting to bend, hand touching thigh.

For some students this asked too much. Usually these were meditators from Jack and Joseph and Sharon's retreats at I.M.S., who were scandalized by this nontraditional approach. Now and then someone would get up quickly, radiating anger, and blunder out the door. Later Ruth would talk with the person, who might stay or leave. The rest of us, who had not had the experience of more conventional vipassana instruction, were willing to sacrifice our dignity to the endeavor of crawling across the floor on our bellies while trying to sustain mindfulness of body. We did not have the larger context of conventional Dharma teaching in which to place Ruth, and from which to judge her. She *was* our context. As far as we knew, this was the Dharma, and if she was outrageous, annoying, unpredictable, frustrating, that was just Ruth. She could also be hugely entertaining, as well as profoundly tender and compassionate. She was a wild woman, a rebel like us who invented as she went along. This we understood, for we had been inventing, during the previous decade of the women's movement, exploring new models of relationship, creating communities, leaving conventionality behind to reshape our lives. We "got" Ruth.

• • •

One ritual that always tried everyone's patience at first was the eating meditation. Probably, as women, we were especially attuned to food, some of us in an addictive way, others in a proprietary way, thinking that we knew best about diet and nutrition. And almost everyone viewed mealtimes as an opportunity to relax, let down our attention, indulge ourselves in sensual pleasure.

In the dining hall recently built onto the little house, we sat on the floor around the walls at the noon meal and waited until everyone had been served. Then Ruth would enter with her own tray and begin to talk to us about mindfulness to eating. We were first to look at the food and be aware of our hunger. I sat gazing at my bowl of vegetables and tofu on rice, watching it cool, aware of my so-predictable frustration beginning to burrow like a scrabbly little animal in my gut. Ruth had us lift the bowl in both hands and smell the food. Then she directed us to pick up the chopsticks or fork, being aware "I now lift my fork." Then she would tell us to spear a bit of food on the fork and raise it. Finally we would put the food in our mouths. Then, having replaced the utensil on the tray, we would refrain from chewing and swallowing as Ruth directed us to be aware of the texture of the food, its temperature, its taste. Very interesting were the looks on people's faces, those folks who had been anticipating the lunch hour all morning, hoping for relief. Now they realized there was to be no letup from our relentless attention to the moment. Ruth asked us to take one bite, hold it, explore it, then to attend to the motion of teeth and tongue as we chewed. And so on. Sometimes my own face expressed that stolid disbelief that I saw among the newcomers. At other times, for no reason I could discover, I surrendered to Ruth's guidance and to the experience, and felt a deep ease and joy in the process of eating.

That evening in the zendo, Ruth might talk about eating, telling a long hilarious story about a sojourn in India when neither she nor Henry nor their Brahman cook could bring themselves to kill a chicken for dinner. Ruth and Henry ended up giving the live chicken to the cook and receiving three eggs in return, in honor of Brahma, Vishnu, and Shiva, the Hindu trinity of divine forces in the universe.

Ruth sat silent for a time, remembering, then shook her head. "Yah, if everyone had to kill their own meat. At least to see how it's done. Many have reported that they cannot anymore eat meat."

And although she did not continue, I knew that passing through her mind were the animals she had shown me pictures of: cows hoisted by one leg on a hook before killing, chickens stuffed in tiny cages, geese force-fed with tubes down their throats, dogs in Philippine markets lying in the blistering sun, their forelegs bound behind them, waiting to be taken away, killed, and eaten. Ruth is willing to look at these cruelties, to care about them, to send money to organizations that work to change the conditions. Once in a Chinese restaurant, as I and others pondered whether to order duck, she told us about how the ducks are so brutally force-fed. When we protested, not wanting to hear, she said quietly, sadly, "You cannot just turn away."

• • •

One of the favorite rituals at a Dhamma Dena retreat was (and is) the excursion to the spa or to the Joshua Tree National Monument. As a reward for our effort, and to give us a new venue for practicing mindfulness, Ruth would offer us these field trips. Usually Thursday was

the day, and as with all events at Dhamma Dena, the outing was preceded by a lengthy organizational and educational morning talk with
Ruth, deciding who would ride in which car, urging silence throughout, demonstrating "driving meditation," finding bathing suits for
those who had forgotten theirs. Then, if it was the baths we were going to, we set off in a caravan to Desert Hot Springs, a town an hour
away. Finally we pulled up into the parking lot of a glossy hotel built
around hot mineral springs. In the central court there are six round
pools of varying temperatures, from extremely hot to bathtub warm.
Ruth came with us into the pools, wearing a bathing cap with rubber
flowers on it, and we kept silence amid the leathery spa regulars, the
servicemen from the nearby air base, and the vacationing middle-aged
couples with children. At some point Ruth gathered all of us in the
largest round pool, arranged us in a circle, and had us move, dip, and
turn in unison, feeling the warm water swirl around us—a ring of
women, dancing in the water, unified by Ruth's intent, delighted face
and softly spoken invitation, experiencing our relationship with
warm liquid and cool air, with sky and palm trees and one another,
immersed in the elements that compose the world and ourselves.
Bemused spectators watched us; now and then a female onlooker
might join our circle. Then Ruth insisted that each of us must take a
vigorous swim in the cool water of the Olympic-sized swimming
pool.

On the drive home in the dark, we held our silence, relaxed and
mellow, and Ruth's head bobbed as she drifted off to sleep in the passenger's seat. Back at Dhamma Dena we ate the soup made by the stay-
at-homes, and went for a short meditation session and talk in the zendo.
Then, released by Ruth's final ringing of the bell, we came out into the
night. Slowly I walked back to Dukkha House, not needing a flashlight, finding with my feet the path among the bushes and down the
sandy road. Above me an extravagant desert sky opened, a small wind
ruffled the sage bushes.

• • •

Over the years, within the community who came to the women's retreats, various knots pulled tight and had to be untangled—questions clarified, conflicts confronted.

Many of Ruth's women students held passionate political views. They opposed the acceleration of the arms race, fought for feminist goals, demonstrated to protect the environment. I myself was arrested twice in 1983 and spent fourteen days in jail, first for opposing the test launchings of the MX missile—which were devastating the Pacific Islands on which the missiles landed—then for protesting the development of nuclear weapons at Lawrence Livermore Laboratories. The women in northern California worked to stop the cutting of the redwoods, and supported other causes.

Then we would come down to Dhamma Dena, to a teacher who was ignorant of all this. In her old age Ruth has begun to pay attention to environmental issues and to support political candidates, but in the early eighties she focused exclusively on the world she could see, touch, and smell. She did send money to animal-rescue organizations, and could talk knowledgeably about the outrages visited on animals, but beyond this she seemed to know nothing of U.S. or world politics. Near neighbor to major air bases and weapons-testing sites as Dhamma Dena is, Ruth did not interest herself in learning what went on there. At a major Buddhist women's conference on the East Coast in 1984, she declared to an auditorium full of people that she was not a feminist. I chastised her afterwards, saying, "Ruth, how can you say you are not a feminist when you were the first teacher to give all-women's retreats, and so many of your students are lesbian-feminists whom you loyally support!" She looked intrigued, and then said, "Well, dahling, why didn't you stand up and contradict me?"

Ruth's ingenuousness was hard for us, her students, to tolerate. We wanted her to take responsibility at least for informing herself about the public sphere. But she seemed utterly ignorant of the larger context of all our lives.

This narrow focus led Ruth into some serious confrontations with her Jewish students. Roughly two-thirds of the women at the early retreats were Jewish, and Ruth's accent, her directive, stereotypically Germanic style, presented a difficulty for them. But there came a further irritant. When Ruth began to lead the holiday retreats, with typical enthusiasm she festooned the cactus in the yard with Christmas lights, hung shiny bulbs on the plant on the altar, lit candles, and played a tape of Handel's *Messiah* in the zendo. The Jewish women, having been confronted all their lives with the Christmas celebrations of the dominant society, while their own Jewish holidays had been ignored, objected.

Then one day Ruth, in telling about her life, in the zendo, casually mentioned that she had belonged to a Nazi youth group and described some of its activities and philosophy. Some Jewish women were so outraged that they left the retreat. Others confronted Ruth right there in the meditation hall, trying to get her to understand how offensive and even threatening this information was to them.

I also struggled mightily with what Ruth had said. I am not Jewish, and had never studied the Holocaust, but as a child I had lived through the Second World War, and at its end (when I was nine years old) had seen the newsreels of the opening of the death camps. I had read *Mein Kampf* and in college had seen Leni Riefenstahl's Nazi propaganda film *Triumph of the Will*. I had also lived in Fascist Spain for a year as an adult. I knew about Spain's alliance with the Third Reich and the use of its cities as targets for the Nazi air force to perfect its techniques of saturation bombing, and I had experienced life under Franco's military dictatorship. The very word "Nazi" struck terror to my heart.

Questions of trust arose. Could a Jewish woman really open herself to Ruth's teachings while knowing of Ruth's participation in the culture of the Third Reich and her seeming unconsciousness of its significance? What we wanted, all of us who attended those retreats, was for Ruth to express a wider view, for her to acknowledge the historical-political picture in which her own experience was embedded. We wanted her to contextualize her experience, to have researched the Nazi past and understood it in relation to the lives and deaths and suffering of millions.

The board of the Berkeley Women's Sangha, many of whom came regularly to Dhamma Dena, wrote a letter to Ruth expressing their concerns. And at the next women's retreat, Ruth met with these women and apologized to them. She thanked them for opening her eyes by letting her know the effect her words and actions had on her Jewish students. And in succeeding holiday retreats she incorporated elements of Jewish religious observance.

When I speak with some of the Jewish women now, so many years after that early eighties event, they acknowledge their own youthful reactivity at the time. With age they have developed a more philosophical attitude to spiritual teachers, having had to learn that a teacher is also a human being with flaws and blind spots.

Now, in April 2003, I want to hear what Ruth has to say about her own attitudes toward the fate of the Jews and others who perished in Hitler's death camps. We are seated once again at the dining table in Las Vegas House. Through the vertical-slatted venetian blinds at the living room windows, I see the fluffy foliage of the palo verde trees in Ruth's garden against the pale tan of the desert earth.

I begin by telling her about the reading I have been doing, learning about the Weimar Republic, the Third Reich, anti-Semitism.

Sixty years have passed since those years in Germany. Ruth speaks from her awareness now, having been a spiritual teacher for three decades. She says of all her students, Jewish and Gentile, White and African American and European, men and women, "I have treated them like myself, I have never made any difference. I was always bringing us back to the human level. I was following the Buddha path, and I think I expressed myself with all of you in compassion and loving, and in sisterhood."

She holds the two realities: her joyful experience of participating with other young people in the Hitler Youth, and her horror at later discovering the devastation wrought by the Third Reich. Both are true.

And also within her experience is the postwar sufferings of Germans under Allied bombing and occupation.

"We got a lot. And I always said, 'Look, we are paying for what we did.' In Germany the Allied bombing, yah, they killed hundreds of thousands, mostly women and children. The Allies also did very awful things. But I understood, I said, 'That is what we had done and we get it back.' On the personal level I paid my dues. For whatever Nazi enthusiasm I had, I paid big, you know. I was always an open subject for the sexual attacks from the Allies. The so-called liberators."

She refuses to be bitter or to blame any group. "This is human. I don't see it anymore Germans. I cannot see that it was only Americans, they did also bad things with the Negroes, and it's still not really what they want. And the Indians. I cannot separate myself from what was done, but I also cannot say, 'You Germans bad bad bad.' I can sit down and cry for the whole of humanity, how they are governing, and the possibilities they have for enlightenment."

Ruth looks down, her face carved in lines of sorrow and determination.

"I have actually emptied my heart from all of it. I see it all *human*. Greed, hatred, and delusion. The only thing I respect is the Buddha's teaching. Believe me, dahling, if we can get with that then we could maybe have a peaceful planet."

As I sat with Ruth in her house, this seemed to me such a clear expression of her perspective and her teaching. She tried over and over again to lead us into this deeper understanding of each human being—beyond gender and ethnicity and cultural identification—asking us to look deeply into our own hearts and to honor the full humanity of every other person. Politics and rhetoric and righteousness fall away before this core perception. This woman whom we had chosen as our teacher was always inviting us to leave our categories behind, to sink into a wider identification with all that lived. She embodied our ideas and aspirations while cutting them at their root to show us a more profound truth, one that could lead us to freedom.

CHAPTER FIFTEEN

Building the
Community Together

Particularly in the early years at Dhamma Dena, I would be caught up in the labor of cleaning out new space, dragging furniture around, painting walls, then standing by while Ruth ruminated on an environment, made a different decision, and coaxed us to undo all the work we had accomplished and begin again. Generally I labored in a state of frustration, or bored acceptance, or amused surrender. Ruth's old students have all experienced the unpredictability of working with her. Perhaps the most extreme example is that of Nick, a student from Hawaii who had decided that he would enlarge the tiny hut in which Ruth slept and build a decent-sized dwelling for her. Ruth's kuti was so small that it accommodated only a desk and a couch, on which she slept, and was crammed with her books and belongings. Nick had offered his services to build an addition. He says, "That was a trip, doing that for her. It was like a Milarepa thing. I was donating all the materials. I laid out this whole structure, about at least a third bigger than it is now. In fact I had the foundation laid out and had the materials for the whole place. She comes and looks at it and she says, 'That is too big for me. I don't want that. I don't want so big.'" So Nick's work was all in vain and he had to begin again.

As he remarked, it was like the story of the great Tibetan Buddhist sage Milarepa, a reformed murderer much in need of purification. His

teacher Marpa directed him to build a tower. When the tower stood tall
and solid, Marpa ordered Milarepa to tear it down and put the stones
and earth back where he had found them. Then Marpa ordered him to
build it again. Then to demolish it again. This maneuver was repeated
numerous times, until Milarepa had to give up his attachment to the
task and its goal—and presumably go through hellish realms of frustration, anger, discouragement, and despair. Only then did Marpa agree
to give him the teachings.

Most old students could take you to a place at Dhamma Dena and
describe a day, or days, or weeks of labor. "I painted that roof, all afternoon one day in the hot sun." "I dug out the cactus garden behind Ruth's
kuti." Ruth's listing for the women's retreat used to read: "All women
welcome for *work* and meditation" (my emphasis). When Ruth bought
the Dukkha House from an unfortunate young family (living in the
desert requires a strength and resiliency that this couple, after many
babies and a struggle with alcohol, could not muster), we women were
called to follow Ruth down the short stretch of dusty road to the little
recently abandoned house. The rooms stood knee-deep in junk and
filth. The young parents had given up trying to maintain cleanliness
and order, leaving the bathroom full of dirty diapers, the sink crusted
with old food and piled with discarded utensils, the walls stained and
splattered.

While we stood uncertainly, holding our pails and rags and scrub
brushes, Ruth waded in and began throwing trash from the living room
out into the yard, while calling encouragement to us. "Come on, dah-
lings, first we pull out everything, and then we scrub!" It was a long,
hot, sticky afternoon in those shadowy rooms. I remember the smell
of shit, the grit on my fingers and under my nails, the dust up my nose,
the bending, lifting, carrying. Ruth worked among us, her long skirt
dragging in the dirt, her sleeves rolled up over her elbows. She directed
us, called someone over to give her a hand, inspected every foot of
cleared floor or wall or counter, and urged us to more effort.

I don't know if this task took one day or many, but my feelings about

Dukkha House were grounded there. In the months that followed, other students built a large new wing and patio onto the little house; Dukkha House was named and designated as the women's dormitory. Dukkha (or suffering) seemed the logical name both as an acknowledgment of the former owners' difficult life and as a reminder to us more fortunate women of the pervasive dissatisfaction that underlies much of our experience. It became my favorite place to stay during retreats at Dhamma Dena. I loved sitting out on the patio looking across the desert toward the mountains. I loved the central room with its old black wood stove on cold winter nights. I loved the small sounds made by women sleeping in the bunk beds in the big room. And I had the satisfaction of knowing I had helped rescue Dukkha House from its neglected condition.

Ruth's willingness to engage in every detail of the creation and maintenance of her center is unusual among Dharma teachers. She remarks on it, "I worked with you like everybody there and then I went into the zendo and was a vipassana teacher. I never was only one thing and let you only work and stood there like an administrator. I was always part of everything, and I did not feel it injures my status as a teacher. We grew, actually, together."

Ruth's continual message was: be here with *what is*, care for this environment— and Dhamma Dena provides numerous opportunities for such care and mindfulness. The sinks all empty into buckets; one has to be aware of full buckets and carry them out into the desert to pour at the base of a thirsty bush. Most of the toilets are wooden outhouses, their interiors plastered with pictures of animals taken from magazines and calendars. One has to remember to shut the door, to turn out the light if there is one, to put toilet paper in the container to be burned rather than dropping it down the hole. Anything left out in the desert sun is soon damaged by the heat and dryness; we learned to take care of faded dish towels and cloth napkins. And, in the zendo between meditation sessions, Ruth would tell us about the plants and animals that surrounded us: the plant world so very delicate and vulnerable because of scorching heat and dryness, the spiders and snakes that coil under trash piles and spin webs in corners, the rabbits who hide and then hop away to hide again, the coyotes who roam the vicinity of the property, calling hungrily in the night, the desert tortoise burrowing into the sand, and the many birds who make their nests in cactus plants and up under the eaves of the buildings.

Everything became a teaching, setting us powerfully in a net of relationships, encouraging us to cultivate that deep caring for all of existence that animates Ruth, and offering us opportunities to look at our own mental habits that cause us to suffer. My resistance to Ruth or to the tasks she set for me, my judgments of her—all this I came to understand as the meat of practice. At first I enshrined my resistance, believed in it, and directed it at Ruth, but gradually I learned to chew it up, really taste and examine it, following it down to that basic dis-ease that rules our lives: wanting things to be other than they are. What she taught us with mop and scrub brush was exactly what she taught us in the meditation hall. Pay attention to what is going on inside you; develop your awareness until you become sensitive to more and more subtle signals. Journey *through* your suffering to the ineffable joy that ordinary life offers.

● ● ●

The story of a spiritual teacher is often recounted as the saga of a towering figure silhouetted alone against the sky—somehow separate from all other beings. But in actuality spiritual teachers are intimately connected to groups of people, and the teaching and learning go both ways. There is, of course, the model of the seeker who sits alone in a cave for years, but for Western Dharma teachers this isolation is rarely an option. Certainly, in Ruth's case, she has been dynamically related to her community at Dhamma Dena over long years. Members tell how Ruth changed their lives, set them on a spiritual path, challenged and charmed them; in turn, the community has educated Ruth in particular ways and contributed to her growth and understanding. Ruth has also been instrumental in establishing centers in Oregon, Canada, and Germany, but she always returns to her home in the Mojave Desert.

Ruth welcomes folks into her world at Dhamma Dena. Some come as lost souls drawn by the magnetism of this woman who was known as *die goldene Mitte*; they simply want to be near Ruth and learn from her. Now and then someone arrives to train to become a Dharma teacher. Others come because they want to offer service. All the major building and maintenance of the physical plant have been done by such people. The organization of retreats and cooking for retreats also fall to these people. Often Ruth pays their transportation; she gives them room and board; she may pay them a minimal amount for their labor. The labor itself, for most people, becomes an avenue for practice.

Not that it is easy to work for Ruth. She may arrive from Hollywood in the middle of the night, wake you up, and insist you help with baking bread for the retreat that will start the next day. Ever vigilant about money and waste, she may criticize you roundly for discarding the outer wilted leaves of the lettuce or tossing a carrot that shows signs of rot. She may ask you to work on a roof in the heat of the midday sun. She may push you past the limits of your energy. Often she will interfere with your task, telling you how to do it differently than the way you began. Working for Ruth is like being a servant on a feudal estate, where you are entirely at the mercy of the mistress.

Her student and helper Margaret Frederick observes, "Dhamma Dena is Ruth's *home*." It is not an impersonal retreat center; in practically every aspect, the buildings, rooms, furniture, and utensils reflect Ruth's esthetics, her austere view of what is necessary for comfort combined with her love of elegance and luxury, her demand that things be carefully arranged and cared for. Serving dishes, drapes, linens, lamps —so many of the accoutrements at Dhamma Dena came from Ruth's home in Hollywood or were gathered from the streets or secondhand shops. Speaking of the furnishing of Dukkha House after we had cleaned it out, Ruth says, "It wasn't a problem, you know, how beds are, you go to the Goodwill, you get some bases, you get some mattresses.

Palm Springs secondhand stores are super, they're really department stores. Elegant, wonderful! Then I went just to the streets in Hollywood on trash night. Hollywood, yah, sure. But we also had so much at home, you know, there was always something, always scavenged."

The buildings at Dhamma Dena fell into Ruth's hands because she knew how to take her opportunities. The zendo had been a weekend hunter's cabin owned by a doctor from Long Beach. When in 1978 the neighbor told Ruth it was for sale, Ruth, with the help of Henry, and some savings she had brought from Germany, was able to amass the $7,500 price. Then she enlisted her students to transform the little cabin into a meditation hall.

About four years later a builder from Seattle offered to extend the zendo, making it twice as long. While Ruth was away in England for her European teaching tour, the builder completed the new spacious and solidly built meditation hall. "The road had to go out," Ruth says, "in order to make the extension, and the roof had to be supported. And that there is not just bricks, dahling, they are cement blocks and inside they hold steel beams so they don't rock, and cement inside, on top of it. That is a very insulated house you know."

I remember the pleasure of arriving at the retreat, following this building project, to find a large zendo, full of light, with ample space for everyone's knees, and with a splendid platform and altar at the front. Above the altar Ruth had hung her mosaic tabletop made of stained glass; a patterned rug from the Hollywood house lay on the wall-to-wall carpet; glass doors opened out onto the concrete apron that surrounded the building.

The next change in accommodations involved the arrival of a large trailer, which was parked behind the Dukkha House and designated as a dormitory space for men. Other smaller trailers appeared in successive years, and were prepared for special guests. Throughout the eighties our retreats coexisted with the lives of Ruth's neighbors, Stevie and her husband and their foster children. With their approval, Ruth built a high wooden fence between the houses to ensure more privacy, and she cultivated cordial relations with the couple, so that when they decided to leave the desert, they let Ruth make the first offer on their house. It was 1989 or 1990. Ruth says, "I paid a high price for that. Oh, sixty-eight thousand. I wouldn't get it now. Also I put in about twenty-five thousand. I made a beautiful addition, the bathroom and the extension of the porch, and the teacher's room. There were only cacti. You couldn't open the door, these big things grew almost in. Yah, we worked two weeks to cut down these cacti."

This became Samadhi House, situated very close to the main house. I remember my first retreat staying there, when it seemed so very luxurious. There was actually a workable indoor bathroom, and I slept in a room with one other person, rather than in a dormitory with ten women. The closets were big; there was a kitchen where one could make tea.

The money that came to Ruth from her teaching she poured back into improvements on Dhamma Dena. In the Theravada tradition the teachings are considered priceless and are given freely. Teachers do not receive payment, but must depend on *dana* (generosity)—offerings of money, goods, and services, the amount to be determined by the giver. The minimal fees paid for retreats (seven dollars per day in the beginning) barely covered the expenses, so that the money that came to Ruth as dana often went to buy the water that was trucked in, to fund repairs, to pay the dump fees for disposing of trash, and other expenses. As well, she was often subsidizing students, housing and feeding the indigent, sometimes paying for a particular student's journey to a monastery in Burma or picking up the tab for another student's graduate study. For years she paid the airfare for an East Indian female medical student to come to the retreats.

Ruth has always been immensely generous, while holding tightly to the purse strings. She abhors waste, and will scavenge for recycled things rather than buy new. Yet she has doled out large sums of money to students who needed it. When I was starting to write *Turning the Wheel*, about American women's participation in Buddhism—a project Ruth approved of—she asked me what I needed to begin work, and promptly wrote out a check for the amount I mentioned. I paid her back later, but there have been other, more spontaneous, gifts over the years, freely given, with no strings attached.

• • •

Sometimes Ruth's tendency to concern herself with every aspect of a retreat can be difficult for the workers. Even in retreats in other locations, she will pop into the kitchen and supervise, as she did at a retreat in Washington. "They tell me we have nothing to eat, the vegetables are gone. I asked, 'Where is all the cabbage we had yesterday?' They said, 'Well we had to throw it away, it was frozen.'

"I see myself hanging in that garbage bin, and pulling the cabbages out of the bin, and brought them back and insisted that we cook it. They were shocked at me that I could do that. They thought always I was a very fine delicate lady. But I am that too. I have many roles played. I can be a bitch, I can be a very refined lady, I can be a real farm woman, even I can be a cowboy woman. And I also can be very keen what is being thrown away!

"They didn't want to cook the cabbages, but I said, 'There comes no penny for more food!' So they did it.

"Oh, I have done that here at Dhamma Dena but I didn't make a fuss. I tell you, what they threw out once on lettuce, the outer leaves which are sometimes very good, I made a whole bowl of salad, and they didn't know I had got it from the garbage."

There is a downside to Ruth's total engagement with Dhamma Dena. Because she sees Dhamma Dena as her home, and wants things exactly as she deems appropriate, she has never been fully open to the good ideas and skills of people who have offered to help manage the place. She is unwilling to hire a manager and delegate the work to him or her.

One result of this is that during retreats she is often overburdened with responsibility, thinking about the outhouses and the water and

what to serve for dinner, while leading the meditations and giving
Dharma talks. And while she seems to have unlimited energy for all
these tasks, sometimes the stress of such wide responsibility creates
frustration in her, and that spills over in irritation at the staff or the students. Two of my good friends, whom I brought to Dhamma Dena,
could not tolerate what they saw as Ruth's harsh treatment of people.
One left in the middle of the retreat, vowing never to return; the other
stayed the course but said at the end that she would not come another
time to sit with Ruth. One day in Las Vegas House I decided to ask
Ruth about this, whether she is aware of her occasional impatience and
sharpness.

"Sometimes it seems you are ordering people around, in a very
harsh way," I begin.

"Do I?" she asks.

"I have seen you do that, during a retreat."

"Yes, I am criticized for that."

"Do you see that in yourself?"

"I notice it. When I notice it I will immediately soften."

"Where do you think that comes from?"

Ruth seems annoyed by my question, and answers forcefully, "What
does it need to come from! It is in every human being! When you're not
enlightened it is there, you bring that whole stuff with you. I don't want
to blame my mother or my father or something like that. It comes because I am frustrated, I want it otherwise, I see it's too slow, then here
I am. Then I go around, you will see me at the same time, 'Listen
dahling, I was too sharp, forgive me. I didn't really mean it, I hope you
don't misunderstand.' I'm just eager to get the thing done, also.

"The people working here for me, they take the old cereal, they take
the cabbage, it's nice and moist, they take it and put it in that indented
place for the coyotes. It's half full with sand. They will not bother to
clean it up. Now *then* I become sharp. When I see a very obvious thing,
and it is the lack of caring for the coyotes, to clean it up and not to mix
the good food with the sand. Then I will be sharp. What it comes from,

from the insufficiency of what the performances are. And the mind is not awake."

Sometimes people expecting a leisurely atmosphere are rudely surprised by Ruth's demanding approach. Ella, a Bay Area musician and librarian, tells about her encounters with Ruth and how she won through to appreciation. She describes herself as having been "emotionally distraught" at the time she signed up for a retreat in 1981, and asked if she might come down early.

I thought I'd spend a few days by myself quietly in the desert. That was my introduction to Ruth, because I got there and the first thing I encountered was Ruth. And I realized immediately that this was going to be anything but a quiet few days by myself.

She started by having me move the furniture around in the dormitory where there were a lot of beds. I guess she thought it wasn't going to fit or she didn't like the way it was. She was standing over me and I was moving these heavy beds and dressers. I remember I had moved them all, the way she said, and then she said, "No, no, no, dahling, this will never do, I don't like it, no we should move it back." This went on and on, all afternoon. Really, it was a workout.

Then I was going to help Julie Wester in the kitchen. So, once again, Ruth was overseeing. I think I was making humus in the blender, and she started to say, about the way I was cutting something, "Don't you think you should cut it differently, dahling?" All I remember was raising this large knife at that point, and she said, "Oh, okay dahling, you cut it the way you want."

My experience of her was that she both drove me crazy and cracked me totally open. That was why it was so powerful to sit with her. She really understood me. I'd come and talk with her and she'd say, "Vy do you resist me so much, dahling?" And that was the key. Coming up against her. So much in my life has been about trying to look at that kind of resistance—that impulse to push away—and let it go. Be suspicious of it rather than endorse it.

Some people complained that she would talk during the meditation, and that this was irritating to them. I just think they didn't *get it*. She was like somebody's meddlesome grandmother, and yet there was so much love in everything she did.

People are so confused, they feel like spiritual practice will remove the disagreeable parts of yourself, and you will sort of waft through life, kind of like Katharine Hepburn or Mother Teresa, you'll look as though you're above it all. It's a whole strategy. And Ruth completely blows the whistle on that. No one wants to believe it: how could you be enlightened and still fuss? Yet it seems so good, so right that way.

She didn't hold herself back or try to protect herself or maintain a façade. She was in authority and she was in command, but almost like a hostess. She didn't try to inhabit some cliché of what it was to be a teacher. It was so clear that she was an authentic, genuine person, who wasn't trying to *be* something.

It was great to be there and be that uncomfortable. I knew instinctively that there was something here. I would think, "Oh I don't want to go there," and then I would go back.

· · ·

Various people stayed to live in the several little houses that Ruth began to acquire. Some of these people suffer from serious mental difficulties, and they constitute another loose community that has developed around Ruth. She also cares for individuals in the center itself. One woman's family deposited her with Ruth, after years of mental illness, and sent a small stipend each month for her care. For two years, Ruth took on the task of helping this woman connect with reality.

First she taught her to pay attention to each of her activities. When she walked, she had to note, "I lift my foot and bring it forward, and now I set it down." I remember this disturbed woman at Dhamma Dena, looking anxious as she sat at the back of the zendo, perching on a straight chair around the side of Samadhi House to smoke a cigarette, chopping vegetables at a kitchen counter, her head down. Ruth included her in all the retreat activities, often having to prompt her or help her understand, and many times the woman fled the scene, rushing away to her solitude. With each retreat I attended, I noticed changes in her: she sat more peacefully, she sometimes spoke quite cogently in a group, she gave up smoking. Ruth worked with her consistently.

"I taught her typing," Ruth says. "I made her a piece of cardboard with two holes with a string, and she had to hold it around so that she couldn't see the keyboard. She would put it on the head and she would be angry and throw it. But she learned. She did wonderful, she did a lot of typing for me. She could cook a little bit, she washed the dishes. Oh, sewing! She did sew, very simple stitches. All this I taught her.

"The time I spent with these people! I let her even drive my car, a hundred feet on the sandy roads where nothing can happen. That made her so proud and gave her courage and trust she will be healthy one day."

Ruth chuckles, admitting that some people say she runs a halfway house. "The fact that I live here and also that it is kind of little funky, maybe it lends itself, whether you want or not, that people like this will find haven here. You need only to start with one. Which I did, and then others come."

Speaking of her willingness to accept mentally ill people into the Dhamma Dena community, Ruth says, "They heal better here. They won't heal when they go to a retreat center, ten days and go out. It doesn't help. It goes above their heads. They only can do it where they have space and can spit at me and run away, yah, and throw the door and all of that. I know where it comes from, it comes from their pain, from their confusion and anxiety."

The most recent disturbed person to reside at Dhamma Dena was a woman I will call Libby. She came from a wealthy family in Los Angeles, and had once been a beautiful, highly intelligent young woman, but according to Ruth she had ingested too many psychedelics during the sixties, "and now her mind is gone, dahling." Ruth settled Libby (now about sixty years old) in a tiny trailer just behind the fence near Samadhi House. Coming from Samadhi we would see Libby sitting naked in the doorway to her trailer, talking earnestly into a nonexistent cell phone. Her white hair flying loose, blue eyes and delicate bone structure hinting at her former beauty, her wrinkled skin tanned a deep brown from the desert sun, she carried on long urgent conversations with important people about the state of the world.

Ruth insisted that Libby wear a dress when she came to pick up her meals in the kitchen. She would pad in barefooted, her nakedness covered by a faded cotton jumper, her eyes darting suspiciously, and she would take her tray back to eat her meal at her trailer. Periodically she wrote to world leaders and movie stars, putting her incoherent messages on scraps of paper and bringing them to the Dhamma Dena office "to be mailed."

Ruth fed and protected Libby, brought clothes and blankets to the trailer. At one point she set Libby up in Samadhi House with videos to occupy her, but Libby took the opportunity to rip out all the window screens in the building in order, she said, to let the flies out. She also stirred the excrement in the outhouses with a long stick to liberate the flies.

People who work at Dhamma Dena and keep it running are often not as enthusiastic as Ruth about caring for mentally disabled folk. The presence of irrational and often hostile people complicates their work and distracts them from their service to the retreats. And when Ruth goes away, they find themselves solely responsible for these residents. Ruth asks them to open their hearts and extend themselves to provide a safe place for these vulnerable people. Some do not choose to do that, and leave. The others will make the effort, seeing it as part of their practice or perhaps just one of the conditions of working at Dhamma Dena. In some instances Ruth may be unrealistic in her expectations that a mentally disturbed person can be helped. In reality not all messes can be cleaned up, not all problems can be solved—and the inability to recognize distinctions between mental conditions can cause problems. Libby, for instance, the most radically disturbed of the residents, was so impaired that she could not be worked with, and became too much of a burden on Ruth's helpers, who persuaded Ruth to situate her on a nearby property. There her SSI check pays for a trailer, and her nudity and strange behavior do not disturb anyone. Ruth goes to visit Libby, brings her clothes, drives her to town and helps her buy groceries, but Libby is no longer part of the scene at Dhamma Dena.

One resident who has clearly benefited from her association with Ruth is the artist Linda Sibio, who came to Dhamma Dena from Los Angeles after suffering a psychotic break. Living in one of the little houses, closely connected with Ruth, Linda has regained stability in her life. She has worked as a teacher at a community school for problem children, is painting again, and has formed an organization of mentally ill people from the surrounding community. This group, called Cracked Eggs, produces plays that explore mental illness, creativity, and American ways of life.

While Linda has established a creative and useful life for herself in the desert, and while medication keeps her relatively stable, she still must struggle with her terrors, and sometimes finds herself in crisis. Then she can turn to Ruth. She tells of one instance in which she became so anxious that she wanted to go to the hospital. She went over to tell Ruth that she was leaving, but encountered Ruth's objection: "No, you can work through it!" Linda continues, "She actually touched my body and said, 'Pay attention to your body and feel the sensations in your body. If you can't feel them, then touch yourself so you can feel them.' She told me to let the thoughts in my mind go and pay attention to my breathing. After a couple of hours I came out of it."

Linda is working, through meditation and Ruth's instructions, to develop the capacity in herself to bring balance to her mind. She is buying the cabin she lives in, and while sometimes she feels lonely and misses the social life of the cities, the performances and art shows, she says. "If Ruth is here it's worth the lack of social life, to study with her and learn the meditation."

• • •

The building of Dhamma Dena has called upon the sum total of Ruth's life experience. The years on the farm with her mother, when she learned to work long and diligently, the terrible privations of wartime and postwar Europe, made her willing to take on menial jobs, to serve others and survive on very little. Living with Henry called for extraordinary patience and self-control. Through her own mental breakdown, she discovered that she could work with mentally deranged people. All these skills and capacities and tendencies have found their use at Dhamma Dena.

Over twenty years, Ruth, and her students—laboring enthusiastically or reluctantly or doggedly or with a sincere interest in work as a way to cultivate mindfulness—have created the Dhamma Dena of today. From a distance, this collection of buildings and trailers blends inconspicuously into the desert environment of flat land and chaparral; up close it reveals itself as a large beautifully furnished meditation hall, a main house of office and kitchen and dining room, the dormitories of the old garage, Dukkha House and Samadhi House, as well as the sleeping-trailers, the shower house, and a large workshop and storage shed. When I drive out the sandy road to Dhamma Dena, I always feel that I am coming home, not just because of my many retreats there but because of the labor I have engaged in, the sweat expended on building, cleaning, painting, rearranging in those structures. It is the same with all the regulars, those of us who return year after year to the desert: like Ruth we have invested something of ourselves in this Dharma center. We are viscerally connected to the place itself, to the immense sky above, the hot desert wind, the splendid sunsets. Dhamma Dena holds us and lives in us much the way that Ruth inhabits and welcomes us. If Dhamma Dena is Ruth's home, as Margaret suggests, it is a home generous enough to shelter us all.

CHAPTER SIXTEEN

A Teaching

We are sitting on the patio of Las Vegas House, having just eaten the light supper we prepared and brought out through the front door. It is one-thirty in the morning, and Ruth is excited about our dining in such a "Mediterranean" way. "Ah, dahling, it is like the Riviera!" Earlier, we worked until 7:00 p.m., when I suggested we stop and begin again tomorrow. Ruth countered, "Why don't you go take a rest and come back at eleven or midnight. We can eat a bit and then go on. I am staying up, I have so much to do, and you can join me." It was a novel idea for me. (Not for Ruth, who routinely stays awake most of the night.) I decided to try it. Back at Samadhi House I fell into a deep sleep, then woke up at eleven and trudged across the desert in the dark, directing my dim flashlight beam at rocks and holes and scraggly bushes, drawn by the brightly lighted patio of Las Vegas House in the distance.

Once there, I found Ruth at work on the garden and patio, having swept the floor, arranged flowerpots and watered plants, cleaned the chairs, and generally puttered happily during the hours when I had been sleeping. Now, in the night, the lights illumine the pots of bright red geraniums at the edge of the patio, the palo verde trees standing in the sandy yard beyond, and the mesh of metal fence. Outside our circle of light, darkness lies deep over the desert, and in that black sea, here and

there a yard light on a tall pole glimmers like a lighthouse. From somewhere close, coyotes yip hungrily.

Margaret had come by earlier, shaking her head in surprise. "A coyote was coming up the road, like he was meeting me. He looked like a
gray fox actually."

And Ruth looked stricken. "Ah, I forgot about it!"

Margaret promised to take the scraps and dog food to the desert
place where the coyotes arrive each night looking for food. And she
disappeared.[52]

Now Ruth and I sit at the table on the patio, relaxed in the still-
warm air. I have brought the tray of coffee things—cups, jar of decaf
coffee, cream in a little white pitcher, and the electric pot, which I
plugged in around the corner. Next to the cups rests a plate with two
slices of crumbly breakfast roll, "for our sweet."

We sit in a bowl of light, afloat on the vast black ocean of desert
night. Ruth is casual in a pink, green, and black muumuu and gold slip-
pers, her hair pulled up on top of her head, little wayward tufts escap-
ing around her face. We are both enjoying the sense of luxury, of food
and ease in the late-night silence that feels special, as if only Ruth and
I, of all people in the world, are awake.

And we talk about community, how closely she lives with the people at Dhamma Dena, how available she is to them, and how she works
to solve the conflicts that arise and soothe hard feelings. Ruth admits
that sometimes it takes her a long time to let go of a particular incident, to forgive the selfish conduct of an individual. I'm happy to talk
about this subject, for I have been wanting to ask about forgiveness. My
former partner is now dying of a brain tumor, and I am conflicted about
what my role will be in her dying. Because of the circumstances of our
breakup, when I was suffering with cancer, and because in my view she
was not able to be present with me in my illness, I have some ambiva-
lence about showing up for hers.

Ruth sets down her coffee cup, and I see by the focused intensity of
her gaze that she is entering this subject wholeheartedly. "You know,

forgiving, you have to understand what it means. It means you don't carry your pain around, your aversion against. Your disapproval, you don't carry that around anymore." That afternoon we had discussed a conflict Ruth was having with a Dhamma Dena resident. Now she refers to our discussion. "That's what you talked me there, about my own problem. You have to have patience and understand with whom you talk. I'm not bitter, and I'm not making any karmic further. . . . The same with you. You have to also stop carrying something around which you have against her. And that comes with the way she treated you, inappropriately to say the least, actually maybe very tough, without really the human warmth which you wanted at that time. And she could obviously not give more."

I nod. "I don't think it was that she didn't want to. She *could not*."

"No. That's it, you don't carry it around. I still carry it but . . . when I see people carrying anger and hatred against their fathers thirty-five years later, I don't do that. Now, with your friend, I think there is very much relevancy to what I am talking about. It still cooks in your heart."

I interrupt, "I think I understand now why she acted the way she did. She just didn't have the strength that one needs to take care of someone when they are sick. And there were unacknowledged problems in our relationship too."

"She was actually afraid," Ruth says.

"Yes, she was terrified."

"That's right. Some people cannot see sick people. You have to overcome a lot."

"So I think I understand that and I have let go of my anger, but there's still this sense that maybe I haven't."

Ruth begins to chuckle.

"You're amused?" I ask her.

"I see *myself* with still that anger," she admits. "But, go along."

"Okay, here's something that happens to me. This person has some behaviors that are very very annoying to me. And. . . ."

Now she's laughing outright.

"That's the same with me," she says. "The one I was angry at—that person's behavior was annoying and deceptive, and that's why I grinded over it."

"Well, suppose I go with an open heart, because she's sick, to help her, and then she does something like she used to do when we were together—she's selfish or critical—and I feel angry. Now, if that was somebody else that I had no history with, I could open my heart, I could see them act that way and think, ah, so what."

"But that's different," Ruth points out.

I tell Ruth about the two visits I have made to this woman since her illness began—once to see her in the hospital before the surgery, the second time to take her to see a spiritual teacher. In both encounters I found her gentle and vulnerable, like a little child. Being with her, my heart opened and I was able to be compassionate and caring.

Ruth nods. "So you sacrificed yourself, really. Or, you took up the challenge."

"I took up the challenge. I went, and it was very touching. But since then I haven't felt it in me. I heard that she spilled some tea on her lap and had third-degree burns, and I thought of visiting her. . . ."

Ruth interrupts, "One thing you said, 'But I don't feel it.' One big rule in the Buddhist Dharma is to not take the feelings as your guideline. They are coming from *I*, what *I* like. They go along what the ego says. And that is the danger—particularly for you now that you are a teacher and a spiritual devotee of the greatest compassionate lady in the world, Kwan Yin."

She refers to the preeminent goddess in all of Asia, the Buddhist bodhisattva of compassion, with whom I have been working in leading retreats and about whom I have written a book.[53]

Ruth explains what she means. "You cannot go to your feelings. Feelings are the turning point. In the twelve links,[54] first comes this this this this, rebirth consciousness, contact then with the object of the experiences of consciousness, then comes *feeling*, Number Seven. And if you don't catch it there you go into craving: liking, wanting, and craving. And in this case it is, 'My feelings say this, I now go along with my feelings for what is pleasant in this way, for what isn't bothersome.'"

I am nodding. "So my feeling is aversion. Mild."

"I know, I know. Mine too, it is also aversion, but I have no action on it. But *you* go on and take it as your guideline. When I am alone I can see and then I smile about me that I'm still on it, hmm? And then I see that the aversion is actually against *me*. Then I am humble. You allowed that person to take advantage of you, I think, and then I let it go into the sound of Shiva, something like that.

"I get great compassion in this case for others who hang on so long in their aversion and their revenge feeling or making even-steven. It's you insisting on your own righteousness, even in the face of death. With this person, you know that *she is dying;* but *you die too;* you have to take that into consideration—that you both have this ultimate goal, given by the natural law of impermanence. So you are on the same level. The righteousness, then, is not any more so important. It mellows down when you take that as your guideline.

"So you have now your choice, you know you are a teacher, you are a representative of Kwan Yin, you tell how she is so compassionate and she has only one thing in mind. She turns around just before enlightenment, and says, 'Go, go, create the foundation of your enlightenment, go more precise and more definite, more precise and more accurate in your efforts toward that.'[55] You have to let that go then.

"Now if you really want to let go, you make an act where you see yourself taking it up as a challenge, for your breaking through this resistance, or this kind of holding, clinging to my feeling that 'I don't feel it to go.' Now you take the risk. I have done that often, you take the risk that she might be the way you saw her before."

I ask, "What do you mean?"

"She might be critical and not appreciative. And then you have a test how much you are attached to your feeling, of your being approved."

I follow her logic. "Because then I could say, Now I have a *reason* not to go."

"Yah, right. You have to cut. But you know, it is not just cut. You can take as your help your disposition. See, you are promoting and a devotee of Kwan Yin, so you have no excuse. You can also recommend the reconciliation and so on. You see that."

"Absolutely," I agree. I am most struck by her observation that the feelings don't matter, lingering over that thought.

Ruth nods, takes a sip of coffee and a bite of cake.

"I give you in Buddha's words, 'Cling not to well-being. In pain are you not perturbed, even-minded in all chances, that is the task.' Equanimity. Equanimity is the second wing of enlightenment. The other one is wisdom. And equanimity means actually on the higher level of focusing, noninterference. Not with the ego in any way. Equanimous in all chances, that is the path.

"You don't go with the feelings. And I see that in me, with that incident I told you. I do see the way that person acted is unpleasant to me and irritating, hmm? But I am aware that I am not acting upon it when I am together with the person, I know that I don't need to contaminate my mind with it and I don't hang onto it, but it's still there, it is floating and it comes. The Buddha says it is natural to all of us, this clinging. Our actions are like our fingers to us, the fingers don't go that way" (she opens her hands away from her). "The fingers go always with me" (she curls the fingers inward). "The rake comes this way and always to me."

We talk for a while about how this person has been humbled by her illness, which has stolen her capacities, and may feel embarrassment because of this. But Ruth will not allow this to become an excuse for my keeping a distance.

"So you go now to more active loving. You have no stand to justify when you take all the points into consideration that I pointed out. And don't forget, it is a credit to your account of Dharma, you took up a challenge very consciously. You see deeply, compassionately, her disposition is now humbleness and embarrassment. People feel embarrassed about being sick."

"And just distress. Generally."

"That is the same thing." Ruth pauses, drinks her coffee, looks up at me. "So now you have a great chance, to do on many levels, to strengthen your Dharma forces."

But I can't let the subject go, yet. I begin to speculate. "Here's a trap for me. I can imagine that when I visit she would at first be very open, and then she would start doing some of the things that always irritated me so much, and I would get annoyed."

"Yah, these patterns remain," Ruth agrees. "Well, then, you stand there and notice your annoyance. That's all. That's the only way to get now into patience and allowing her, more so than before, to do what she does. When you are conscious, you break through a lot of attachment to like and dislike. You now stay through that discomfort, stay faithful to what the experience is in you. Your irritation is saying, *I want her other than she is.* According to my like right now, see? This feeling arises with each experience, and the thing is always to go to *your experience.* In this case you want her other, you see that, then you see there is no point of wanting her other. Your training is now to detach from 'I like' and 'I want it other than it is.' That's the clue. That is depth of Dharma now. Become more refined, and see more your experience rather than her behavior that irritates you."

I tell her, "I wouldn't even care about this except I think she and I, because we had been lovers for four or five years...."

"Was it good time?"

"Some. I very much loved this person, and there's still that in me."

"Yah, you loved things which were pleasant to you. And then you said, 'She irritated me.' So you see there is already actually the call for this training, from the beginning. You have to keep that more in mind, what is pleasant and unpleasant, and then see it in yourself. You communicate with that person in a different quiet way instead of being reproachful or enlarging this resentment in you. Make sure you don't act it out but take it as a guideline for your next action. If you don't act on it, then you have the door open for another challenge. Otherwise you close that door."

I ponder, "It would seem that it might be easier now that she is very humbled."

"Right, but you have to be sensitive to that humbleness. That isn't a deep humbleness which I can experience and maybe you too when you go a little bit beyond everything, where you see the equality, the evenness, the source of all of us that illuminates us. But she is not humbled from that source. She is humbled because her attachments, that nurtured her, are gone. Her powers are gone on which she made her life and which she values. And that is very terrible humbling. That's ashamed actually. You should consider that, and take that into account when you communicate with her, that you don't humble more by talking about your success and where you were, and all of that. Maybe you offer her greetings from Ruth, and say I invite her to come. I give her a nice little cottage here and she can be quiet—you don't know whether a little meditation would be helpful for her. They say that the quiet mind is healing mind. So then she cannot argue, and that is not humbling her anymore."

She nods. "You know, it's nothing absolute in this Dharma, because it always depends upon fifteen different other points. And that is called Diamond Mind."

I offer, "Different facets, yeah?"

"Yah, you have to view how it fits into the Dharma, into ethics, into right speech, into right effort. It's a complicated thing. You see, that's what I mean when I say what Karma is—that *you don't get away with anything anymore.* You have no justification available anymore, because you weigh it against all the guidelines of the Dharma."

I point out that if I were to stay away, no one would blame me.

"Right. But that is not you. That is not anymore in your guideline. You can actually not, from your heart and from your Dharma, do that. You see, like I did. After I married, my sponsor was very bad to me, but I gave him each week one full day to clean his house, as a gratitude for help me come to America. He did something good to me. And that goodness is lasting, because I'm still here, hmm? You learn through every hard time, you learn through everything, through goodness or difficulty. So if you want to do justice to your heart, you have to do justice not just through words but through this good deed which came to you and which was a big steppingstone and a great shift in your life, and sometimes small, doesn't matter, one should always have available appreciation for what was done good. And even not for you maybe so good, but for the person who gave you that goodness.

"It's a nice subject. But it is not that easy to accomplish. Remember Kwan Yin. Go, go more intensely forward. *Gate, paragate,* go more accurately, *parasamgate,* more precise now. *Bodhi svaha.* To build up your foundation for your enlightenment. That is a purification, actually."

I talk about this person's need for compassion now, and Ruth agrees, but then corrects me on the main point. "Yah, she does, that she goes peacefully. But that is not so important, dahling, in the Dharma, that she gets comforted. It is important that *you* cut deeper into *your* system, so that you have a better, clear discernment: what is my path here in this situation. 'Cling not to well-being,' not giving the karma the next level to act out. That is number one, because that's what we need in the Dharma so that it will continue to live in its purity.

"Sometimes you cannot do anything about it because it could cost your life. They crucified Christ for that. They killed Moggallana, the first disciple of Buddha. He was very accomplished with even supernatural powers and had a great wisdom, but that wisdom doesn't sit well in ignorant minds. It is always scratching on the ego-centered disposition. And if you are not careful, they stone you. They beat Moggallana up, and just before death he goes to Buddha and says, 'Look what they did to me!' The Buddha said, 'Moggallana, this is your last chance,'" Ruth laughs, relishing the scene, "'and if you can move through this unattached and take it, then this will be your last round on earth. There's no more reincarnations, it means enlightenment you can get now. So don't worry.'

"Now you see the immensity of the Dharma, how it opens up in your consciousness. You know, the Dharma in response to a poem was written down. The poem was 'The world is so entangled, who can disentangle the tangle?' When you see it first you don't see the tangle. At first you thought you understood. *Now* you look backwards and see how you have to disentangle the tangle. Here a little more friendliness, here a little bit more forgiving, here a little bit more alertness and seeing a different view, and that view, and so on. It comes by stretching and pulling apart this faculty called attention. It becomes then conscious attention, it becomes concentrated attention, it becomes penetrating attention, it becomes more precise attention. It is now able to see more aspects of one thing called 'my anger' or 'my resentment.' Nothing, we work with nothing, but we work with life, and that is all."

The night has deepened around us, the silence grown more continuous. We regard the coffee cups, the empty cake plate. From inside comes the snuffling of the little dog Tara, and Ruth smiles at me, welcoming.

"We take in the dishes, dahling, and then you come with me to walk the doggies a little bit. They need it."

I agree. I have surrendered now to the night and whatever it may bring.

• • •

In the weeks following this conversation, when I had returned to the Bay Area, I was able to be present with my former partner in her dying process. Although her speech was impaired by the brain tumor, and it was often hard to determine whether she fully understood what was said to her, I believe, judging from her facial expressions and attempts to communicate during the several visits we had together, that she joined me in opening to forgiveness and reconciliation before she took her last breath.

PART IV

The Elder:
Reaping the Fruits

CHAPTER SEVENTEEN

Impermanence

Through the eighties and nineties, Ruth was growing in her teaching capacities, developing Dhamma Dena as a retreat center, and participating in gatherings like the Women and Buddhism conferences taking place throughout the country, as well as the conferences of Western Buddhist teachers. As the eighties progressed, instead of finding a room full of beginners in her retreats, she could work with numbers of returning and experienced students. Vipassana meditation in the United States was coming of age, with many meditators having practiced for long periods. In these years Ruth refined her approach, became subtler and more universal in her guidance. And yet she retained her concern for those just coming to meditation, always lavishing special attention on them.

She explains how she perceives her teaching now. "You cannot capture me. Even in a retreat, when I go through a day, I bring many things. And I also realize now I do teach on different levels. I start on the level of giving instructions, hmm? Then I shift and talk about the effect of that, and the result. Then I sometimes connect it to an incident, to some happening and event out in the world. Then we can go out and see the whole effect, like seeing the suffering all over and the ignorance. And then we see from where it comes, from where it arises, since we have had deep touch with ourselves, so that we no longer need to criticize and to judge what is wrong there. You have rather to bow, because in that bowing you understand maybe your gratitude that you have a little clarity. Then that is very touching.

"Everything has a greater depth for me now. It puts me more in wonderment. I see, number one, that everything that we call problem or dissatisfaction, it is having only one cause, and that is absence of mindfulness, of attention. I don't see anymore bad people or great people, or [ask] how could they do this? It's just the unawareness actualizing itself. There's always the absence of your higher faculty which is able to be the ultimate authority, the only effective authority too, when that comes through.

"I see that everywhere. And then, dahling, I am overwhelmed. Not in a sad way, or in a kind of defeated way overwhelmed. I have sometimes tears in my eyes when I see the immensity of the ignorance and the immensity of the Buddhadharma, how it always fits wherever you want to look at it. There is nothing that you cannot explain and see with the Dharma eyes.

"It is so natural. You have some kind of evaluations and criticism, but it is light, then you see down underneath that it couldn't be other. At such moments when I realize the power of destructiveness in unawareness I wonder why they are not killing themselves more! Actually I am grateful when I see—I see a dog, and I see nobody. Then suddenly comes a gentleman with a leash, then I am so happy, like you have given me a thousand dollars. My real inner joy comes when I see something ethical very good, some kind of an aspect of lovingkindness, I am grateful for every little thing which is positive in the direction of the Buddhadharma, in the direction of basic human goodness, like love, and care.

"What I understand in it, what comes through because I am very happy that moment and grateful, I take a breath and it is the fourth factor of enlightenment, joy. A real joy when you see goodness happening, another contribution to our potential being actualized, even if the person doesn't know what he does."

She continues to develop her capacity to bring full attention to the activities of daily life, and to teach that to her students. "You stand at the sink and wash dishes, or you sit at your computer. There is an attention necessary and a mundane knowledge of which button to push. The transcendent in it would be that you are very relaxed, you trust, and bring a certain kindness to it, and understand that you have the ability to do that, can see yourself functioning with understanding.

"If you feel irritated, accept it and feel it more deeply. Stop. Stand up. Take a breath. Take refuge. Renew your whole system. Lose anger. Accept discomfort. You have a mind to notice it. That's a great delight when you are awake to that. A renewing of consciousness. Every moment you touch something, it can be new and real."

• • •

During the days when I came down alone to Dhamma Dena to interview Ruth, walking to Las Vegas House, or sitting outside the zendo to watch the sunset, or using the outhouse behind Dukkha House, I often felt the weight and progression of my many years of association with Ruth. And I remembered some of the experiences that had let me break through my resistance and criticism to appreciate how very precious and unique she is. During the early years, this came often from her meticulous guiding in the body, when I would touch in to the basic life-energy that sustains us all, and realize the fragility and changeability of my own physical being, and of all life. Or her leading us in joyful movement would open my heart and release a flood of grief and delight, emptying me to meet life as it came to me. In many ways she touched me, moved me, frustrated me, and turned me in to look at my own clinging mind. During those years I sometimes squirmed in agonies of resistance, criticizing Ruth, wanting her to be perfect, wishing that I could escape her constant instruction, her meddling in everything. But I was always drawn to come back to Ruth and Dhamma Dena, to experience the discomfort again.

Sometimes at a retreat I would stew in frustration because Ruth had apparently discovered or surmised that the majority of the students had never meditated before. She would pitch her teaching at the most elementary level, explaining what meditation is, carefully attending to the needs of each newcomer, asking gentle questions, offering advice.

But I, enamored of my view of myself as an experienced meditator, would want more advanced instruction, and would begin to feel restless and dissatisfied. At one such retreat I grumbled internally for several days, criticizing Ruth. By midmorning of the third day, I was growing weary of the suffering I was causing myself. I decided I must change my attitude, but went on silently fuming, wanting Ruth to teach differently. By the fourth day I was driving myself crazy and felt utterly defeated by my own mind. Meditation became impossible. So at last I gave up.

I decided to step back psychologically. I would stop trying to meditate and would just watch Ruth in every smallest action, expression, and word, just see who she was, without demanding anything for myself.

I watched her, without judgment; I listened to her without critiquing her grammar and conciseness; I allowed myself to be present for her coquetry, her persuasion, her crisp commands, her soft voice speaking of our connection to all life, her micromanaging of every detail of the retreat; I brought my whole observing self to our dancing, following Ruth, who floated Isadora Duncan–like before us in a voluminous skirt while issuing commands, praising good effort, and chastising the halfhearted or stiffly resistant among us. She came close to them, touched them, charmed them, until they began to smile, and then to follow her lead. We stood in a circle afterward, and I watched the tears pool in Ruth's eyes as she spoke of the Dharma, these teachings that can dig away the foundation of suffering in our life.

Again and again over those many years, I would be defeated by the constriction of my limited persona and all the discomfort I caused myself, and then I would surrender to just observing this human being called Ruth Denison. And what I saw was a person of depth and almost superhuman energy who was using all of her powers, in each moment, to contact the human beings before her and wake them up to their aliveness. I saw a human being acting from enormous life-force, giving with profound generosity, holding nothing back. The more I watched and listened, the better I saw the bright steady light she shed in the room. She was relentless in her pursuit of the opening that would release each person into this present moment, into connection with him- or herself.

As the years and my own Dharma practice progressed, I came to understand that it really didn't matter if Ruth met my esthetic standards, or lived up to my opinions about optimum behavior in a teacher. What mattered was what I could learn from my own elaborate mental cage of "fixed views," and whether I could let go of all that to open to each moment as Ruth does, give it every ounce of my attention and heart. To desire Ruth to be other than she is, I realized, was pointless and exhausting; to allow her full, brilliant, flawed complexity is freedom, and can provide a model for accepting my own so-less-than-perfect humanity.

This acceptance may seem a risky business. Most of us have heard about people's "surrender" to a spiritual teacher who later emerged as a scoundrel. But I have observed and related with and learned from Ruth for two decades. I did not leap into an easy reverence for her. Whatever her shortcomings, I have come to see her continual motivation and to recognize its purity. Ruth's intention, in any situation, is to give the gift of the Dharma, to plant the seeds of awakening in any human being she encounters. This I can trust.

• • •

And she continues, in her own journey through life, to learn from each new challenge. She is in her eighties now, facing the infirmities and inevitable losses of age. Death becomes more of a reality, creeping closer as it claims the lives of her contemporaries. One difficult passage that Ruth has had to navigate was the decline and death of Henry Denison.

It drew upon her persistence and her loyalty, and it has taken her more deeply into her Dharma practice, strengthening her resolve to wake up completely.

Ruth's union with Henry had been an unconventional, often trying marriage, but she never thought of breaking their long and, as she put it, "deeply loving" connection; and she cared for him with great tenderness during his dying. Always she felt gratitude for his taking her to her teacher U Ba Khin, and for encouraging her to follow her own path.

In the early nineties, Henry began to suffer from dementia but would not tolerate having an attendant, and when Ruth suggested that he come to live out at Dhamma Dena, he adamantly refused. She would come to Hollywood regularly, driving in from the desert to check on him, and she never knew what she would find when she arrived at the house.

One day she saw on his desk a notice of foreclosure on the Creston Road property. He had taken out a loan and not made the payments. The checks were written and filed away, not sent. Ruth had four days to intervene to save their home.

"Another time I came home, I go in the kitchen, wanted to use the oven, pull the door open and the maggots jump out. There was inside a leg of lamb permeated by maggots. And I said, 'Look, Henry!' He said, 'Well, don't you see what is there?' That's when he would walk away. Then I knew he had cooked for his group that used to come to meditate there . . . leg of lamb and salad, being gracious. But the group wasn't there anymore."

She tried to convince him to go to the desert. "I talked and talked, and he would say, 'Shut up. I'll never come to the desert.' Then when I come home and I see that the curtain is drawn and I pull the curtain to the sides and the big sliding door is out, the glass is in front of it, I said, 'Dahling, what happened here?' He said, 'Don't you see what happened?' 'Yes, I see.' I knew he was probably confused and ran through the glass."

Ruth's efforts to help Henry created more and more stress in her, until the tension nearly ended her life and sabotaged her teaching. Henry set the kitchen on fire. Hearing about this, in great distress, Ruth drove from Joshua Tree to Hollywood. But during the trip she fell asleep at the wheel. "From the fast lane I woke up in the slow lane and there was a big truck almost ramming me. There was the off-ramp and I went down and stopped and got into a cry which I never heard myself. It was like I realized where I was, that I could have been dead.

"In Henry's house, I saw the ashes, and the kitchen had no roof. I hadn't really comprehended the immensity of that fire. And Henry sitting there not knowing what to do. It was horrible, dahling." When she drove to Oregon the next day to lead a retreat, she found herself so wracked with stress and worry that at first she could not even speak, and had to be treated by a doctor.

Now she knew she must find a way to lure Henry to the desert, even if she had to trick him or kidnap him. Henry had alienated all his friends, so that almost no one came to visit him. He had thrown out the students and live-in attendants Ruth had hired. He was utterly alone and mentally incompetent, having been diagnosed with dementia and told that he needed twenty-four-hour care and supervision.

Meanwhile, at Dhamma Dena, Ruth had acquired the house a short walk away across open country, where an old couple had lived for decades. This was not a hunter's cabin or trash-filled cottage but a nicely appointed, spacious house with large living room, patio, and fenced yard for the dogs. She called this house Las Vegas House[56] and prepared it for Henry, with a bed in the living room for her to sleep on when she took care of him. The regulars at Dhamma Dena, some of whom had known Henry for a long time, agreed to help with his care.

But how to get him out there! First she went to live with him for some days, massaged his feet, babied him, until he let down his guard. Then she made up a story about taking him to see her doctor where he would not need to pay, coaxed him into the car, and drove him to Dhamma Dena. There, with the comforts of steak dinners, vodka and orange juice drinks, his dogs around him, Margaret and Ruth warmly welcoming him, and videos of spiritual teachers to entertain him, he began to feel at home, until he had forgotten that he used to live in Hollywood.

This was 1995. For five and a half years, Henry lived in Las Vegas house, spending his waking hours seated in his big chair, drink at his elbow. When Ruth would finish teaching in the evening she would come to Henry, cook him dinner, sit and talk with him, massage him, pet and comfort him. When she went away to teach, Margaret, hired as his principal caretaker, would continue his care.

When retreats were in session, Ruth sent her older students to visit with Henry, and anyone arriving to work in Las Vegas House or yard would have a conversation with him. Ruth remembers a fall retreat when the women were working in the garden. "This woman was from Florida, I think. She opens the front door where he is sitting, that big chair, and he sees her and she sees him, and Henry says, 'Who are you?' She says, 'Well I came to clean up the weeds, Ruth sent me here.' He said, 'She did? Does she pay you for the work?' She tells us in the class this and she described it so nicely. Then she says, 'No, she doesn't.' 'That's a strange arrangement,' he tells her. Maybe he said, 'Typical Ruth' or something, I don't remember... 'and you work, despite?' And she said, 'Yes.' 'Why?' he asked. He would go on, you see. He followed up. And then she said, 'Well I get from Ruth what I really want.' Henry said, 'Baby, then go for it!'

"Then he could be *for* me and he knew what I'm doing. He was then devoted. He was also very beautiful. So in many ways I miss him, you know, just to tell him again. He would ask, 'What are you going to do today?' I said, 'Dahling, you want to hear about impermanence? Can I tell you, can I share what I have in mind?' Sometimes he would even tune in so that he could make a comment to it, and then sometimes he was just gone."

During his last years Henry survived a number of medical emergencies. Ruth sometimes saw her spiritual practice as revolving around his care. There were lessons to be learned in seeing her old lover-rival-friend-enemy drifting off into someplace undefined. In the midst of the hard work of sickroom care, there was an intimacy and sweetness to their time together. On the desk next to his chair Henry had arranged a group of photographs of Ruth, and when she was not with him he would gaze at them. She was his anchor, still, to the so-called real world. He was her elegant man, even in rumpled pajamas, his long torso upright in the contour chair, looking like a Biblical prophet peering in stern wonderment out at the world. In her Dharma talks Ruth spoke often about Henry's dying and what it taught her.

But she was saddened by his condition. She saw him as a man who had had everything: intelligence, the freedom of time and choice, a burning desire for spiritual practice, and many supportive, like-minded friends. But his disease had not only denied him friends and meaningful human contact, but also separated him from himself and his lifelong search for spiritual fulfillment. There were times when he recognized and felt this loss. In periods of depression he confessed to Ruth that he saw himself as a "loser." These were the most poignant moments for her.

Then, on September 1, 2000, when Ruth was in Massachusetts leading a retreat at the Insight Meditation Society, she received word that Henry had died. She was shaken, and she cried. But she decided to continue the retreat and go back to California only when it was over.

When she returned, she held a memorial ceremony, to which old friends and the Dhamma Dena community came. And then she took Henry's body to the crematorium in Palm Springs for the ultimate goodbye.

• • •

When she talks about impermanence now, Ruth sometimes evokes Henry's death. She wants to make people realize that death is real, and to help us stop being so afraid of it. Impermanence, she sees, is the force of change—"something coming into being, something going out."

As we talk about this in Las Vegas House, the dogs snore in their basket next to Henry's old chair. Ruth tells me about a talk she gave in Colorado Springs a few days before. "I asked the question, 'Are you agreeing, can we believe now that we have to die?' and then I would make a little joke about it, hmm? And I had the skeleton there and so on [the small white plastic skeleton that she sometimes dangles before us in the zendo, to remind us of mortality]. 'Can we become friendly to this guy?' I asked. I was light, and then I became again with the deepest sincerity. I talked about Henry, how he went into the cremation device, and I opened the door. On a patio in Palm Springs, looked from outside like a big oven on which the old people bake bread. I open the door and the one who was *forty-two years my companion* was now laying dead in a cardboard coffin. It slided off the gurney into the oven. Then I got help in closing, and I pushed the button, and I listened at the first flames. I thought, That was my husband. Forty-two years of life together.

"They were just stunned. I told them, 'Not one tear was running from my eyes.' I was so deep identified with that and the wish that he may have a new wonderful beginning. I heard myself saying, 'I follow you soon.' I was standing a little while there, with Margaret. Then we went into the most ancient hotel in which Greta Garbo and all these old actors were having their hideout. Remember, this is Palm Springs. We had two hours there waiting, then we get an eight-pound package. Which is there."

She indicates the package that sits on the windowsill behind Henry's chair. "It's still untouched as it came to my hands, packed in brown paper. I decorated, even some strings of pearls from the Christmas tree, and people are always enchanted when they see this little package so decorate, they say, 'Oh did you get a present?' 'Yah,' I said, 'I haven't unpacked it yet.'

"In my lecture I would say, 'Are we knowing that it is for real that we are going to die? Then you must feel more this body so you can appreciate this present moment deeper, in gratitude. And that will give you more joy for being in contact with that what is around you. And you will not have this accumulated anxiety as you are starting to age, that you think, What is now?

"I said, 'Let's celebrate now. Impermanence is a wonderful thing. We should really bow to it because it gives us space, it doesn't overpopulate the world. It's like you have a room and you buy always furniture, you don't throw any out: that's the same with the people. We're already doing not so good with it.'

"I read *Don Juan* to them.[57] There is a scene where he says to his student, about the subject of death, 'We cannot stress this point enough, we cannot contemplate enough the fact that we are all going to die.'

"Then I found a wonderful quote from a man who lived through the blast at Hiroshima. He comes from his work, very full of ideas what he is going to present into his working place. And he comes from the Kobe line and moves away from the train station. Suddenly there is a siren going, everyone runs now, and then he said everything was around him penetrated by dark clouds, dark clouds with green and red fire. Then the next what he felt was pieces of glass and metal hit him. So he describes that and then suddenly it was dark. And he was unconscious. I took now, the words came to me. I said, 'Today is September 11—two years ago we had something similar going on, when thousands of people were met by death unexpected, unplanned—who could have written the same thing.' (I didn't say it was just the reverse on the political level— *we* were the ones who did it to the Japanese. Dahling, that was not appropriate in that moment.)

"Then I said, 'I have a very special relation to this moment, because I had the ticket for September 11 and it was changed—United Flight 175 from Boston to Los Angeles." Ruth had been set to come back from her teaching at the Insight Meditation Society, with a ticket on that flight. The day before, she decided to delay her departure in order to do some sightseeing in Boston. "I missed that plane." On September 11, 2001, at 9:03 a.m., Flight 175, carrying sixty-five people, crashed into the south tower of the World Trade Center in Manhattan, next to the billowing black smoke coming from the north tower, which had already been hit. "I could be in the rubble," Ruth says, "and I still live that. I look up and see the tower and the rubble, see a finger in the rubble—could be my finger. It's not a drama. It's light coming through my mind. Because I was very close. Then I realize I am here. I have a mind, and my eyes can see. Then at next level I know that I see my mind seeing. It gives a freshness in the perception and authenticity of the experience.

"It has shifted my consciousness ever since. Quite radical. I often connect to that event, but mainly to the last five minutes to all those who sit in that plane and they know they will die. I hear the screams, I hear the confusion, I hear the anxiety moving through and upsetting the whole situation, and then it was a big bang and it was silence.

"I hear that and look down to me, my consciousness shifted, and I have to touch me to realize I am alive, I am not there. The shift is that there is enormous gratefulness, unexplicable appreciation of the present moment wherever I am. I am alive, hmm? That is not that I glorify just life, but it gives me the opportunity that it is a gate to my ultimate realization. Ever since, I know that it can happen to me every minute—death, unplanned, unexpected. Knowing that, I make a new resolve to live in that way that I can attain complete realization."

Ruth shakes her head, smiles at me. "You see?" she asks.

And then, in a little coda, she adds, "Anyway, this is my life. It was a colorful life in a way. I don't realize it. It was not so . . . *noblesse oblige.* You have to pay for it, *everything,* with effort, with sometimes stepping back, you have to go back and you have to be gracious and sometimes it isn't what you want to do but then because of the situation. . . ."

She nods, shifts her shoulders, lifts her hands as if to illustrate. "Yah, dahling, I could always kind of dance that way."

Sources

INTERVIEWS

Daryl Bailey, April 24, 2003
Robert Beatty, February 14, 2003
Susanna Brinnon, March 7, 2003
Joan Buffington, February 3, 1984
Margaret Cormier, March 13, 2003
Ron DeHart, February 3, 2003
Doshin (Houn Houtman), May 28, 2003
Fanshen Faber, February 18, 2003
Russell Fieber, February 18, 2003
Margaret Frederick, October 28, 2002
Joseph Goldstein, January 27, 2003
Lucinda Treelight Green, January 16, 2003
Jain Hein, October 25, 2003
Nick Herzmark, February 26, 2003
Ella Hirst, January 23, 2003
Cindy Hoffman, February 17, 2003
Jim Hopper, February 13, 2003
Robert Hover, March 14, 2003
Nellie Kaufer, January 27, 2003
Jennifer Keane, February 24, 2003
Paul Koppler, June 16, 2003
Jack Kornfield, April 4, 2003
Frank Leder, February 3, 2003

Kathy Lewis, February 18, 2003
Dana MacDonald, October 28, 2002
Jacqueline Mandell, March 13, 2003
Isha Mayim, January 28, 2003
Maria Monroe, March 14, 2003
Alan Morinis, April 25, 2003
Carol Newhouse, January 21, 2003
Wilhelm Polert, April 5, 2003
Caitriona Reed and Michelle Benzamin Miki, February 21, 2003
Ulrike Ritter, February 2, 2002
Marion Saltman, February 9, 1984
Sharon Salzberg, February 9, 2003
Sarada (Doreen Spencer), February 13, 2003
Rhea Shapiro, February 20, 2003
Seimi Shiba, January 31, 2003
Linda Sibio, February 2, 2003
Shanti Soule, February 27, 2003
Beverly Spring, May 13, 2003
Katherine Tate, February 2, 2003
Denise Taylor, March 26, 2003
Michelle Tellier, February 17, 2003
Arinna Weisman, January 14, 2003
Julie Wester, January 14, 2003
Hope Winthrope, February 1, 2003
Nina Wise, February 5, 2003
Annabelle Zinser, October 28, 2002

BOOKS

Arendt, Hannah. *Antisemitism:* Part One of *The Origins of Totalitarianism.* New York: Harcourt, Brace and World, Inc., 1968.

Bhatt, Mahesh. *U. G. Krishnamurti: A Life.* Delhi: Penguin Books India, 1992.

Brecht, Bertolt. *The Jewish Wife and Other Short Plays.* New York: Grove Weidenfeld, 1965.

Bridenthal, Renate, Atina Grossman, and Marion Kaplan, eds. *When Biology Became Destiny: Women in Weimar and Nazi Germany.* New York: Monthly Review Press, 1984.

Brooks, Charles V. W. *Sensory Awareness: The Rediscovery of Experiencing Through Workshops with Charlotte Selver.* Great Neck, NY: Felix Morrow, 1974, 1986.

Butterfield, Stephen T. *The Double Mirror: A Skeptical Journey into Buddhist Tantra*. Berkeley, CA: North Atlantic Books, 1994.

Elon, Amos. *The Pity of It All: A History of Jews in Germany, 1743–1933*. New York: Henry Holt and Company, 2002.

Fest, Joachim E. *The Face of the Third Reich: Portraits of the Nazi Leadership*. New York: Da Capo Press, 1999.

Feuerstein, Georg, Ty Koontz, and David Dykstra, eds. *The Adept: Selections from Talks and Essays by DA FREE JOHN on the Nature and Function of the Enlightened Teacher*. Clearlake, CA: The Dawn Horse Press, 1983.

Fromm, Erich. *Escape from Freedom*. New York: Henry Holt & Co., 1941.

Furlong, Monica. *Zen Effects: The Life of Alan Watts*. Boston: Houghton Mifflin, 1986.

Garraty, John A. *The Great Depression*. New York: Harcourt Brace Jovanovich, 1986.

Gidlow, Elsa. *Elsa, I Come with My Songs: The Autobiography of Elsa Gidlow*. San Francisco: Booklegger Press, 1986.

Goldhagen, Daniel Jonah. *Hitler's Willing Executioners: Ordinary Germans and the Holocaust*. New York: Alfred A. Knopf, 1996.

Handke, Peter. *A Sorrow Beyond Dreams: A Life Story*. New York: Farrar, Straus & Giroux, 1974.

Heiden, Konrad. *Der Fuehrer: Hitler's Rise to Power*. New York: Houghton Mifflin Co., 1944.

Herman, Judith Lewis, M.D. *Trauma and Recovery*. New York: Basic Books, 1992.

Höss, Rudolph. *Death Dealer: The Memoirs of the SS Kommandant at Auschwitz*. New York: Da Capo Press, 1996.

Huxley, Laura Archera. *This Timeless Moment*. New York: Farrar, Straus & Giroux, 1968.

Isherwood, Christopher. *Diaries, Volume One, 1939–1960*. New York: HarperCollins Publishers, 1996.

———. *My Guru and His Disciple*. New York: Farrar, Straus & Giroux, 1980.

———, ed. *Vedanta for Modern Man*. New York: Collier Books, 1962.

Jeffrey, Francis, and John C. Lilly, M.D. *John Lilly, so far....* Los Angeles: Jeremy P. Tarcher, 1990.

Kent, Stephen A. *From Slogans to Mantras: Social Protest and Religious Conversion in the Late Vietnam War Era.* New York: Syracuse University Press, 2001.

Kindleberger, Charles P. *The World in Depression.* Berkeley, CA: University of California Press, 1986.

Koontz, Claudia. *Mothers in the Fatherland: Women, the Family and Nazi Politics.* New York: St. Martin's Press, 1987.

Kornfield, Jack. *Living Buddhist Masters.* Kandy, Sri Lanka: Buddhist Publication Society, 1977.

Leary, Timothy. *Flashbacks: An Autobiography.* Los Angeles, CA: J. P. Tarcher, Inc., 1983.

Lerner, Eric. *Journey of Insight Meditation: A Personal Experience of the Buddha's Way.* London: Turnstone Books, 1977.

Lilly, John C., M.D. *The Center of the Cyclone: An Autobiography of Inner Space.* New York: Julian Press, 1972.

Mann, Golo. *The History of Germany Since 1789.* New York: Praeger, 1968.

Miller, Alice. *For Your Own Good: The Roots of Violence in Child-rearing.* London: Virago Press, 1987.

Mitscherlich, Alexander, and Margarete Mitscherlich. *The Inability to Mourn: Principles of Collective Behavior.* New York: Grove Press, 1975.

Niewyk, Donald L. *The Jews in Weimar Germany.* Baton Rouge and London: Louisiana State University Press, 1980.

Owings, Alison. *Frauen: German Women Recall the Third Reich.* New Brunswick, NJ: Rutgers University Press, 1994.

Ramacharaka, Yogi. *Science of Breath: A Complete Manual of the Oriental Breathing Philosophy of Physical, Mental, Psychic and Spiritual Development.* Chicago: Yogi Publication Society, 1904, 1905, 1932.

Schmidt, Amy. *Knee Deep in Grace: The Extraordinary Life and Teaching of Dipa Ma.* Lake Junaluska, NC: Present Perfect Books, 2003.

Scholl, Inge. *The White Rose: Munich 1942–1943.* Middletown, CT: Wesleyan University Press, 1970, 1983.

Shainberg, Lawrence. *Ambivalent Zen: One Man's Adventures on the Dharma Path.* New York: Random House/Vintage Books, 1995.

Shattock, E. H. Rear Admiral. *An Experiment in Mindfulness: An English Admi-*

ral's Experiences in a Buddhist Monastery. New York: E. P. Dutton & Co., Inc., 1960.

Sherrill, Martha. *The Buddha from Brooklyn.* New York: Random House, 2000.

Trumbo, Dalton. *Night of the Aurochs.* New York: Bantam Books, 1979.

Van de Wetering, Janwillem. *The Empty Mirror: Experiences in a Japanese Zen Monastery.* New York: St. Martin's Griffin, 1973.

Vipassana Research Institute Historical Research Project. *Sayagyi U Ba Khin Journal: A Collection Commemorating the Teaching of Sayagyi U Ba Khin, Published to Mark the Twentieth Anniversary of His Demise.* Maharashtra, India: Vipassana Research Institute, 1991.

Watts, Alan. *In My Own Way: An Autobiography.* New York: Pantheon Books, 1972.

FILMS

Aimee & Jaguar, Max Faerberboeck, director, 1999. German film set in 1943 Berlin; lesbian relationship between a Jewish woman and a Nazi wife.

Blind Spot: Hitler's Secretary, Andre Heller and Othmar Schmiderer, directors, 2002. Documentary featuring interview footage of Traudl Junge, one of Hitler's personal secretaries during WWII.

Cabaret, Bob Fosse, director, 1972. Musical about an American young woman caught up in prewar Berlin decadence.

Judgment at Nuremberg, Stanley Kramer, director, 1961. Drama based on the Nuremberg trials after WWII.

Paragraph 175, Rob Epstein and Jeffrey Friedman, directors, 1999. Documentary about the treatment of homosexuals in Nazi Germany.

The Pianist, Roman Polanski, director, 2002. Drama of a Polish Jewish musician struggling to survive the destruction of the Warsaw Ghetto in WWII.

The White Rose, Michael Verhoeven, director, 1986. German story of Munich students who launched an anti-Nazi uprising in 1942 and were executed.

NOTE: For more information on Ruth and Dhamma Dena, contact Dhamma Dena Desert Vipassana Center, P.O. Box 183, Joshua Tree, CA 92252. Tel: (760) 362-4815. Films about Ruth Denison have been created by two filmmakers, Annie Hershey and Merry Song Caston, and are available for purchase from the filmmakers. *The Book of Ruth,* a collection of quotations by Ruth, has been compiled by Jain Hein and Lucinda Treelight Green, Ph.D., and can be purchased from Dr. Green.

Notes

1. Watts, *In My Own Way: An Autobiography*.

2. Quoted in Alice Miller, *For Your Own Good: The Roots of Violence in Child-rearing*, p. 28.

3. Peter Handke, *A Sorrow Beyond Dreams: A Life Story*.

4. One account of life in the Third Reich that touched me deeply and helped me understand how irresistible and nearly universal was participation in the Hitler Youth, is the story of the White Rose. This was the name of a small group of university students in Munich who, in 1942 and 1943, printed leaflets denouncing Hitler and urging German citizens to sabotage the war effort. They were caught by the Nazis and were executed. Hans and Sophie Scholl, brother and sister, who were at the center of this effort at resistance, themselves had previously joined the Hitler Youth, entering into it "with body and soul." See *The White Rose: Munich 1942–1943* by Inge Scholl.

5. A fascinating compendium of such answers is found in Alison Owings, *Frauen: German Women Recall the Third Reich*.

6. From Golo Mann, *The History of Germany Since 1789*.

7. As horrendous as these figures are, they must be balanced against the six million Jews, the countless thousands of Poles and Russians, and other people murdered by the Third Reich. The Allies, in response to the German war crimes, retaliated with extraordinary ferocity.

8. Cited in Alison Owings, p. 146.

9. Owings, p. 471.

10. A. L. Basham, *The Wonder That Was India* (New York: Grove Press, 1959), as quoted in Stephen A. Kent's *From Slogans to Mantras.*

11. Isherwood, a British author who moved to Hollywood in 1939, was the author of numerous novels and nonfiction books, among them *The Berlin Diaries (Goodbye to Berlin),* which provided the inspiration for the play *I Am a Camera* and later the Broadway musical and the film *Cabaret.*

12. In Isherwood, Christopher, *Diaries, Volume One, 1939–1960,* p. 408.

13. Watts, British philosopher, teacher, and mystic, became famous for his books on Eastern forms of spirituality. They include *The Wisdom of Insecurity; The Way of Zen (The Spirit of Zen); Nature, Man and Woman; The Joyous Cosmology; The Two Hands of God; Beyond Theology;* and *The Book: On the Taboo Against Knowing Who You Are.*

14. Watts, *In My Own Way,* p. 236.

15. Watts, *In My Own Way,* p. 317.

16. Other important books by Huxley include *Brave New World, The Perennial Philosophy, Heaven and Hell,* and *Brave New World Revisited.*

17. Watts, *In My Own Way,* p. 317.

18. Quoted in Isherwood, ed., *Vedanta for Modern Man.*

19. Quoted in "Sensory Awareness: The Work of Charlotte Selver" (brochure). The Sensory Awareness Foundation, Mill Valley, CA.

20. Watts, *In My Own Way,* p. 196.

21. Bulletin #15, Summer 1999, the Sensory Awareness Foundation, in Charlotte Selver, *Collected Writings, Volume I: Sensory Awareness and Our Attitude Toward Life,* p. 10.

22. Ibid., pp. 18–19.

23. Charles Brooks, *Sensory Awareness,* p. 23.

24. From "Sensory Awareness: The Work of Charlotte Selver" (brochure), p. 5.

25. Gesshin was later ordained in the Vietnamese Zen lineage to become Gesshin Prabhasa Dharma roshi (mentioned in previous chapters).

26. Watts, *In My Own Way,* p. 316.

27. Theravada, or the Way of the Elders, is the oldest form of Buddhism, its practices taught by the Buddha himself in India 2,500 years ago and continuing mostly

in Southeast Asia in the twentieth and twenty-first centuries. Vipassana meditation practice, popular in the West, is the practice followed by Theravada meditators.

28. These "memoirs" were later read by other sojourners in Asian meditation centers. Sharon Salzberg, senior teacher at the Insight Meditation Society, recalls finding them a source of inspiration in the early seventies. A typed copy was kept at Dhamma Dena for years, but my efforts to find it yielded nothing. Residents at Dhamma Dena think that an overzealous retreat manager threw it out with other papers for recycling. Ruth told me she had given a copy to U Ba Khin, but the International Meditation Center in Burma did not respond to my queries about it.

29. The light at the tip of the nose, called *nimitta,* a tiny glowing disk, is recognized as a sign of the mind's strong concentration.

30. In Vipassana Research Institute Historical Research Project, *Sayagyi U Ba Khin Journal: A Collection Commemorating the Teaching of Sayagyi U Ba Khin,* p. 57.

31. Millbrook's builder must have been a fancier of medieval lore, for a sallyport is an opening in fortifications from which defenders may rush out, and a portcullis is a heavy iron grating lowered on chains to bar the gateway to a castle or fortified town.

32. Timothy Leary, *Flashbacks: An Autobiography,* pp. 187–188.

33. Leary, *Flashbacks,* p. 190.

34. Leary, *Flashbacks,* p. 196.

35. Leary, *Flashbacks,* p. 189.

36. Richard Alpert, who later became the celebrated Ram Dass, author of *Be Here Now.*

37.   Sentient beings are numberless, I vow to save them.
     Desires are inexhaustible, I vow to put an end to them.
     The Dharmas are boundless, I vow to master them.
     The Buddha Way is unsurpassable, I vow to attain it.

38. Not until many years later did Ruth find a book in Henry's library that helped her understand her loss of vital connection. *The Hindu-Yogi Science of Breath,* by Yogi Ramacharaka, defines prana, the subtle life-force carried on the breath; delineates its working in the human body, mind, and psyche; and offers breathing exercises to cultivate physical and mental health. It also describes the negative results when prana is blocked or diminished.

39. Watts, *In My Own Way,* p. 376.

40. Dharma combat: the tradition in Zen of student and teacher debating points of doctrine.

41. Ruth gives the date of her authorization by U Ba Khin as 1971.

42. Ajahn Dhiravamsa was a Thai Buddhist teacher.

43. Sri Aurobindo was a Hindu seer recognized as an embodiment of divinity, and a visionary who posited a transformation in world consciousness.

44. Author of *Journey of Insight Meditation.*

45. *San Francisco Examiner,* April 3, 1985.

46. The Pali form of "Dharma." Pali is the sacred language of the Theravada Buddhists, while Sanskrit [as in Dharma] serves for most other forms of Buddhism.

47. Ayya Khema, a German-born Theravada nun who taught with Robert Hover in Los Angeles, was a friend of Ruth's, and later became an internationally recognized meditation teacher and champion of women's equal rights in Buddhism.

48. I. B. Horner, *Women Under Primitive Buddhism* (Delhi: Motilal Banarsidass, 1930), p. 254.

49. Recently, Goenka apparently changed his mind, for Ruth was graciously received at one of his centers.

50. Ajahn Sumedho is the Western head monk of Amaravati, a monastery in England.

51. The term "Lesbian Nation" was coined by Jill Johnston in her 1974 book of essays of the same name.

52. As more houses are built in the desert, the habitat of the coyotes shrinks, and they have increasing difficulty finding food. Their days are numbered, but for now, Ruth feeds them every night.

53. *Discovering Kwan Yin* (Boston: Beacon Press, 1999).

54. The great Wheel of Life, called *Pratitya-samutpada,* is created by the twelve links of dependent origination that lead from one to the next, binding us to the unsatisfactory world of Samsara. The links are (1) ignorance, (2) willful actions, (3) relinking consciousness, (4) body and mind, (5) the six senses, (6) contact or sense experience, (7) feeling: pleasant, unpleasant, or neutral, (8) craving, (9) grasping, (10) becoming, (11) birth, and (12) old age and death and the continuation of suffering.

55. She is quoting the last lines of the Heart Sutra, attributed to Kwan Yin (Chinese

name of the Buddhist bodhisattva Avalokitesvara), *Gate, gate, paragate, parasam-gate, bodhi svaha.* "Go, go, go beyond, go utterly beyond, awake, so be it."

56. The name came because trees grew in the yard of the house, giving it a relatively lush look, and the previous owner had installed many bright outside lights. At night the house glittered like an oasis in the desert.

57. The Mexican shaman presented by Carlos Castaneda in a series of famous books, including *The Teachings of Don Juan, The Power of Silence, The Journey to Ix-tlan,* and *A Separate Reality.*

Acknowledgments

As the teachings of the Buddha are priceless, so Ruth Denison's teachings and her inimitable personality are given freely, and gratefully received. For many years she has taught the Dharma with steadfast patience to this sometimes surly student, repaying obstinacy with gentle concern and humor. I can never thank her enough, just for being herself, and, as one of her students put it, bringing so much light into this world. During the research for this book, Ruth responded to my sessions of tiresome questions with unfailing energy and good humor. Without her gracious cooperation, this book could not exist. When we read the finished draft together, she found it faithful to the spirit that motivates her and the contribution she is still making to American Buddhism.

In the late nineties, several of her students suggested that I write a biography of Ruth. Annabelle Zinser of Berlin and Jain Hein of Scarsdale, New York, were the principal enthusiasts. At the same time, they talked to Ruth, persuading her to abandon her natural reticence and allow me to present her in a book. Apparently their arguments succeeded, for at the 1999 autumn women's retreat at Dhamma Dena, Ruth asked me to come talk with her. She surprised me by telling me that she would like me to write her biography. We talked until 1:30 a.m. as I cautioned her that I would attempt a truthful, unvarnished view of her life and teachings. Ruth listened carefully, and agreed. Early in 2002, the year of her eightieth birthday, I began research for this book.

Particularly Annabelle Zinser helped in the early stages of the work, encouraging me, hosting me in her home in Berlin, supporting me in crucial ways. I am grateful to her for that help, and for her belief in this project and the rightness of my doing it. Jain Hein, Ruth's faithful devotee, I thank for her unflagging devotion to our teacher and her enthusiasm for this writing. Jack Kornfield let me know how delighted he was that I was undertaking this project. The Berkeley Women's Dharma Foundation offered support in the form of a generous grant.

Ruth's colleagues and students gave generously of their time, telling inspiring, often hilarious, wonderfully perceptive stories of their encounters with Ruth over the years, as well as performing some checking of the often slippery facts and dates. Their experiences have provided background and texture to this work.

Although their names appear in the Sources section, I want to thank especially the people who live with Ruth in the desert, who were wonderfully helpful with transportation and information. They include Ron DeHart, Hope Winthrope, Seimi Shiba, Katherine Tate, and Linda Sibio. Margaret Frederick good-naturedly picked me up many times at the Palm Springs airport, brought me to Dhamma Dena, and days later cheerfully drove me back; she swiftly answered my e-mailed or telephoned questions about details such as names and dates—and whether the coyotes are fed dog food. She is a gem whose contribution to this book I sincerely appreciate.

To all those friends, librarians (Judy Clarence most especially), and bookstore clerks who sent me to just the right book or article or online biography, I give thanks. So the reader will know whereon I base my history, these materials appear in "Sources."

Old friends Sandra Butler and Nan Gefen both performed invaluable, close readings of the manuscript. Sandy's comments on the psychology of abuse helped me assess the significance of some difficult material. The Reverend Maurine Lewis, visiting from Wisconsin, curled up in my living room to read the book and comment insightfully. Eva Herzer checked my German phrases and German history. Jennifer Boesing explored some implications of the text with me and shared her very useful perspective.

I thank other friends for listening to me talk about what I was finding out, particularly the disturbing details of the Third Reich; and those of my friends who know Ruth, for discussing with me the significance of some behavior or quirk that puzzled me. Among these I count Carol Newhouse and Annie Hershey, who besides reading the manuscript, always inquired how it was coming and, in discussions over good dinners, commented upon its content.

My Beacon editor, Amy Caldwell, saw the value early on of my doing a book on a major woman Buddhist teacher, and it was her suggestion that I also explore my own experience as a student in relation to that teacher. I thank her for her wisdom in suggesting what I believe was the right approach, and I thank her also for her intelligent guidance in cutting and polishing the manuscript.

I want to reach out with my gratitude to all the people who are participating in the great adventure called the creation of American Buddhism. We have established an unprecedented presence and efficacy of women in Buddhist practice in the United States, and this context has encouraged the Ruth Denisons of the world to continue giving of themselves, sometimes against considerable odds.

Lastly, I bow in gratitude to my dear partner, Martha Boesing—playwright, theater director, and social activist—for her willingness to engage with me in seemingly endless discussions about the subject of this book over many months, read every word of it in several drafts, and meticulously point out the places that needed more thinking, a sharper perspective, a more focused approach. The contribution of her keen mind and generous spirit can be found on nearly every page. I am unendingly thankful for it, and for her loving presence in my life.

Index

Printed in the United States
By Bookmasters